New
Coop

New York Loves Them, Cooperstown Snubs Them

*Great Mets and Yankees Who
Belong in the Hall of Fame*

TOM VAN RIPER

McFarland & Company, Inc., Publishers
Jefferson, North Carolina

All photographs are from the National Baseball Hall of Fame and Museum, Cooperstown, New York.

LIBRARY OF CONGRESS CATALOGUING-IN-PUBLICATION DATA

Names: Van Riper, Tom, 1963– author.
Title: New York loves them, Cooperstown snubs them :
   great Mets and Yankees who belong in the Hall of Fame /
   Tom Van Riper.
Description: Jefferson, North Carolina : McFarland & Company, Inc.,
   Publishers, 2020. | Includes bibliographical references and index.
Identifiers: LCCN 2020016065 | ISBN 9781476679655 (paperback :
   acid free paper) ∞
   ISBN 9781476640358 (ebook)
Subjects: LCSH: New York Mets (Baseball team)—Biography. |
   New York Yankees (Baseball team)—Biography. | Baseball players—
   New York (State)—New York—Biography. | National Baseball Hall
   of Fame and Museum
Classification: LCC GV875.N45 V36 2020 | DDC 796.357/64097471—dc23
LC record available at https://lccn.loc.gov/2020016065

BRITISH LIBRARY CATALOGUING DATA ARE AVAILABLE

ISBN (print) 978-1-4766-7965-5
ISBN (ebook) 978-1-4766-4035-8

Front cover: Keith Hernandez and Ron Guidry (Jerry Coli/Dreamstime);
New York City skyline (TTStudio/Shutterstock)

Printed in the United States of America

McFarland & Company, Inc., Publishers
   Box 611, Jefferson, North Carolina 28640
   www.mcfarlandpub.com

Dad, thank you for the trips to Shea.
May 30, 1970, July 25, 2008,
and every one in between.

Acknowledgments

Thanks to the following noted baseball experts for taking the time to be interviewed for this book. Their voices add much value:

Marty Appel
Ken Davidoff
Peter Golenbock
Brian Kenny
Rob Neyer
Howie Rose
Erik Sherman

Table of Contents

Prologue

When it comes to success and recognition, in sports or in life, New York is it. It's the place to be and the place to play. The big stage, the bright lights. Make it as a baseball star anywhere else, and you're pretty well set. Make it in New York, and you're golden. Throw in a championship ring or two, and you're platinum, on to the Hall of Fame. Or so the thinking goes. But that doesn't mean you can't be overshadowed, even under the brightest of lights. It's happened to the best of them. Maybe they came up short on some traditional lifetime stats (wins, homers, etc.) that Hall of Fame voters love, or maybe they were nudged out of the limelight by higher profile teammates. Perhaps they lacked big-time personalities and tended to shy away from publicity. Maybe it was because they played before anyone was paying attention to advanced metrics. Or maybe some combination of all of those things.

Keith Hernandez belongs in the Baseball Hall of Fame. So do Ron Guidry and Bernie Williams. So do Graig Nettles, Willie Randolph, Jerry Koosman and David Cone. So why aren't they? They seemingly hit all the criteria: they were stars, they won championships, and they did it while enjoying that (allegedly) built-in public relations advantage of New York.

Fans and media in other baseball towns love to complain about New York as the great magnifying glass, where good players are deemed great and great players are deemed legendary for no reason beyond the extra attention that comes from playing there. But the historical evidence suggests that only the latter is true. Obvious Hall of Famers like Derek Jeter (just inducted in 2020) and Reggie Jackson become lionized beyond their achievements. Even Joe DiMaggio, according to today's advanced metrics, is a bit overrated relative to his legend. As great as the Yankee Clipper was, the numbers for WAR and OPS-plus would place him clearly in arrears of noted peers Ted Williams and Stan Musial as

well as the man who succeeded him in center field at Yankee Stadium,
Mickey Mantle (and that would hold true even if you factored in DiM-
aggio's three missed years due to military service and assumed he'd have
produced similarly to the years right before and after). But when you
play most of your career before the days of television and you have Er-
nest Hemingway referencing you in *The Old Man and the Sea*, you have
an almost mythical aura that grows alongside your accomplishments on
the field.

The point here isn't to be critical of DiMaggio, Jeter and Jackson, but
to demonstrate that for those players not perceived to be that top alpha
dog on championship teams, the New York spotlight doesn't seem to
help them much. Less obvious Hall of Fame choices like Cone or Nettles
fail to pick up that extra lift that might get them over the top. That wasn't
always the case. Before mass media began evening out levels of exposure
across the country, baseball history begat more than its share of questionable New York–based Hall of Famers. Most of them are old-timers
from the city's original baseball power, the Giants, who were selected by
a friendly Veterans Committee. Go ahead and check the career numbers
of Roger Bresnahan, Freddie Lindstrom, Ross Youngs and George "High
Pockets" Kelly, and you'll scratch your head trying to figure out why they
have plaques hanging in Cooperstown. And let's not even get started on
Phil Rizzuto, a fine Yankee shortstop in the 1940s and '50s but also a
.273 hitter with little power whose .351 career on-base percentage was
good but not all that far above the league average of his era. No doubt
the Scooter benefited from a lengthy career as a popular announcer in
the Yankee TV booth after his playing days ended, a platform that provided him with years of visibility as his fans argued his case. After peaking at 38 percent of writers' ballots through 1976, barely more than half
the 75 percent needed, Rizzuto was suddenly waved home by a relenting
Veterans Committee in 1994, a full 38 years after his last game.

But by and large, the Big Apple stage tends to inflate the reputations
of those seen as leading men at the expense of those perceived (often
inaccurately) to be supporting players. As veteran baseball author Rob
Neyer puts it: "I don't think there is an advantage to playing in New
York. The only thing is it does give you a chance to distinguish yourself
in October."

What we see it boil down to is this: the biggest litmus test for New
York sports legend status is being perceived as that "main man" on multiple championship teams. DiMaggio certainly had that. Jeter also had

it to a degree, the numbers showing that he was the top player on three of the five Yankee title teams that he played on. Jackson wasn't the top player on either of his two Yankee title teams, but his pre–Yankee stardom with the Oakland A's already had him well on his way to Cooperstown, and his big-time hitting performances in two Yankee World Series wins (1977 and 1978) cemented his reputation as a big-game player. At the same time, Reggie's outsized personality boosted his Yankee image beyond his numbers. Teammates who scored better Yankee numbers without the outsized personalities—like Randolph, Guidry, and Nettles—were beloved in their own way but never fully appreciated by Hall of Fame voters.

Also overlooked was Bernie Williams, who never quite seemed to capture the New York crowd's fancy as much as his teammate Derek Jeter did. Jeter, of course, was a genuinely great player who holds the distinction of spending his entire 19-year career with the Yankees. But let's be honest—he was also deified a bit beyond his accomplishments at the expense of teammates like Williams. A statistical audit of Jeter's career (both offense and defense) shows him to be about even with Alan Trammel, the longtime Detroit Tiger shortstop who was shut out of the Hall for 15 years before a Veterans Committee did the right thing by voting him in in 2018. Clearly one ring in Detroit doesn't bring the buzz of five in New York. During the Yankees' great run of four titles in five years from 1996 to 2000, Jeter's production didn't quite match that of Williams, who fell off the Hall of Fame ballot after two years. Ultimately, Williams' long-term career wasn't as productive as Jeter's was, but it's still right up there with several Hall of Fame outfielders. Of course the quiet Williams wasn't a man about town making the social scene, and he never had the chance to dive into the stands after snagging an extra-inning foul pop in a rivalry game against the Red Sox. He never ran all the way to the first base line to alertly cut off a throw and flip the ball to his catcher to nail a runner at the plate in a playoff game. Jeter was simply bestowed with more "main man" status on those championship Yankee clubs by the fans and press than Williams was, even though that status isn't backed up by production on the field.

At the same time, David Cone, while he was much-appreciated during the Yankees' 1996–2000 run, always seemed to be a bit lost in the shuffle on deep Yankee staffs that included David Wells, Andy Pettitte, Orlando Hernandez, Roger Clemens and Mariano Rivera. Cone's Yankee run was almost a carbon copy of his earlier Mets days in that regard, his greatness shaded a bit by sharing a rotation with Dwight Gooden, Ron Darling, Bob Ojeda and others. The fans always loved Cone, but he wasn't quite perceived as that clear top dog in Queens or in the Bronx.

Speaking of the Mets, all-time pitching great Tom Seaver still stands as the only Hall of Famer to have spent the bulk of his prime with that franchise. Seaver won only one World Series ring, but his career body of work is so obviously Hall of Fame worthy that additional titles don't matter so much. What Seaver's enormous presence also did: cast a big shadow over Jerry Koosman, Seaver's no. 2 for much of the late 1960s through the mid–'70s who might have gotten less attention than any pitcher in history who amassed more than 200 wins and 2,500 strikeouts.

Overshadowing Keith Hernandez a bit was the late, great Gary Carter, who is most notably remembered for helping the 1986 Mets to a World Series title, even though Carter's career included just one superstar season in New York (1985) after eight of them in Montreal. Magnetic and camera-friendly as well as talented, Carter finally got his full recognition when he became a Met. Like Seaver, Carter got only one New York ring. But there was another factor at work. The Mets, after seven years of struggles during the late 1970s and early '80s, had finally been rebuilt into a contender by 1984. They acquired Carter before the 1985 season as the coveted "last piece of the puzzle" that could catapult them to a championship. When that happened in 1986, Carter seemed to receive the lion's share of the credit despite a .255 batting average and defense that, at age 32, was no longer elite. Carter finished third in the 1986 National League MVP voting despite a 3.6 WAR that was sixth-highest on the Mets. The team's best player in 1986: Keith Hernandez, with his .310 batting average, .413 on-base percentage, great defense, and 5.5 WAR. While Hernandez was certainly a fan favorite and got plenty of acclaim on that Mets team, he really wasn't awarded that "difference maker" tag as much as Carter was, if only because he had arrived in town two years before Carter had and had already become an ingrained part of the club. When a high-profile star comes over and a championship soon follows, outsized tributes are usually the result. Carter and the Mets were very much the baseball version of Mark Messier and the New York Rangers. A huge star in Edmonton who was brought in to lead the Rangers to a Stanley Cup and end their famous "1940" curse, Messier is remembered as the main man of the 1994 championship team, even though the Rangers' best player that year was defenseman Brian Leetch. It's not

that Carter and Messier weren't instrumental in their clubs' championships—obviously they were. But all in all, based on their career peaks,
they were more Canadian sports legends than New York sports legends.
Hernandez, like Leetch, received plenty of credit but probably not as
much as he deserved.

Absorbing the lion's share of attention from the late '70s Yankee
clubs of Guidry, Nettles and Randolph was one Reginald Martinez Jackson. Just as with Carter-Mets and Messier-Rangers, Jackson's move to
the Yankees in 1977 also coincided with a championship. There's a narrative that has existed for years that the Yankees' excellent 1976 club (on
which Nettles and Randolph both had big years) that took the American
League pennant but dropped the World Series to the Reds was vaulted
over the top to a championship after Reggie signed on the following year.
And in a way it's true—Jackson did have a good year in 1977 and the
Yanks did in fact take the whole enchilada. What gets lost is the pretty
much indisputable fact that the Yankees were a better team in 1976 than
they were in 1977. The 1976 Yankees led their division all season and
wound up winning handily. In '77, they pulled out a dogfight over Boston and Baltimore on the final weekend. Baseball's two-team expansion
in 1977 that brought the 107-loss Toronto Blue Jays into the A.L. East
clearly inflated the win totals of the division's better teams, producing
three with 97 or more victories. The Yanks' 100 wins that year were only
three more than the previous year, before the expansion. In other words,
not as good a year, all things considered. And why did they get over the
hump and win the World Series in 1977 after failing the year before? To
be sure, part of it was Jackson having a big series, most famously his historic three-homer night in the Game 6 clincher. Part of it is the random
luck which dictates that anything can happen in a short series between
two quality teams. But don't forget this: the Los Angeles Dodger club
they faced, as good as it was, wasn't the equal of the 1976 Big Red Machine, one of the great teams of all time. Given the dominant four game
sweep, does anyone really think that the Yankees would have beaten the
'76 Reds even with Jackson added to their lineup?

None of this is to say that Reggie wasn't a great player—he was. But
he was a great player in Oakland. In New York, where he played from
age 31 to age 35, he was a good player with a big personality, enough to
take the spotlight away from many of his teammates. Let's take a close
look at his career for a moment. Jackson was an annual average six-win
player across eight years with the Oakland A's from 1968 to 1975, with

four top-five MVP finishes. After a season in Baltimore which was also outstanding (league-leading .502 slugging percentage, 27 homers, 5.3 WAR), Jackson signed his lucrative deal with the Yankees amid much fanfare. In five years there from 1977 to 1981, he was never a six-win player, or even a five-win player. Reggie's 17.1 WAR (3.4 per year) in New York not only fell short of Randolph and Nettles during the same period, it didn't quite match the 18.3 WAR that Wade Boggs later put up in his five Yankee seasons from 1993 to 1997. But of course Boggs's number 12 isn't on the Yankee Stadium wall alongside Jackson's number 44. His Cooperstown bust doesn't have him donning a Yankee cap, as Reggie's does. Boggs is remembered as a decent late-career Yankee after a superstar run with the Red Sox. His .313 average in pinstripes seemed run of the mill compared to his .338 average and five batting titles during his nine years in Boston. Boggs did win a World Series in New York, but not until his age 38 season when he was seen as one cog in a long line of solid contributors, not so much as a major force.

So Jackson and Boggs share very similar achievements—both were superstars with previous clubs who came to New York for five years and did well, though without replicating their best seasons. But of the two, it's only Reggie who holds a rep as a "Yankee great." Shows what charisma and one big World Series night can do. Wade Boggs, much like Willie Randolph or Graig Nettles, simply wasn't "the straw that stirred the drink," as Jackson was. Or at least as Jackson proclaimed himself to be and was largely perceived to be. Reggie didn't hit line drives, he hit home runs. He hit some of them very far. He hit them with swagger. He hit three of them in a single World Series game against the Dodgers, a one-night feat that had fans understandably screaming themselves hoarse with "Reg-gie" and that practically guaranteed legend status (but a one-night feat nonetheless). He feuded with Billy Martin, Thurman Munson, and George Steinbrenner, keeping him on the back pages regularly. Reality is that on both of the Yankee world championship teams he played on in 1977 and 1978, Reggie, by the advanced numbers, was the team's sixth-best player, trailing Nettles, Guidry, and Randolph in both seasons.

If this seems like a lot of harping on Reggie, there's a reason—while some players like Jackson have that quality that allows them to take advantage of the New York spotlight, plenty of others don't. Willie Randolph's 13-year run as the quiet glue of the Yankee infield may have been appreciated by his managers and coaches, but it didn't get him "Will-ee" chants from the stands. This book focuses on those like him. We pay tribute to those players who stand as the most underrated in Yankee and Met history over the past 40 years or so, at least from a Hall of Fame perspective. Why those who seemingly had all the bases covered—genuinely great careers, World Series titles and the big stage—still managed to get hosed by Hall voters. As much as it may seem illogical to include World Series rings as measuring devices of a player's value in a team sport, most pundits do seem inclined to give it some weight. So we'll focus on those who have won the hardware in New York.

As for our featured seven, we mostly know the reasons for the snubs beyond the big shadows of Carter, Jeter, Jackson and Seaver. Hernandez? Not enough homers for a first baseman. Guidry and Cone? Not enough wins. Koosman? Nice pitcher, but never really an ace, exactly. Williams? His peak ended too abruptly. Nettles and Randolph? Complementary pieces, not straws that stirred drinks. And it's all nonsense. We'll show the genuine greatness of these players in a few ways: advanced stats (sabermetrics), which weren't around when they were playing but eye-opening to look at in hindsight. Even if you're not particularly a SABR person, the traditional stats (batting average, home runs, earned run average, etc.) look much different when you place them in the context of the era in which they occur. Examples: Starting pitchers didn't win (or lose) as many games in the 1990s and 2000s as they did in the 1960s and 1970s when bullpens weren't used as extensively. Offensive output has always ebbed and flowed in different eras, with the 1970s and '80s emerging as a pitcher-friendly period with low wattage offense. That would mean that Graig Nettles, who hit an impressive but not eye-popping 390 homers in his career, would have likely hit the 500-homer mark had he played two decades later, when many more home runs were flying out of big-league ballparks. That offensively fueled era of the 1990s was when David Cone was pitching for the Yankees, leading him to a career 3.46 ERA that seems high for the Hall of Fame but looks a lot better in context. And so it goes for many others.

These days, teams value on-base percentage, slugging percentage and WHIP more than batting average, RBIs and wins. We're more enlightened about what makes a great player. Does it not make sense to take a look back at those who played under the old-school metrics and consider their careers in a new light? There's a group of players out there that deserve their due.

1

Ron Guidry

You've seen and heard it many times. The pitcher for the home team gets two strikes on a hitter, and the noise begins. The rhythmic clapping starts up, and then gets louder as the crowd rises to its collective feet, trying to will their pitcher toward that third strike. If he gets it, the crowd gets to let out a big scream. The two-strike clap fest has been going on for so long now that an entire generation of fans has come to know it as the norm, a routine part of the night's entertainment.

But if you've ever wondered whether the custom has an origin, it does. It was born on June 17, 1978, at Yankee Stadium. That night, Yankee lefthander Ron Guidry took his 10–0 record and 1.57 ERA to the mound against the California Angels. An uneven start to the season had the Yankees seven games behind the Boston Red Sox in the American League East, a repeat of their 1977 World Series title looking ominous. Leadoff hitter and catalyst Mickey Rivers had just hit the disabled list that morning. Manager Billy Martin was a month away from his first firing by George Steinbrenner. Reliever Sparky Lyle, the 1977 A.L. Cy Young Award winner, was throwing flat sliders to the tune of a 4.00 ERA as he moped over his reduced role in the wake of George Steinbrenner's signing of Rich ("Goose") Gossage the previous winter. Lyle's book *The Bronx Zoo* would reveal much of the team dysfunction when it came out the following year. With things looking off kilter in Yankee Land, fans were latching onto Guidry's first half dominance as the main show.

And he was only getting better as the 1978 season moved along. Guidry had reeled off double-digit strikeouts in his past three outings as he piled up innings, Ks and wins. Still, he wasn't particularly feeling it on this night after his pregame warmup. As he grabbed his jacket and left the bullpen, he told Lyle to be ready early.

Sure enough, things didn't start well.[1] The game's first batter,

Bobby Grich, laced a double to left field. Guidry got a strikeout when no. 2 hitter Rick Miller failed on sacrifice attempt and then and foul tipped a two-strike pitch into catcher Thurman Munson's glove. Then came a hard smash up the middle by Dave Chalk. The spry Guidry was able to deflect Chalk's shot with his glove and then chase the ball down

Ron Guidry earned Cy Young Award votes in six seasons and won five Gold Gloves as the American League's best fielding pitcher.

in time to get him at first. Three batters, two hard-hit balls. But with veteran Joe Rudi at the plate, Guidry threw a vicious slider that hit the inside corner at the knees for strike three. Guidry gave up a walk in the second inning but struck out Brian Downing on a hard swing at a high fastball to escape trouble. Two more hits came in the top of the third, but so did three more strikeouts. Through three innings, he had six Ks. Then in the fourth, Don Baylor, Ron Jackson and Merv Rettenmund all went down swinging. The Yankees already had a 4–0 lead, and Guidry was getting stronger.

By the end of the sixth inning, he'd struck out every Angel hitter at least once after Chalk, Rudi, and Baylor all whiffed. The mix of low sliders and high fastballs was just too much. The K count was 14 and growing. As Guidry faced Downing with two out in the top of the seventh, an unmistakable phenomenon was taking shape. The 33,162 fans in attendance were having so much fun watching Guidry blow away the Angels that they weren't waiting for a third strike to make noise. The strikeout was no longer just a pleasing result, it was now the expectation. And the Stadium crowd didn't merely want to see it, it wanted to be part of it. With two strikes on Downing, the noise grew. People stood and put their hands together, wanting to believe they were transferring their energy to their skinny (5–11, 160 pounds) left-hander. When Downing flailed at another high fastball for strike three, the place exploded as Guidry sprinted off the mound.

The only real drama remaining over the final two innings was over Guidry's chase of the all-time record of 19 strikeouts in a nine-inning game. He came up one short when Ron Jackson bounced one to third for the final out, leaving Guidry with 18 strikeouts. His record was 11–0. Going back to August 10, 1977, his record was 19–1 with a 1.75 ERA and 166 strikeouts over 195 innings. You may know the rest of the 1978 story. The Yankees fell 14½ games behind the Red Sox by mid–July, stormed back to a 3½ game lead, fell back into a tie, and then beat Boston in a one-game tiebreaker at Fenway Park on a home run by Bucky Dent off Mike Torrez. Then they repeated their 1977 series wins over Kansas City and Los Angeles to take a second straight title. Guidry won the tiebreaker in Boston on three days' rest to finish the season 25–3 with a 1.74 ERA, .946 WHIP and a 9.6 WAR. His 248 strikeouts and nine shutouts are still Yankee single-season records. Guidry followed with one win apiece against the Royals and Dodgers in the postseason. It was one of the great pitching seasons in baseball history.

Barely more than a year had passed since Guidry had been a Yankee afterthought while Tom Seaver, Steve Carlton, Jim Palmer, Bert Blyleven and a few others reigned as baseball's dominant pitchers. Now, seemingly out of nowhere, he was better than all of them. The Louisiana native with the dark hair and thick Cajun accent was a third-round draft pick by the Yankees out of the University of Southwestern Louisiana (since renamed the University of Louisiana at Lafayette) in 1971, the same draft that produced Mike Schmidt, Jim Rice, Keith Hernandez and George Brett. Thirty-two pitchers were taken ahead of Guidry, only two of whom, Frank Tanana and Rick Rhoden, went on to make any real noise in the major leagues.

He didn't exactly fast track his way through the system. By age 26, Guidry had appeared in all of 17 major league games, mostly getting knocked around to the tune of 18 runs in 32 innings in 1975 and '76. Guidry had always been able to throw hard dating back to his American Legion days in Louisiana.[2] But his path to the majors was slowed by two things: lack of a potent secondary pitch that could complement his fastball, and an inability to throw strikes consistently. In his first year of A-ball in Ft. Lauderdale in 1972, he struck out 61 hitters in 63 innings but also walked 50. At Double-A West Haven two years later, it was 79 Ks and 53 walks in 77 innings. Later, his cameos with the Yankees brought the same mix of promise and disappointment. A call up in August 1976 illustrated perfectly. Brought in by Martin to face the Baltimore Orioles in the fifth inning at Yankee Stadium with his team behind 4–0, Guidry excited the crowd by pumping a third-strike fastball past future teammate Reggie Jackson for the first out. But the good vibes didn't last. Lee May singled, Ken Singleton walked, Doug DeCinces and Dave Duncan both doubled. Three runs were in before Guidry was out of the inning, the game now out of hand. Five years into his pro career, he thought about quitting.

Peter Golenbock is a veteran New York writer and author or co-author of several baseball books, including *The Bronx Zoo* with Sparky Lyle. He got to know Guidry very well while doing a book with him in the early 1980s (*Guidry*—1983). He recalls at least one reason why the pitcher hung in there as his career teetered. "The second baseman from Ron's Little League team was his closest friend and wound up becoming his financial advisor," recalls Golenbock, who now lives in Florida. "But he wound up losing a good bit of money and had to go back to the minors for at least one more year."

The financial bath turned out to be a blessing. Sticking it out gave Guidry a chance to improve his slider with the help of Lyle, a fellow left-hander who used the pitch almost exclusively to dominate as a reliever for much of the '70s. Lyle's pointers helped Guidry's slider break down more sharply, giving him a legitimate out pitch to mix in with his heat. Using essentially just those two pitches, his confidence and his control improved quickly. His alarming 5.4 walks per nine innings as a minor leaguer would ultimately drop all the way to 2.4 per nine as a major leaguer. The low-key Lyle has never spoken much about his mentor role with Guidry, which doesn't surprise those who know him. Golenbock remembers that Lyle never sought attention for helping a teammate, which he saw as something a veteran ought to do. And Marty Appel, the Yankees' public relations director from 1973 to 1977 and later an executive producer of Yankee telecasts for WPIX, recalls that "Lyle was like that, he was very affable. But the effect on Guidry of having Sparky mentor him was tremendous." Lyle's observation of potential greatness in his young teammate and Guidry's respect for Lyle's expertise "says a lot about both of them," Appel says.

There was also Guidry's unwavering work ethic, which extended past the diamond and into the gym. Golenbock claims to have seen the rail thin Guidry bench press 500 pounds. Even if Golenbock's memory exaggerates a bit on that one, the point is clear. "Ron looked like a string bean, but he was very powerful," he says.

Guidry's improvement came just in time to help the Yankees, who came very close to losing him just as he was about to put it all together. Steinbrenner, never known for his patience, was ready to trade the late blooming pitcher. Luckily his main baseball man, Yankee president Gabe Paul, never wavered as a Guidry believer. "George was ready to trade him, and he was also prepared to lose him in the [1977] expansion draft," says Appel. "But Gabe Paul talked George into trusting the scouting reports."

Guidry wound up sticking with the Yankees when the 1977 season opened. Pitching under Martin, a manager who was never particularly inclined to trust rookies, he got into just a handful of games during the first month, all but one of them in relief. But when he got a second spot start in Oakland on May 17, he pitched a five-hitter into the ninth in a game the Yankees would win in extra innings. At the same time, issues were popping up among some veteran Yankee pitchers. Ken Holtzman was ineffective early before being yanked from the regular rotation in late May, and then Don Gullett and Catfish Hunter later missed time with injuries. Guidry had an opening as a regular starter the rest of the way, and he took advantage. His first win as a starter came on April 29 when he shut out Seattle for eight-plus innings with eight strikeouts, with his new mentor Lyle picking him up for last two outs. Guidry's first complete game was a three-hit shutout over Kansas City on June 16, followed three starts later by a complete game, nine-strikeout shutout of Detroit on July 3. For the first time in his young career, Guidry was rolling. Good-bye, fledgling major leaguer, hello Louisiana Lightning.

He wound up the 1977 season 16–7 with a 2.82 ERA in 210 innings, closing with 10 wins in his last 13 starts as the Yankees rallied to take the division from Boston and Baltimore. A season that he'd begun as a little used reliever wound up with a handful of Cy Young Award and MVP votes next to his name. Despite a delayed entry into the rotation that limited him to 25 starts, Guidry finished ninth in the league in strikeouts (each of the eight pitchers ahead of him started 30 or more games). He followed the regular season with a complete game three-hitter over the Royals in Game 2 of the A.L.C.S., and, after stumbling in the decisive Game 5 when he put the Yankees into an early 3–1 hole before an excellent long relief job by Mike Torrez allowed the team to rally back and win, beat the Dodgers on a four-hitter in Game 4 of the World Series to give his team a commanding three games to one lead. Later, memories of Guidry's pivotal Game 4 performance in L.A. were mostly drowned out by Reggie Jackson's famous three-homer night in the Yanks' clinching Game 6 victory, but it was certainly just as important. The table for Guidry's big 1978 season had been set—his tremendous year should not have particularly been a surprise, even if the extent of it was. Appel isn't sure he agrees. "It was shocking to me," he says. "The combination of his cunning and his ability was fun to watch."

Add up Guidry's tear from late July of 1977 through the end of 1978, including the two postseasons, and this is what you get: 39–5, 1.89 ERA, 419 innings, 362 Ks. His thorough dominance in '78 that led that led the Yankees to a second straight championship assured Guidry a place in the history books. But in a way it was probably his curse as well. The dreaded bar had been raised—Guidry was never going to top 1978. When he led the American League in ERA again in 1979 while going 18–8 and finishing second to Nolan Ryan in strikeouts, people mostly yawned. When your ERA goes up by a full run per game—to 2.78 from 1.74—there's a natural disappointment. That it still ranked as tops in the league seemed secondary. So went the next eight years of Guidry's career, a body of work destined to live in the shadow of 1978.

Ron Guidry's Yankee career officially ran from 1975 to 1988. Putting aside the brief partial seasons at the beginning and the end, it ran from 1977 to 1987, an 11-year stretch that saw him go 168–87 with a 3.25 ERA over an average of 210 innings a year. His .659 winning percentage outdistanced his team's winning percentage by 89 points, a spread that's right up there with, and in many cases superior to, those of several Hall of Famer pitchers.

Some may also remember that Guidry's pinstripe career coincided with the truly zany days of George Steinbrenner's reign, when managers and coaches were well advised to rent in New York rather than own, when a player bobbling a grounder in a key situation had to prep for a public scolding from The Boss. While the Bombers usually had plenty of talent and won plenty of games in the late 1970s and 1980s, Steinbrenner's haphazard style kept them in the news as much for being a carnival act as a baseball club. Guidry wound up playing for seven Yankee managers—eight if you count his two games under Bill Virdon in 1975 (Guidry debuted in the big leagues on July 27, 1975, at Shea Stadium with two scoreless innings against the Red Sox, six days before Virdon was fired and replaced by Billy Martin, who would come and go five separate times). He worked under 11 different pitching coaches, five of them in 1982 alone. The revolving door for Yankee pitching coaches became more comical than the one for managers—Clyde King and Art Fowler came through three times apiece. In the middle of all the chaos came the worst part of all—the sudden and shocking death of Guidry's catcher, Thurman Munson, in a 1979 plane crash. It's a wonder that Guidry managed to keep his mind and his mechanics together for a full decade.

Guidry pitched through constant starting rotation turnover, when the Yankees were trying to fill post-championship gaps with aging versions of Luis Tiant, Gaylord Perry, Phil Niekro, and Joe Niekro. Mediocrity in the form of Dennis Rasmussen, Shane Rawley and Bob Shirley came and went, along with the disaster of Ed Whitson, a right-hander signed as a free agent who not only once beat up Martin in a Baltimore bar, he became so shaken by the fans' reaction to his 5.38 ERA in pinstripes that the team took to sometimes limiting his home games. But through it all, Guidry just kept pitching. He carried himself like a modern-day model for Rudyard Kipling—keeping his head when all about him were losing theirs. Amid so many distractions, a Guidry start seemed like a return to normalcy every five days.

So how does Ron Guidry compare to some fellow Yankee greats?

For a big stretch of the 1930s and early '40s, Lefty Gomez and Red Ruffing were the co-aces of a Yankee club that won six World Series titles. You could call them something of a lesser version of a Koufax-Drysdale tandem of their day, anchoring the pitching staff of a league power-house. Gomez captured three A.L. strikeout titles and two ERA titles while turning in four 20-win seasons. Ruffing, who had suffered through seven miserable years in Boston during his early career when he went 39–96 (yes, you read that correctly, 39 wins and 96 losses) pitching for awful Red Sox teams, was paroled to the Yankees in a May 1930 trade and promptly went 15–5. He became a Yankee mainstay, compiling a 231–124 record with 40 shutouts over 15 years. Ruffing was a 20-game winner on four straight Yankee World Series champs from 1936 to 1939.

Both Ruffing and Gomez are in the Baseball Hall of Fame. They weren't slam dunk choices—both waited 20 years or more to get there—but they're in. Were either of them any better than Ron Guidry? Not really. It's Gomez whose career compares more directly with Guidry's based on length and numbers. Gomez went 189–102 with a 3.34 ERA in 14 seasons, very close to Guidry's run. Putting each pitcher's career stats into the context of their respective eras shows a very close call. Gomez pitched to an ERA that was 27 percent below the A.L. average during his career, a bit better than Guidry's 18 percent. Gomez was a big strikeout pitcher in his day, whiffing hitters at a rate per nine innings that was 54 percent better than league average, topping Guidry's still-excellent 36 percent rate. Guidry had the slight edge in WHIP (walks and hits allowed per inning), 14 percent better than league average to Gomez's 11 percent. Guidry's career 3.27 mark in Fielding Independent Pitching (FIP—the now widely-used measure of how effectively a pitcher avoids walks and home runs while amassing strikeouts, factors he can control independent of his team's defense) was 19 percent better than a typical pitcher during his era, topping Gomez's 3.88 FIP that was 12 percent better than his peers, who pitched in the relatively hitter-friendly decade of the 1930s.

Ruffing? His one legitimate advantage over Guidry is the breadth that comes from a longer career, which certainly ought to count signifi-cantly. Ruffing won 103 more major league and pitched some 1,900 more innings that Guidry did across a two-decade career. But his year-by-year performance doesn't compare very favorably. He comes in behind Guidry in all of the major measurement categories by besting the league average in FIP, ERA, strikeouts and WHIP by lower margins than Guidry did.

Checking Wins Above Replacement, Guidry's 48.1 career WAR ranks ahead of 11 of 63 starting pitchers currently in the Hall, including Gomez (43.1). Ruffing, who pitched eight more seasons than Guidry did, put up a higher career WAR (55.4) but with a lower annual average and a lesser peak. Guidry was a four-plus-win player six times, Gomez five times and Ruffing just four, with a couple of near-misses (a 4.0 WAR is generally considered All-Star level). Most everyone agrees that some balance of dominance and longevity is the best way to rate a player's ultimate value. Where people differ is exactly how to break the two down—if you lean toward more durability over a period of time, you'll take Ruffing. For more big seasons, it's Guidry and Gomez, with Guidry getting the edge by a hair. One thing is for sure—there's little to choose among the three. With Gomez and Ruffing both in the Hall, Guidry should be too.

The man who later succeeded Ruffing and Gomez as an ace of a Yankee dynasty was, of course, Whitey Ford, who burst onto the scene in as a 21-year-old in mid–1950 and went 9–1 with a 2.81 ERA to help the Yankees take the A.L. flag by three games over the Detroit Tigers. Ford then beat the Phillies in Game 4 of the 1950 World Series, the clincher in the Yanks' four game sweep. After a two-year military hitch, Ford made it back to the Yankees in 1953 and immediately took over as the staff ace, a notch above aging veterans Vic Raschi, Eddie Lopat and Allie Reynolds. Ford went on to a stellar career in which he went 236–106 with a 2.75 ERA through 1967.

A left hander and New York City native who got to pitch for the Yankees during their dynasty days of the 1950s and early 1960s, Ford became of a major face of that dynasty, right up there with Yogi Berra and Ford's close friend, Mickey Mantle. Ford pitched in 11 World Series, starting 22 games. For much of America tuning in every October, watching Whitey Ford pitch in the World Series was like an annual rite of autumn. He was "the Chairman of the Board," as the press tagged him. Ford's 10 World Series wins still stand as an all-time record, a stat that earned him a reputation as a big-game pitcher. He made it into the Hall of Fame on his second try in 1974, enshrined alongside his buddy, Mantle.

Ford's quick election to the Hall stirred some minor controversy initially, when a lot of people questioned his status over that of Robin Roberts, a clearly superior pitcher of the same era whose winning percentage and postseason resume didn't match Ford's only because of the inferior Phillies teams he pitched for. But that talk died down quickly, especially after Roberts got his due two years later. The Roberts comparison aside, there's never been much debate over the Cooperstown credentials of Whitey Ford, the best pitcher on baseball's best team for many years. But if Whitey Ford was any better than Ron Guidry, it was by an eyelash. First some quick perspective on the World Series numbers: Ford did win a record 10 series games, but he also lost eight others. His 2.71 career Series ERA essentially matched his 2.75 regular season mark. In other words, Ford was basically the same pitcher in the postseason that he was during the regular season, pretty much what you'd expect once the postseason workload grows to a significant sample size. You do have to give him a little bonus for the higher concentration of talent he was facing in series play, but the numbers aren't too surprising over 22 games and 146 innings. Guidry didn't get the chance to pitch in nearly as many World Series games as Ford did, but when he did get there, he was stellar. In four series starts across 1977, '78, and '81, Guidry went 3–1 with a 1.69 ERA, striking out 26 in 32 innings.

As for career body of work, Ford naturally gets a lot kudos for his spectacular .690 winning percentage, the third-highest ever among pitchers with at least 1,000 innings. And yet—the spread between Ford's winning percentage and the winning percentage of the great Yankee teams he pitched for was virtually identical to Guidry's spread with his clubs. Digging through the nitty gritty of the career numbers shows a virtual tie between the two lefty aces. Guidry was a far better strikeout pitcher, his rate of fanning hitters at 36 percent better than league average dwarfing Ford's 15 percent clip. Ford had the advantage in WHIP, 26 percent better than the league compared to Guidry's 14 percent. Ford also had a slightly better ERA compared to his peers—26 percent below league average while Guidry was 18 percent below (that comparison corresponds closely to ERA-plus, which factors in ballpark conditions in addition to league average; Ford had the ERA-plus edge 133–119). The Fielding Independent Pitching edge goes to Guidry, 19 percent better than league average to Ford's 15 percent.

Ford's advantage in breadth—both pitchers had a couple of brief, pre or post-prime years that left Ford with 14 productive Yankee seasons to Guidry' 11—explains his edge in career WAR over Guidry of 53.9 to

48.1. Quite close. And as with the comparison to Red Ruffing, breadth is only part of the story. The numbers show that Guidry had a better peak than Ford, averaging 5.7 wins in best six seasons compared to Ford's 4.9 wins. Broadening the peak to each pitcher's 10 best years, Guidry still holds a slight edge of 4.9 to 4.6 wins per year. Ultimately, a few additional solid seasons pushed Ford's career WAR a few points higher, but the dominance-longevity balance leaves almost nothing to choose between the two—Guidry a hair better over 10 years, Ford adding a little more at the end. Yet Ford hit 67 percent of the Hall of Fame vote in his first year on the ballot, and then got over the 75 percent hump in his second year. Guidry? Not even double digits—he peaked at 8.8 percent of the vote in 2000. If only Guidry had control over getting his team to the World Series more often, he could have become a national face of October, too. And probably gotten himself into the Hall of Fame.

Stepping outside of the Yankee world for a moment, another Hall of Fame pitcher whom Guidry compares closely to is Dizzy Dean, the St. Louis Cardinal great from the 1930s. Like Guidry, Dean had a relatively brief career peak. Not because he was a fellow late bloomer but because of a fractured toe he suffered from a line drive off the bat of Earl Averill in the 1937 All-Star Game. Dean compensated for the toe injury with altered mechanics, leading to arm woes that eventually ended his career four years later at age 31 (not including a one-game comeback in 1947 that ended with a pulled hamstring). Looking through the numbers, Dean's signature 1934 season (a 30–7 record including four wins in relief, a 2.66 ERA, a league leading 195 strikeouts, 8.5 WAR) doesn't quite match Guidry's monster 1978 season. Dean's six-year peak between 1932 and 1937 looks better than Guidry's best six years, but not by much— Dean outperformed the league average in strikeouts, ERA and WHIP by just slightly larger margins than Guidry did while averaging a 6.4 WAR to Guidry' 5.8. Considering Guidry's handful of solid "tack on" seasons beyond his peak that Dean lacked, Guidry's overall body of work looks better (his 48.1 career WAR beats Dean's 42.7). In other words, Dean was better for six years, Guidry was better for 10 years.

So why was Dizzy Dean voted into the Hall of Fame with 79 percent of the vote in 1953 while Ron Guidry failed to hit the 10 percent mark before falling off the ballot after seven years? Part of it may be sympathy for Dean's injury that robbed him of some potential prime years. Had it not been for the fluke bad luck of Averill's line drive, Dean surely would have had better career numbers, right? Well, probably.

But since when do players get elected to the Hall of Fame for numbers that might have been? There's no telling when Dean's decline may have begun—that's a variable that differs widely with different players. In the end, the numbers are the numbers, and Dean's are no more Hall of Fame worthy than Guidry's are.

But sometimes the way in which the numbers are compiled can create what MLB Network's Brian Kenny calls "a perception problem." That is, a general perception that Guidry was less than a Hall of Fame pitcher because, unlike Dizzy Dean, he didn't particularly have a large number of great years right in a row. Guidry did have a couple of high ERA years sprinkled between some of his better seasons during the first half of the 1980s, making his "peak" a bit difficult to locate. "You have a little slump in the middle, so you sort of have to piece it together" to find Guidry's Hall cred, says Kenny, a noted sabrematrician and baseball historian who likes to study the Hall worthiness of myriad players across different eras. His comparative analysis shows that players from 1980s and 1990s are very much underrepresented with barely more than 10 percent of all Hall inductees. A good example of a notably snubbed player on Kenny's list: former Indians (and briefly, Yankees) outfielder Kenny Lofton, a four-win player per year over 17 years and a six-win player in his 10 best.

Kenny's theory is that aside from a patently obvious case like Randy Johnson or Ken Griffey, Jr., it's difficult for many of us to think of those relatively recent players we saw with our own eyes as being in the same place as those we read about from history, who seem almost mythical. Could Kenny Lofton really have been as good as Duke Snider, the legendary Brooklyn Dodger? To some the question might seem almost blasphemous. We're talking about the Duke of Flatbush, the man immortalized in song as part of the "Willie, Mickey, and the Duke" trio after the years he spent roaming centerfield in New York at the same time Willie Mays and Mickey Mantle were. But tuning out the sentiment, the numbers show that yes, Lofton was just as good, his speed and defense countering Snider's power. So it goes with Ron Guidry and Dizzy Dean. Of course, to today's younger crowd, Guidry is very much an old-timer himself. But there are still plenty of fans and voters around who remember him. Guidry isn't quite as high on Kenny's snub list as Lofton is, but the numbers say that he would certainly fit comfortably into the Hall of Fame's lower to middle class, sharing space with Burleigh Grimes, Early Wynn, and Addie Joss in addition to Gomez, Ruffing, Ford, and Dean.

Says Kenny: "Vastly underrated, I like Guidry a lot. I'd have no problem voting for him."

The Guidry-Dean comparison is much like Lofton-Snider—it conjures up that "lore" factor that infests professional sports history. Dizzy Dean wasn't just a top pitcher of his day, he was "Ole Diz," one of baseball's great personalities. The Depression-era "Gashouse Gang" Cardinals, playing before the days of television, carry a certain lore in baseball history, with Dean leading a cast of colorful characters that included Leo Durocher, Pepper Martin, and Joe "Ducky" Medwick. It was a club whose gritty style personified the tough times of the 1930s. Dean, who supposedly coined the phrase "it ain't braggin' if you can back it up," went on to a broadcasting career during which he charmed audiences with his Arkansas drawl and butchery of the English language. One widely-quoted story had him telling a local school teacher who had asked him to improve his grammar for the sake of the children tuning in: "Teach, you learn 'em English and I'll learn 'em baseball."

Ron Guidry was never immortalized as a great character during baseball's radio days. Ron Guidry was boring. His team certainly had plenty of characters, but he really wasn't one of them. He was the bland one, the guy who shied away from controversy and self-promotion. When asked once about his memorable 18-strikeout game years later, he described it as "just something that happened."[3] Perhaps some Hall of Fame voters believe that when it comes to assessing a player's value to his sport that showmanship counts, which is their prerogative. But if we're just talking about baseball, there's really no rationale for Dizzy Dean over Ron Guidry.

Another obvious mark against Guidry: "only" 170 career wins, without the mitigating factor of a significant injury like Dean's as an excuse (Dean finished his career 150–83). But one problem with tallying up career wins is that statistical norms change across different eras. Through the years, as four-man rotations yielded to five-man rotations and bullpens began carrying heavier loads, win totals for starters naturally decreased. Both Lefty Gomez and Red Ruffing pitched to a decision in more than 90 percent of their career starts. For Guidry it was just over 80 percent. For most pitchers since Guidry's day, it's been even less. It's no coincidence that of the 50 pitchers with the most wins in MLB history, only eight began their careers after 1975, when Guidry broke in. But more important than tracking win opportunities is this: the statistic itself has always been quite overrated when it comes to evaluating a pitcher. Think about it—the "win" is really nothing more than a derivative stat that's based as much on the quality of a team as it is on the quality of the pitcher. Go out and give up, say, two runs over seven innings? That's a good outing. But whether you walk away with a win, a loss or a no-decision isn't something you can control. It depends, obviously, on the run support you got from your team. Anyone who pitches that well consistently is bound to win more often than he loses, but that fact just strengthens the view that won-lost record is more of an indicator than a performance metric in and of itself. You won because you pitched well (and got run support), you didn't pitch well because you won.

A lot of modern baseball pundits have taken to downplaying wins and losses for measuring pitchers. None more so than Kenny, who has been railing against them for a while now with a campaign he calls #killthewin that's drawn a ton of followers on twitter and even spawned a t-shirt. Some might find Kenny's prescription of tossing the stat altogether a bit radical, but many fans and pundits have casually downplayed the won-lost stat for years. Among many examples, those old enough to remember the 1987 season may recall Nolan Ryan going 8–16 for the Houston Astros even as he led the National League in both ERA and strikeouts. People mostly dismissed his poor won-lost record as one of those fluke things, a simple case of bad luck. And they were right— pitching for the league's second-lowest scoring team, Ryan lost seven games in which he allowed two or fewer runs. Yet it's hard for many of us to let go of wins altogether—just too much history.

Progress has been sporadic in recent years. The new age thinkers made some headway as far back as 2010 when writers voted the American League Cy Young Award to Seattle's Felix Hernandez, who finished that season with a 13–12 record. When you lead the league in innings, ERA and fewest hits allowed per nine innings while missing the strikeout crown by one K, it's tough for anyone to argue that you weren't the deserving winner. Still, Hernandez's victory was seen as a sign of progress, since the voters could have easily gone the traditional route and latched onto the 19–6 record put up by Tampa Bay's David Price, whose all-around stats weren't too far behind Hernandez's.

Things regressed in 2016 when the A.L. Cy Young Award went to Boston's Rick Porcello, who went 22–4 that year but finished fifth among pitchers in WAR, fifth in ERA, fourth in innings, and eighth in strikeouts. Porcello had a very nice year, and he did finish no. 2 in the league in WHIP, but how many people would really doubt that Justin Verlander or

Cory Kluber, who both finished in the top five in WAR, innings pitched, ERA, strikeouts and WHIP, were the American League's two best pitchers in 2016?

Then modern thinking made a comeback in 2018 when the Mets' Jacob deGrom came away with the National League hardware despite a 10–9 record, setting a mark for the fewest wins ever by a Cy Young Award-winning starter. DeGrom's thorough dominance in 2018–1.70 ERA, 0.912 WHIP, 269 strikeouts in 217 innings and a 9.6 pitching WAR that matched Guidry's 1978 mark—may wind up as the big breakthrough that finally decouples wins from strong pitching altogether. We'll see.

With modern thinking focusing on overall effectiveness more than wins, does it not make sense to give pitchers from yesteryear a fresh look? Whether in the 1970s, 1980s or 2010s, strong outings don't always show up in the win column. In 1982, for example, Guidry (under the tutelage of his five pitching coaches) put up a solid but unspectacular 14–8 record. What that record doesn't show are the five starts that year in which he went at least seven innings while giving up three or fewer runs without getting a win. Those quality starts were reflected in Guidry's 222 innings and in his 162 strikeouts, fourth-most in the league. But they weren't reflected in his won-lost record. So, really, how much do the wins mean? Guidry's 4.1 WAR in 1982 was only a bit behind his 4.5 WAR in 1985, when he went 22–6 for a far better Yankee team. Glancing at the wins and losses, you'd think that Guidry was merely decent in '82 and outstanding in '85. In reality, there was little difference between the two seasons. Career win total? What does it matter? For a decade, Ron Guidry was one of the best in the game at pitching large numbers of innings and keeping opponents off the scoreboard. That's what matters, because that's what he could control. On that score, Guidry's numbers stand strong against some of the all-time greats from his era. His 119 ERA-plus is slightly better than Bert Blyleven, Steve Carlton and Nolan Ryan, and not far behind Tom Seaver and Jim Palmer. The same with Guidry's 1.184 WHIP—better than Carlton, Blyleven and Ryan and close to Seaver and Palmer. Not to say that Guidry compares favorably to anyone in this group. He doesn't, because his numbers weren't compiled across nearly as many games or innings. But his ability to match some of the top pitchers in history for a not-insignificant period of time says a lot.

Actually, it may be the presence of guys like Seaver, Carlton and Palmer before (and partially during) Guidry's run that may have been the biggest craw in Guidry's side. Rob Neyer is a longtime baseball reporter and author who once analyzed statistics at the side of Bill James. He observed that the glory days of aces in the 1960s and '70s—Koufax, Marichal, Gibson, Seaver, Carlton, Palmer—set a standard that was pretty much impossible for the next group to reach. "The '80s were kind of a black hole, you had guys like Lamarr Hoyt and Willie Hernandez winning the Cy Young," said Neyer, who could have thrown in John Denny, Steve Bedrosian and Mark Davis. It's a good point that the 1980s were sporadic when it came to pitching stars—Fernando Valenzuela and Dwight Gooden didn't sustain their early excellence for a whole lot of years and Roger Clemens didn't really get going until the latter half of the decade. But of course it isn't Guidry's fault that he came along on the heels of a handful of all-time greats. Not meeting the Seaver-Carlton standard doesn't necessarily mean you don't meet the Cooperstown standard. Says Neyer: "He falls in line with a lot of guys who are in."

As strongly as Guidry pitched through most of the 1980s, his star seemed to fade just a bit from the spotlight as the decade went along. The Yankees won more games than any team in the majors during the '80s but they didn't see the postseason after 1981. The mid-'80s clubs of Rickey Henderson, Don Mattingly and Dave Winfield competed strongly but could never take the division as A.L. East foes like Toronto, Boston and Detroit alternated strong seasons to finish first. After pitching in three World Series in his first five full seasons, Guidry never got a chance to go back. He was largely perceived simply as the steady holdover from the Yankee championship teams of the late '70s as the primary national spotlight moved on to pitchers like Bret Saberhagen, Roger Clemens, Frank Viola and Dave Stewart in the American League and to Fernando Valenzuela and Dwight Gooden in the National League. When Gooden, Guidry's New York counterpart with the Mets, burst onto the scene as a flame-throwing 19-year-old in 1984 with a rookie record 276 strikeouts, what did the delighted fans at a rejuvenated Shea Stadium do? They took up the Guidry-inspired practice of standing and clapping at every two-strike pitch he delivered. Shea even added a little twist every time Gooden got the third strike—the birth of the "K Corner" as fans by the mezzanine railing accompanied the roar by hanging a big "K" sign after each strikeout. The tradition continued as Gooden followed with his historic 24–4, 1.53, 268-strikeout season the following year, the Mets' answer to Guidry's 1978 magic. That Guidry was still going strong himself with a 22–6 record across town seemed secondary. There was clearly a new king of the New York hill—Dwight Gooden was the man. Guidry was steadily adding to his Hall of Fame case, but he had to settle for doing it quietly.

Ron Guidry's final appearance on a major league mound came on September 27, 1988, at Baltimore's Memorial Stadium. His opponent was a promising right-handed prospect making his third big-league appearance named Curt Schilling. At age 38, Guidry was clearly at the end of the road. He came into the game with 49 innings and one win for the season. But with the Yankees still mathematically alive in the A.L. East race with a week to go in the season, he came through with a final vintage performance, stymieing the Orioles for seven innings in a 5–1 win. Schilling gave up two early homers to Don Mattingly before he was pulled after four innings. He'd finish his 1988 September call up season 0–3 with a 9.82 ERA. By the end of the 1991 season, he'd have all of four major league wins. By the end of the 2007 season, he'd have 216 wins, 3,116 strikeouts (15th all time) and a resounding 80 WAR that ranks in the all-time top 25 for pitchers who are in the Hall of Fame or eligible to be voted on. Putting aside the disputed career numbers of PED suspect Roger Clemens, Schilling is probably the best pitcher in baseball history who is not in the Hall of Fame.

His struggle for proper recognition is similar to Guidry's—a career win total that impresses but maybe doesn't scream Hall of Fame. There's also a 3.46 career ERA that seems a bit high compared to past greats. What gets lost—again—is the perspective. If you do like wins as a metric, you still need to put them in the context of team quality. Schilling pitched for several mediocre Phillies teams in the 1990s, turning in winning records for losing Philly teams five separate times. Then upon his late career escape to better conditions in Arizona and Boston, Schilling put up a combined winning percentage of .661—quite close to Whitey Ford's historic number during his Yankee dynasty days. And his ordinary-looking ERA was actually outstanding in the context of the hitter-friendly era in which he pitched, when league averages were well over 4.00 year after year. With apologies to Clemens, Schilling's case is basically Guidry's case on steroids. It's doubtful that Ron Guidry and Curt Schilling commiserated over the flaws of Hall of Fame voting when their paths crossed for one game in 1988. But they could commiserate now.

2

Graig Nettles

On Friday night October 13, 1978, Graig Nettles jogged out to his position at third base, the same way he'd done it hundreds of times to kick off a game at Yankee Stadium. This time, though, the stakes were as high as they get. It was Game 3 of the 1978 World Series, essentially a must-win game for the Yankees, who trailed the Los Angeles Dodgers two games to none. Lose tonight, and a repeat of their 1977 championship would be virtually impossible. Nettles hadn't been much of a factor in the Yankees' two losses in Los Angeles, going 1-for-8, his only hit a meaningless RBI single late in a one-sided Game 1 loss.

The good news: the Yankees were back on their home turf in front of their boisterous fans, including VIPs Woody Allen and Mariel Hemmingway, co-stars of the upcoming movie *Manhattan*, right behind the home dugout. They also had their stud, Ron Guidry, going in Game 3. But as encouraging as Guidry's 25–3 record and 1.74 ERA were, there were those subtle signs that the heavy workload was catching up to him as the season wound down. Including his clinching Game 4 A.L.C.S. victory over Kansas City, Guidry hit the World Series with 282 innings under his belt for the season. He hadn't registered a double-digit strikeout game since August 4. On September 20 he'd been knocked out in the second inning at Toronto after giving up five runs. Working on short rest in the A.L East tiebreaker game in Boston on October 2, Guidry had battled hard while dancing around six hits and a walk over six and a third innings before turning the game over to Goose Gossage. Now here he was in the World Series on Friday the 13th, being asked to propel his struggling team back into it. Guidry was game, but he was tired. And as it turned out, he really didn't have it that night, allowing eight hits, several more hard-hit balls, and an almost unheard of seven walks. Normally those numbers would be catastrophic in such a big spot, nearly

2. Graig Nettles 27

ensuring a 0–3 series hole. But on this night they weren't. Guidry's third baseman had his back.

After the Yankees took an early lead on a Roy White homer in the first, Nettles led off the bottom of the second with a base hit off Dodger veteran Don Sutton and came around to score to make it 2–0. Throughout most of the 1978 season, an early two-run lead with Guidry on the

Graig Nettles played third base better than anyone in the 1970s and bashed 390 home runs in a pitching-friendly era.

mound was practically money in the bank. But not tonight. Guidry's struggles had already begun to show as he allowed three base runners in his first two innings, though he'd avoided damage thanks to Thurman Munson throwing out Bill Russell trying to steal in the first and Lee Lacy grounding into an around the horn double play started by Nettles in the second. Guidry began the top of the third by walking the speedy Bill North, who stole second and went to third on a groundout. With Dave Lopes at the plate, three of the four Yankee infielders played back, conceding the run in exchange for an out. Not Nettles, who positioned himself even with the third base bag, daring Lopes to hit one past him. The in-your-face approach was vintage Nettles, whose unwavering confidence in the field had a way of getting inside opponents' heads. "He had a presence when he was on the field," remembers Marty Appel. "It was 'hit your best shot at me.'"

Sure enough, that's just what Lopes did, drilling a laser beam right to third that left little time for reaction. But Nettles, almost casually, stuck his left gloved hand into the air to snag it. The run wound up scoring anyway when Russell followed with an infield single, but further potential damage had been minimized. Then Russell looked like he might be in position to score the tying run from first when the dangerous Reggie Smith hit a hard smash on one hop down the third base line that seemed destined for extra bases. But there went Nettles—diving to his backhand side, full extension, smothering the ball and popping up quickly to throw out Smith at first. He ran off the field to a huge roar. The Yankees still had the lead, 2–1.

Still down by just that one run in the top of the fifth, the Dodgers put runners on first and second with two down. Smith hit a hard in-between hop to third base that again tested Nettles' cat-like reflexes. He ranged to his right near the line and almost in self-defense managed to get his glove in front of the ball to knock it down. He wasn't able to make a play after the ball trickled a few feet away, so Smith wound up with an infield single. But as NBC announcer Tony Kubek noted, Nettles had certainly saved a run and possibly a double into the corner by keeping the ball in the infield. The game's biggest moment was now at hand with the bases loaded, two down, and Dodger cleanup hitter Steve Garvey at the plate. Garvey swung at a 0–1 slider from Guidry and hit one exactly where he didn't want to—toward third base. Once again there was Nettles, so quickly to his right toward the line that he almost overran the ball as he went to his backhand, which forced a split-second readjustment as he brought his extended glove hand back closer to his face before fielding the ball. A quick pivot and throw to second beat a sliding Smith by an eyelash for the inning-ending force play. Guidry, who had just allowed his fourth and fifth walks of the night, was out of another inning.

Nettles' glove had saved at least three runs, and he wasn't finished. With the Yankees still clinging to their 2–1 lead, Guidry's struggles continued in the sixth when he allowed two singles and another walk around a pair of flyball outs. For the second straight inning, the Dodgers had the bases full with two out. Lopes, who'd been making great contact all night, was up. Almost as if on cue, Lopes hit another hard smash down the third base line. Also on cue was Nettles, pouncing again to his right to backhand the ball on his knees and again pop up instantly for a throw to second for the force. At this point, it was hard to decide whether to be even more amazed by Nettles' latest gem or to just chalk it up as routine by now. Exclaimed Tom Seaver in the NBC booth: "I sit here and shake my head, he's incredible."[1]

The Yankees eventually earned some breathing room with a three-run seventh, an inning that ended with Nettles flying out to the warning track in right-center field. In a scenario that would never happen now, Guidry wound up going all the way in a 5–1 win. On a night when the lefty ace struck out only four, a night where he'd battled hard without his good stuff, Nettles had saved him at least five runs. The Yankees were now back in it, trailing two games to one. After pulling out a 10-inning win the following day to tie the series, they completed their four-game comeback by blasting the Dodgers by scores of 12–2 and 7–2 in the next two games. Guidry, seemingly going on fumes at this point, was spared a Game 7. For the second straight year, the Yankees were champions.

Nettles was quiet at the plate during the series, finishing 4-for-25. His partner on the left side of the Yankee infield, shortstop Bucky Dent, took series MVP honors by hitting .417 with seven RBI in the six games. Normally a light hitter, Dent had already been riding the charmed wave of sports celebrity following his huge three-run homer off Mike Torrez to beat Boston in the American League East tiebreaker and push the Yankees into the postseason. While Nettles' sparkling glove work against the Dodgers got its share of attention, it was Dent—the Fenway Park hero and World Series MVP—who was the toast of the town.

The 1978 World Series scored an average of 44.3 million viewers per game for NBC, still the highest rated series ever (and without a climactic Game 7, no less).[2] While those numbers raised the national profile of Nettles' superior fielding abilities, they didn't particularly surprise Yankee fans, who had been witnessing them since 1973. If anything, the '78 series had sold Nettles short—his glove had been on full display, but not his bat.

Mostly forgotten after Ron Guidry's historic season and Bucky Dent's postseason heroics was the enormous role that Graig Nettles had played in bringing the Yankees back from a 14½ game deficit to catch the Red Sox in the A.L. East. On July 17, with the Yankees in fourth place, Nettles' batting average stood at .239. He had two hits against the Kansas City Royals at Yankee Stadium that night, including his 17th homer, though the Yankees lost 9–7 in extra innings. But on the ensuing road trip through Minnesota, Chicago, and Kansas City, Nettles went 13-for-27 as the Yanks won six of seven. They pulled to within six and a half games of the Red Sox by early August before two losses to Boston dropped them to eight and a half back. But then the Yankees continued winning. From August 27 to September 4 they took nine out of ten as Nettles went 16-for-38 (.421) with no errors. Three days later began the four-game "Boston Massacre" sweep at Fenway Park which pulled the Yankees even with the Red Sox and set up their eventual win in the one game showdown on October 2.

From July 17 on, when the Yankees went 53–22 to snatch the division from the Red Sox, Nettles made exactly two errors at third base while hitting .315 to bring his season average to .276 with a .343 on-base percentage. His 27 home runs tied for ninth-most in the league. He drove in 93. Nettles' 5.7 WAR ranked number seven in the A.L. among everyday players.

And it's not as if 1978 was a career year for Nettles. It was actually right in line with what he'd been doing since the early '70s. An athletic San Diego native who played both baseball and basketball at San Diego State, Nettles was selected by the Minnesota Twins in the fourth round of baseball's inaugural 1965 draft. Six spots earlier, the Yankees had passed on him in favor University of Nebraska pitcher Stan Bahnsen, who turned in a few good years for them before he was dealt to the Chicago White Sox in 1972, the year before Nettles got to New York. Nettles got his first decent playing time for Minnesota in 1969, when he hit just .222 in 225 at-bats for a strong Twins team that won the A.L. West behind a manager named Billy Martin and the bats of Harmon Killebrew, Tony Oliva, and 23-year-old batting champion Rod Carew.

Killebrew, who blasted 49 homers in 1969, played mostly at third base that year, but he shifted to first for 66 games in part to make some room for Nettles, who divided his playing time between third and the outfield. No one could have known it at the time, but Nettles' limited rookie season wound up as a small-scale model for the rest of his career. There was the low batting average, which back then could make people dismiss you as an offensive force. Less noticed was Nettles' ability to draw walks that led to a .319 on-base percentage, right in line with the league average. And his seven homers translated to going deep once every 32 times up, better than the league average of that pitching-friendly time. As a small sample, those numbers didn't particularly mean much, but they turned out to be prescient.

After that '69 season, the Twins, not sold on Nettles enough to move Killebrew to first extensively just yet, dealt Nettles to the Cleveland Indians in a multiplayer deal that brought Luis Tiant—one of Nettles' future antagonists of the Yankees-Red Sox rivalry—to Minnesota. The trade gave Nettles his first chance to flourish. As Minnesota ran to its second consecutive division title in 1970, Nettles took over as the regular third baseman in Cleveland where, in the relative anonymity of fifth place and about 9,000 fans a game, he quietly became one of the American League's top players.

On the face of it, Nettles' 1970 season was nothing more than decent. He did hit 26 home runs, but he also batted .235 with 16 errors at third base. It's easy to guess what people said at the time—ok, he's got some power, but otherwise ... eh. What few people were looking at in 1970: Nettles 81 walks gave him a .336 on-base percentage, a bit better than league average, which essentially negated his mediocre batting average. And his superior range in the field saved 21 runs, according to FanGraphs estimates. His 2.6 defensive WAR (baseball-reference.com) was fourth-highest in the American League behind a pair of Washington Senators' infielders, Aurelio Rodriguez and Ed Brinkman, and Baltimore outfielder Paul Blair. Nettles' overall WAR of 5.2 left him just outside the league's top 10. The exceptional defensive WAR far outdistanced that of the Orioles' Brooks Robinson (0.8), who nonetheless took the Gold Glove at third base, no doubt thanks to the sterling reputation he'd earned over the previous decade (and of course Robinson would go on to shine in the 1970 World Series against the Reds with several head-turning plays, showcasing his defense for the national audience much the same way that Nettles would in 1978).

But while Robinson still held the big defensive rep at third base, the early '70s was actually the start of the transition to Graig Nettles as baseball's top defensive third baseman. "He was as good as anybody," says Peter Golenbock. "He and Brooks Robinson were the definitive third basemen." Nettles played the position with a style all his own, confident enough in his quick reflexes toward his right that he liked to position himself deep and toward the shortstop, the better to get to all those balls to his left. Nettles generally eschewed guarding the line, the favored strategy for preventing extra base hits, in favor of playing the percentages of plugging the third base—shortstop hole. For Yankee pitchers, the reward was the closing of most of the left side of the infield to opposing hitters. He had his own way of concentrating—Nettles liked to say that he would envision the ball being hit to various spots to his left or right and then envision how he would go after it and make the play. It's tough to argue with the results: by the time he retired in 1988, Nettles had accumulated more assists and had started more double plays than any third baseman in history other than Brooks Robinson (all these years later Robinson and Nettles still stand 1–2 in career assists at third, with Adrian Beltre jumping to the number two spot in double plays started, leaving Nettles third).

His second year in Cleveland was even better than his first. Nettles' batting average and on-base percentage improved to .261 and .350, respectively, both better than league average. His 28 homers and 86 RBI were both top 10. As for the stellar defense: Nettles' whopping 3.9 defensive WAR in 1971 led the American League by a wide margin, easily eclipsing the still-excellent 2.8 registered by Robinson, who still (naturally) took the Gold Glove. Robinson's perception advantage wasn't just based on his prior years of excellence—he was also helping to lead a powerhouse Orioles team to its third straight World Series while Nettles toiled for a last place Indians club that hadn't played a postseason game since 1954. Overall, Nettles' 7.5 WAR in 1971 was tops in the American League among everyday players. If you're a firm believer in WAR, then your obvious conclusion is that Graig Nettles was the American League's best player in 1971. And even if you're lukewarm on it, there's no denying that he was something very close to that. Where did Nettles finish in the American League MVP voting? Try 28th, behind the likes of sub-three-win players Pat Dobson, Mike Cuellar, and George Scott. Brooks Robinson, whose six-win season was excellent but not as good as Nettles, finished fourth in the MVP voting, including three first place votes. Like the tree in the forest—when you star for a 102-loss team in Cleveland in the pre–ESPN, pre–Internet era when no one saw you, did it really happen?

After another strong season in 1972 (17 homers, .325 OBP, 4.8 WAR), Nettles became the main man in a big trade between the Indians and Yankees, a trade that would raise some eyebrows a little while after it happened. The six-player deal sent Nettles and backup catcher Jerry Moses to New York for John Ellis, Jerry Kenney, Rusty Torres and Charlie Spikes. Why did the trade raise eyebrows? The initiator from the Cleveland side, Indians president Gabe Paul, wound up leaving the team two months later and joining George Steinbrenner's group that bought the Yankees in January 1973. Whispers of sabotage emerged when Paul wound up as Yankee president right after he'd sent Nettles there. That doesn't mean the whispers were true—as great as the deal worked out for the Bombers, the trade was defensible from Cleveland's perspective. The Indians hadn't been making any noise in the American League East despite Nettles' strong play for them. It was a club in need of a rebuild. The key to the trade for them was Spikes, a highly regarded outfield prospect whom the Yankees had drafted in the first round (number 11 overall) in 1969. And Spikes did show some early promise in Cleveland, hitting 23 and 22 homers, respectively, in his first two seasons. Had Spikes continued trending up, the deal would have looked reasonable for them. Instead he fizzled, battling injuries and inconsistency that led to just 65 career home runs and a .246 batting average before he retired at age 29.

Graig Nettles, entering his fourth full season at 28, was about to begin the 11-year run that would define his career. Yankee pinstripes. Five post seasons; four World Series. Before he moved along in 1984, he would establish himself as the best third baseman in Yankee history, since surpassed only by Alex Rodriguez. But it was also the era of the George-Billy-Reggie zaniness. An era largely defined by a Nettles quip that became famous: "Most kids want to grow up to play in the major leagues or join the circus. With the Yankees I got to do both" (or some such variation—the widely-used quote took on a few slightly different forms over the years). Not that the Yankees were a circus when Nettles first got there in 1973. Martin's arrival was still more than two years away; Jackson's was four years away. Steinbrenner, the new owner, was not yet in peak bombastic form—that wouldn't really come until he returned from a 15-month suspension that commissioner Bowie Kuhn hit him with in 1974 for questionable contributions to Richard Nixon's 1972 presidential campaign.

Nettles joined a rather bland and very average Yankee club that was getting set to play out its final season in the original Yankee Stadium before a major two-year remodel had them sharing Shea Stadium with the Mets in 1974 and 1975. Just as he'd been doing in Cleveland, Nettles put up the type of year that looks a lot better in today's enlightened, advanced-stat hindsight than it looked at the time. As the team finished fourth with an 80–82 season, Nettles batted .234. His 22 home runs seemed pretty impressive, but didn't quite land him the league's top 10. Nonetheless, Nettles' .334 on-base percentage and usual great defense produced a 5.5 WAR, his fourth outstanding season in a row. The trend continued during the Yankees' two seasons at Shea Stadium in 1974 and 1975, where Nettles totaled 43 homers and outhomered the league average by 42 percent (going deep about every 26 times up) despite the loss of Yankee Stadium's short right filed porch during those two transient seasons. For the fifth and sixth years in a row, he was either above or close to a five-win player (4.9 and 4.7 WARs in the two Shea Stadium years).

Then came 1976, a breakthrough year in several ways for the Yankees and for baseball. That year, ABC had signed on to a national TV deal with Major League Baseball, giving the league a second major network alongside its traditional partner NBC. Marvin Miller won free agency for the players, a game-changing development that would alter the sport's landscape forever and that George Steinbrenner would come to take advantage of quickly. At the same time, the Yankees were moving back home to the Bronx into their newly renovated Yankee Stadium, having assembled a club that was ready to shoot to the top of the American League. Gabe Paul, the man who had pushed Nettles to New York from Cleveland, showed that he could work the magic from the Yankee side of the fence too. After bringing in the likes of Chris Chambliss and Lou Piniella in 1974 and signing Catfish Hunter In 1975, Paul really went into overhaul mode as the new stadium awaited. Lineup regulars Mickey Rivers, Willie Randolph, Oscar Gamble and Carlos May were all new Yankees in 1976. So were pitchers Dock Ellis, Ed Figueroa, Ken Holtzman, and Grant Jackson. Nettles was among the key holdovers that also included catcher Thurman Munson, outfielder Roy White and reliever Sparky Lyle. Together, the new-look Yankees led the A.L. East virtually wire to wire and won it by 10½ games. They then captured their first

A.L. pennant in 12 years on a memorable ninth inning homer by Chambliss off Kansas City's Mark Littell in the fifth and deciding game of the A.L.C.S. The Yankees were swept out the World Series by the powerful Reds in four straight, but the season was a resounding success. The Bronx Bombers were back.

What's interesting is which players the fans and the local press looked at when dishing out most of the credit. It started with Munson, the beloved Yankee captain who had been enduring bumps and bruises behind the plate since 1969. He was the gamer, the resilient catcher who'd battled day in and day out for several average Yankee teams before he was finally rewarded with his first pennant winner. Sure enough, Munson was voted American League MVP in 1976, an honor that at the time felt more like a cumulative award for his years of effort at a physically demanding position than for truly being the league's best player. Then there were newcomers Rivers and Figueroa, who had come over from the California Angels the previous winter in a big trade for Bobby Bonds. Figueroa led the pitching staff with 19 wins. Rivers was an immediate asset as the new catalyst, hitting .312 and stealing 43 bases from the leadoff spot. Both had terrific seasons, but they also benefited from that perception advantage that falls into the laps of players that switch teams. With the Yankees jumping from 83 wins to 97 wins, the focus naturally moved toward what was different about the roster from one year to the next. Rivers represented a change in the lineup from 1975 to 1976, a new force at the top of the order that had been missing in the past. That's probably why he wound up third in the MVP voting behind Munson and Kansas City's George Brett.

But being the new kid in the lineup doesn't necessarily mean you did more to help the team than a holdover who also had a big year. In 1976, Graig Nettles led the American League with 32 home runs. His rate of homering once every 18 times up was a whopping 69 percent better than league average (the average A.L. player homered just once every 59 times up in 1976). He finished ninth in the league in both OPS and (ballpark adjusted) OPS-plus. His .254 batting average and .327 on-base percentage were right in line with the league averages. And again there was the tremendous defense—Nettles' 3.6 defensive WAR ranked a close second in the American League to Baltimore's slick fielding shortstop Mark Belanger. Once again, there you had it—Nettles' superstar level of power and defense was neither boosted nor undermined by his neutral on-base numbers. Add it all up, and Nettles' 8.0 WAR was the highest in the American League among everyday players and second overall to the Tigers' pitching phenom and pop culture sensation Mark (The Bird) Fidrych. For the second time in six years, Nettles was the league's top day-to-day player (at least by WAR). And for the second time in six years, no one noticed, even though he did it on the biggest baseball stage in the country this time.

Nettles did not make the American League All-Star team in 1976. He didn't win the Gold Glove at third base, losing out to Detroit's Aurelio Rodriguez, whose 0.3 defensive WAR didn't come within shouting distance of Nettles, and whose Fangraphs estimate of one run below average at his position contrast with Nettles' 27 runs above average. Of course things like WAR and zone ratings weren't part of the baseball vocabulary in 1976, so voters did the easy thing. They looked at Rodriguez's error total—only nine—and decided it looked better than Nettles' 19 errors.

And then there was the MVP voting. Graig Nettles, probably the most deserving player in the league and certainly among the top few, finished tied for 16th in the writers' balloting. He finished fourth among Yankees, behind Munson, Rivers and Chambliss, all of whom certainly had excellent years. Rivers turned in an impressive 6.4 WAR, Munson a 5.3, and Chambliss a 4.1. They just weren't as good as Nettles. But once again—perception. Batting average was a very big thing in the 1970s. Rivers (.312), Munson (.302) and Chambliss (.293) all looked a lot better than Nettles did at .254. No one particularly noticed that Nettles' .327 on-base percentage put him a bit ahead of Chambliss, just slightly behind Munson, and dead even with Rivers (that's right, Nettles got on base at the same rate as Rivers, who hit 58 points higher but whose one big flaw as a leadoff hitter—very few walks—didn't get much attention in the batting average-obsessed 1970s. If you hit .300 with speed, you were considered a top leadoff man). Given Nettles' clear superiority in power and defense over the others, it's easy to see in hindsight that he was the top player on the team and probably the top player in the league. On the 1976 Yankees, though, Nettles didn't have the distinction of being a dynamic new addition like Rivers or a grimy, beloved spiritual leader and .300 hitter like Munson. He was caught in between—a holdover of the previous few years whose full value wasn't as obvious as Munson's given the so-so batting average and the perceived good fortune he had to be a lefty hitter swinging at Yankee Stadium's short right field porch, which had people downplaying his home run total somewhat (more on that in a bit).

When the Yankees won it all in 1977, Nettles again flourished as one of the league's top players. His 37 homers were two behind league leader Jim Rice while his .333 on-base percentage topped the league average slightly. His 1.4 defensive WAR and nine runs above average at third were a dropoffs from his best seasons, but still strong (Nettles started 155 games at third base and committed 12 errors). His overall 5.5 WAR ranked ninth in the American League among everyday players. His bat was mostly quiet during the 1977 postseason, but his "in your face" presence on the field, as Marty Appel put it, was on display in the decisive Game 5 A.L.C.S. victory over Kansas City. When George Brett blasted a triple in the bottom of the first inning, the big hit that helped the Royals to an early 2–0 lead, his hard slide into Nettles at third base culminated in a forearm to the midsection. Nettles responded with a kick into Brett's shoulder, igniting a bench-clearing mini-brawl until cooler heads prevailed. Maybe it was coincidental, but Brett, the main Yankee antagonist during the playoff battles of the era, wasn't a factor for the remainder of the game. He wound up going 0-for-2 with a walk the rest of the way, got thrown out stealing in the fifth inning, and made an error in the ninth that scored the Yankees' final run in a 5–3 comeback victory. The exciting game and series ended on a grounder to third by Kansas City's Fred Patek that Nettles scooped up and turned into a double play.

When he repeated virtually the same season in 1978, as the Yankees repeated as champions, Nettles had wrapped up a nine-year run during which he averaged just under six wins per year from 1970 to 1978. How many everyday players in the American League did better during those nine years? Exactly one: Rod Carew, Nettles' teammate from the 1969 Twins. And that was by a nose. Fittingly, the Yankees' 1978 American League championship clincher over Kansas City featured a Nettles game-tying homer in the second inning and then a diving, full extension grab off a bullet hit by Hal McRae in the eighth to save a double and preserve a 2–1 win for Ron Guidry. Shades of things to come in the '78 World Series.

But through it all, few people perceived Graig Nettles as a genuine superstar. First off, he really didn't look the part. At 6-foot and 180 pounds, he wasn't big and powerful. He wasn't particularly fast. His throwing arm, accurate as it was, wasn't a rocket. To the average fan, Nettles came off physically more as the guy in the next office than as a super athlete. Then there were those '70s statistics. Nettles didn't hit .300. His power was impressive, but no doubt it was helped by the short right field wall in his ballpark. The WAR stat, driven by things like on-base percentage, slugging percentage, and defensive range, wasn't around yet. His personality didn't attract a crowd—Nettles was generally content to keep things low key while using his occasional humorous zingers to keep his teammates loose. Yankee pitchers would later tell stories of Nettles approaching the mound during tough situations and asking, "Hmm, how are you going to get out of this one?" Think back to those Yankee championship teams of the late '70s, and who do you think of? George, Billy, Reggie, and Thurman. Steinbrenner's bombast, Martin's intensity, Jackson's flair for the dramatic, and Munson's grouchy yet genuine leadership. And of course, the seemingly never-ending back page feuds among all of them. Nettles? "More of an observer than participant," remembers Marty Appel of the team feuds. "But he was someone who kept the team loose in tense situations, very good for team chemistry." Amid a handful of high maintenance types on those Yankee clubs, Nettles was a rock. George Steinbrenner didn't fluster him. Nettles once blew off a team luncheon and didn't particularly seem to care whether The Boss was upset. His widely-quoted response to a small fine: "If they want somebody to play third base, they have me. If they want somebody to go to luncheons they can hire George Jessel." That was Nettles—a little flap, a little joke about it, and then back to the grind. No ongoing drama.

But by and large, the fans and the press didn't see Nettles as a main man on those Yankee clubs as much as they saw him as part of the good, solid supporting cast. The reliable guy penciled into the lineup every day who made the plays at third and popped his share of homers over the friendly right field porch. A nice player, for sure, but a Hall of Famer? Nah. Nettles even received the ultimate dis from his own team. Look out at Yankee Stadium's outfield and you will in fact see the no. 9 Nettles wore among the multitude of retired numbers. The problem is that the number is retired for Roger Maris, not Nettles. Of course Maris did make history in 1961 by breaking the single season home run record, an achievement to be celebrated in its own right. But there's not much of an argument to be made that his Yankee career was as productive as Nettles' was.

Hindsight in today's enlightened era shows that the view of Graig Nettles as a good-but-not-great player was all wrong. Take a look at how he compares to other all-time third basemen, and it's clear that his ticket to Cooperstown should have been punched a long time ago. Start with the man Nettles succeeded as the A.L.'s top defensive third baseman, Brooks Robinson. Was Nettles' career as good as Robinson's? No, but it wasn't far behind. For his entire 22-year career, FanGraphs credits Nettles with 141 runs saved, while baseball-reference.com gives him 20.2 defensive WAR. For Robinson, whose career dates back to 1955 and who had his best seasons in the mid to late '60s, it is a whopping 294 runs saved and a 38.8 defensive WAR over 23 years. Clearly, he wasn't called "the human vacuum cleaner" for nothing. But Nettles was the better offensive player, scoring an edge in offensive WAR, 52.3 to 47.4, and out homering Robinson 390 to 268 with an OPS-plus edge of 110 to 104. In overall career WAR, Robinson outpaced Nettles 78 to 68. Robinson's peak beat Nettles by just a bit—he averaged 6.0 wins in his ten best seasons compared to Nettles' 5.5 wins.

Setting the bar even higher, how does Nettles stack up against another peer from his era, Mike Schmidt? No one would compare Nettles favorably to Schmidt, who is generally regarded as the greatest third baseman of all time. Offensively, it's really not close. Schmidt's 548 homers and 147 OPS-plus pretty much blow Nettles away. Schmidt was also a true defensive ace in his day—he was awarded 10 Gold Gloves—with a 17.6 defensive WAR and 127 runs saved that come up not all that short of Nettles' numbers. Schmidt averaged 5.9 wins over his full career to Nettles' 3.1 wins, a good-sized gap. Their respective peaks were a bit closer, with Schmidt averaging eight wins in his ten best seasons to Nettles' five and a half wins.

So to compare Graig Nettles to two of the best to ever play third base, this is how it looks: Nettles was clearly in arrears of Robinson defensively and Schmidt offensively, but netting out all the numbers for career WAR averaged against 10-season peak WAR shows him to be about two-thirds of the player Schmidt was and 90 percent of the player Robinson was. That's clear Hall of Fame territory. When the numbers say you're two-thirds as good as the best guy to ever play your position, you're pretty much golden, or ought to be. Take a look at the other positions on the field. Using the same measurements—averaging career WAR against 10-season peak WAR—Tom Seaver was two-thirds the pitcher that Cy Young was. Behind the plate, Hall of Famer Gabby Hartnett was two-thirds of Johnny Bench. In the outfield, take two-thirds of Babe Ruth and you get Mickey Mantle. And it keeps going around the infield—Charlie Gehringer was two-thirds as good as Rogers Hornsby at second, Frank Thomas two-thirds of Lou Gehrig at first, and Arky Vaughn two-thirds of Honus Wagner at short.

And to put Nettles' 68 career WAR in perspective: it doesn't beat Robinson or Schmidt, but it beats more than half of the 232 former MLB players currently in the Hall of Fame, including six third basemen. But alas, there's a reason beyond just the passage of time as to why memories of Nettles' career are fading—more top notch third basemen coming along. Says Rob Neyer: "Nettles has a good case, though he would have had a better case twenty years ago when the list of all-time great third basemen was shorter." No doubt, the likes of Wade Boggs and Chipper Jones, both now in the Hall, along with Scott Rolen and now Adrian Beltre, both strong future candidates, push Nettles further down the third base chain. That doesn't make Nettles any less deserving for Cooperstown, but it makes it tougher for people to see him in quite the same light.

The closest comparison to Nettles among Hall of Famers who played his position is probably represented by Paul Molitor, who played close to 800 games at third base before ultimately settling in as a DH during the latter part of his career. How does this matchup look? Very, very close. Both had long careers that lasted a little beyond 20 seasons. Nettles had far more home run power, while Molitor's all-around offensive game was a bit better, which he showed by getting on base 11 percent more often than a typical player during his era (Nettles was 1.5 percent better). Molitor also outslugged the league by the same 10 percent that Nettles did despite way fewer homers, thanks to his extra base power that yielded over 800 combined doubles and triples, far more than Nettles' 356. But most baseball players don't just swing bats, they wear gloves too. Molitor, though, wore a glove in barely more than half of his 2,683 career games from 1978 to 1998. And when he did, he wasn't especially good. Baseball-reference gives him a -8 defensive WAR, while FanGraphs says he saved eight total runs at third base, due almost exclusively to one strong defensive season in 1983. In other words, not in Nettles' league.

So the comparison is pretty clear cut—Nettles blasting home runs and flashing his glove, Molitor spraying hits all over the field. It nets out to nearly a draw. Overall, Molitor put up a 75 career WAR to Nettles' 68, a difference of about 0.3 per season that's mainly attributable to Nettles' defensive decline by age 35 in 1980 that had him tacking on less production during the tail end of his career than Molitor did. Nettles had the slightly better peak, his 5.5 average WAR in his 10 best seasons edging Molitor's 5.2. So what happened in the Hall of Fame voting? Molitor sailed in with 85 percent of the vote in his first year of eligibility in 2004, much the same way that Brooks Robinson did with 92 percent of the vote in 1983. Nettles, whose career was on par with Molitor's and quite close to Robinson's, settled for a four-year run on the ballot during which he maxed out at 8.3 percent of the vote.

The mismatch of career numbers to balloting numbers among these players seems bizarre. Yet it's probably easily explainable. Paul Molitor and Brooks Robinson did those things that traditional voters grasp easily. For Molitor, it was the nice round numbers he surpassed—the .300 career batting average and 3,000 career hits, pretty much guaranteed tickets. For Robinson, it was the 16 Gold Gloves that earned him the "best fielder ever at his position" distinction, a strong narrative which, combined with solid offense, was also a surefire ticket. And make no mistake, both are certainly deserving Hall of Famers.

Nettles' value takes a bit more effort to piece together, something that Hall voters have never been willing to do. Maybe it's laziness, or maybe it's just the locked in mindset that's difficult for traditionalists to break. Recently a New York sports radio host made a general comment about prospective but non-obvious candidates that echoed some fans on social media sites: "if you have to think about it or start analyzing a lot of numbers, he's not a Hall of Famer."

Really? That's a pretty lazy approach. Electing Mike Schmidt, Greg Maddux and Frank Thomas is easy. To be unwilling to take a closer look at someone who isn't the most obvious choice at first blush doesn't inspire a lot of confidence in your voting accuracy. Mention Graig Nettles, or some of the others in this book to some people, and you invariably get the usual tired line, that the Hall of Fame is for truly elite players, that it's not the "Hall of the Very Good." Well, yes. The point isn't to open up the Hall for the merely "very good" but to show that Graig Nettles and others were in fact truly elite despite not accumulating the traditional career benchmarks that lazy voters love to latch onto, like 500 home runs or 3,000 hits.

A quick example: every Hall-eligible player with 500 career homers who isn't seen as tainted by the PED scandal is in the Hall of Fame, while Fred McGriff and his 493 homers never topped 39.8 percent of the vote. Given that pattern, it stands to reason that if McGriff had hung around for another year and popped at least seven homers to hit the 500 mark, his plaque would be on the wall in Cooperstown even though his career wouldn't have been any better than it already was. McGriff is pretty much the poster boy for voters' obsessions with numbers that end with multiple zeroes.

To be fair, of course, today's common measurement tools weren't common back when Nettles and others were playing, or for several years after they retired. So it's understandable that voters would miss the boat on them initially. But where is the current baseball press—particularly in New York—to beat the drum for these guys? It's long overdue.

Putting aside the "sabermetric" numbers like on-base percentage and other measurements that make up WAR, even players' more traditional numbers are often viewed out of whack. A player's stats need to be viewed in the context of the era in which they were accumulated. To treat a number like 500 home runs as a uniform plateau across all eras doesn't make sense when you consider the way statistical norms change from one era to another. On the face of it, Graig Nettles' career home run total of 390 doesn't feel like a Hall of Fame number. But Nettles played in the dead ball era of the 1970s and '80s, when 30-something homers often led the league. His ratio of at-bats to home runs outdid the league average by 43 percent during his career, a rate that would have netted him 500 homers in a more hitter friendly era like the 1990s or early 2000s. As it stands, Nettles' 390 home runs rank 63rd on baseball's all-time list. Of the 62 players ahead of him, only a few had careers that overlapped strongly with Nettles' career during the dead ball era—Schmidt, Reggie Jackson, Darrell Evans, Dave Kingman—along with a handful of others who overlapped partially. What does that mean? It means that Graig Nettles was one of the premier home run hitters of his time, a much stronger indication of his level of play than a raw total, which is as much a product of the time period as it is of the player.

There is the matter of Yankee Stadium and its generosity toward lefty power hitters. Yes, the short porch in right field helped Nettles, the same way it helped Babe Ruth, Lou Gehrig, Mickey Mantle and Reggie Jackson, among others. But again, perspective. Nettles didn't play his entire career at Yankee Stadium, and his home run frequency there (48 percent better than league average) wasn't much better than it was during his other seasons. Playing in Cleveland from 1970 to 1972, he outdid the American League in home run to at-bat ratio by 44 percent. Playing for the Yankees at Shea Stadium in 1974 and 1975, he did it by 42 percent. When Nettles went to the San Diego Padres in 1984 his 20 homers in 395 at-bats gave him one for every 19.8 times up, which meant that he homered more than twice as often than the typical N.L. player who went deep just once every 52 at-bats that year. He went on to outperform the league by 36 percent and 49 percent, respectively during his two following seasons in San Diego in 1985 and 1986. Yes, even in his early 40s without a short porch, Nettles was still reaching the seats.

One other interesting tidbit on the lefty-hitter-at-Yankee-Stadium issue: because many of the Yankee lineups of the mid–'70s through the early '80s featured a lot of dangerous left-handed hitters—Nettles, Jackson, Chambliss, Rivers, Carlos May, Oscar Gamble, at various times— opposing teams saw that their best chance to beat the Yankees was to throw left-handed pitching at them. During his 11 years in pinstripes, Nettles saw lefty pitching in 45 percent of his at-bats, much higher than the norm. In the team's three-year A.L. pennant run from 1976 to 1978 it was even higher than that—Nettles saw lefties just about half the time yet still finished first in the league in homers in 1976, second in 1977, and ninth in 1978. By comparison, Nettles' contemporary George Brett, a fellow left-handed hitter and one of the great offensive players in baseball history, faced lefties just 33 percent of the time during the same stretch from 1973 to 1983. Of course Brett was a great hitter anyway, and his career rates statistically ahead of Nettles' by a bit more than Brooks Robinson's does (though less than by what Mike Schmidt's does), but he did hit a relatively modest .280 against left-handed pitching compared to .318 against right-handed pitching. Had Brett seen as many southpaws as Nettles did, his offensive edge would have been less pronounced, most likely.

Nettles' Yankee career did end a bit unceremoniously. A book he did with Peter Golenbock called *Balls*, which came out in early 1984, presented, among other things, a very unflattering portrait of George Steinbrenner. In part because of the book, and probably in part because he was 39, Nettles was shipped to the San Diego Padres for a low-level pitching prospect just days before the 1984 season started. But even as his career moved beyond its peak, Nettles teamed with his former World Series rival, Steve Garvey, to help San Diego to its first National League championship in 1984 with his 20 homers in 395 at-bats. During his late career return home he wound up tacking on 51 home runs and a 5.9 WAR over his three years with the Padres at the ages of 39, 40, and 41.

Graig Nettles' final major league home run came at Olympic Stadium on April 16, 1988, as a pinch hitter for the Montreal Expos. With his club trailing the Philadelphia Phillies 1–0 in the bottom of the eighth and Phillies starter Kevin Gross working on a two-hit shutout, Nettles got the call with two out and nobody on and blasted his 390th career homer to tie the game. The Expos went on to win 2–1 in 10 innings. Nettles didn't homer again during his final season on the Montreal bench. He started nine games at third base, the last three of which came after his 44th birthday on August 20. He finished at .230 (.323 on-base percentage) and 14 RBI in 93 at-bats.

There was no great exclamation point stamped onto his great career, but his final appearance is kind of interesting to look back on now. On October 1, 1988, with the Expos and Phillies tied 3–3 in the bottom of the sixth, manager Buck Rodgers called on Nettles to pinch hit in the pitchers' spot with the go-ahead run on second base. Nettles failed to get the run home, flying out to Phillies center fielder Bobby Dernier. His career was over. The Phillies would win the game 5–4. The Montreal starter Nettles hit for: a young hard throwing lefty named Randy Johnson, who was making his fourth career start exactly four days after Curt Schilling had made his third career start against Ron Guidry in Baltimore. Two historically underrated Yankees had gone out just days apart alongside a pair of future aces who would combine to shut down the Yankees in the World Series for the Arizona Diamondbacks 13 years later, denying them a fourth straight championship in 2001. Johnson, who of course came to be known as "The Big Unit," went on to win 303 games with 4,875 career strikeouts, second all-time to Nolan Ryan. He's also one of only eight pitchers in baseball history to accumulate a career WAR of over 100. Johnson, who had 25 career strikeouts in 26 innings when Nettles pinch hit for him, got his Hall of Fame plaque in 2015. Schilling, Guidry, and Nettles are still waiting.

3

Willie Randolph

On the night of October 11, 1977, the Yankees took the field to open the World Series at home against the Los Angeles Dodgers. It would be the ninth meeting of the two storied franchises in series play, but the first in 14 years since the Dodgers rode a pair of complete game gems by Sandy Koufax to sweep the Yankees in four straight back in 1963.

The two clubs were statistically quite even in 1977, though most figured the Dodgers as a slight favorite. Their 98 wins were two fewer than the Yankees, but that could be chalked up to cruising through much of the season after a blistering 22–4 start had them leading the National League West by 10½ games a month into the season. It was quite a head-turning season in Los Angeles. All five pitchers in their vaunted starting rotation—Don Sutton, Tommy John, Burt Hooton, Rick Rhoden and Doug Rau—had surpassed 200 innings while leading the staff to a MLB-best 3.22 ERA. Reggie Smith, Steve Garvey, Ron Cey and Dusty Baker all hit the 30-home run mark, making the 1977 Dodgers the first major league team ever with four such players. Never really challenged all year, L.A. finished 10 games ahead of its divisional nemesis, the Cincinnati Reds, reversing the Big Red Machine's two-year dominance of the N.L. West on their way to back-to-back World Series titles, including a sweep of the 1976 Yankees.

Meantime, it had been a successful but tumultuous year in the Bronx. It was the year Reggie Jackson arrived during the first winter of free agency and almost immediately clashed with Billy Martin and Thurman Munson. Martin also clashed with George Steinbrenner and narrowly avoided a June firing after he humiliated Jackson at Boston's Fenway Park by pulling him off the field during the bottom of the sixth inning after he thought Jackson had loafed retrieving a base hit that landed in short right field. Martin and Jackson had to be separated in the dugout; the Red Sox would embarrass the Yankees with a three-game weekend sweep by a cumulative score of 30–9.

The pitching became complicated when the Yankees' other big free agent fish, Don Gullett, was limited to 22 starts by nagging shoulder soreness. Still, the club got enough strong performances from other people to avoid ever falling more than a handful of games out of first place. Then things really began to click in early August when Jackson shook off

Willie Randolph's 53.9 WAR as a Yankee from 1976 to 1988 led all major league second basemen.

his early struggles and distractions to lead the Yankees on a white-hot run of 24 wins in 27 games between August 6 and September 4. They took the A.L. East by two games and then squeaked out an A.L.C.S. victory over Kansas City with a three-run, ninth inning rally in the final game.

Now the World Series was at hand against a very tough Dodger club. Veteran Don Sutton, a 32-year-old future Hall of Famer who by 1977 had thus far compiled 190 of his 324 career wins and who owned a lifetime postseason mark of 4–0 with a 1.62 ERA, was up in Game One against Gullett. Underlying all of it was the pressure to bounce back from last season's humiliating sweep at the hands of the Reds, which had infuriated Steinbrenner. Billy Martin, having guided the Yankees to the A.L. pennant the year before, knew that his chances of getting a coveted contract extension from Steinbrenner probably hinged on winning it all this time. Getting a leg up by winning the first game would go a long way. And despite all the veterans lining both rosters, it was the youngest player on the field, 22-year-old second baseman Willie Randolph, the cool customer who hadn't so much as dipped a toe into the 1977 Yankee soap opera, who would do it for them.

Gullett was shaky to start, walking three and allowing a triple to Bill Russell that led to a pair of first inning runs. Long reliever Dick Tidrow was already warming in the Yankee bullpen before the inning was done. The first inning could have been worse if not for Reggie Smith stopping and starting on a steal attempt and ultimately getting tagged out in a rundown for a big second out before the final walk of the inning. Gullett then got Dusty Baker on a grounder to escape further damage. The Yankees got one back in the bottom of the first on a Chris Chambliss RBI single to make the score 2–1.

That's the way it stayed into the middle of the game as Sutton and Gullett both settled in to pitch well. Willie Randolph wasn't much a factor early, grounding out and striking out in his first two at-bats. But there was one play in the fourth inning that won the praises of Howard Cosell and Tom Seaver in the ABC television booth—not spectacular on its face, but a play that, if you look closely, showed how Randolph had already mastered the subtleties of playing the infield.[1] With one out and Baker on first base, Dodger catcher Steve Yeager hit a slow roller toward second. It was clearly too slow for a double play, and clearly Randolph would have to charge in and get to the ball quickly to have a chance at throwing Yeager out at first. Complicating the play was Baker running right into Randolph's path as he sprinted toward second. After taking his first couple of steps in toward the ball, Randolph intentionally hesitated for a split second to let Baker cross in front of him before hustling the rest of the way to field the ball on the infield grass. Knowing that by now he had little time, he unleashed a lightning-quick sidearm throw to first to get Yeager by a step. Instead of two on and one out, it was one on with two out. Gullett got out of the inning by fielding Sutton's attempt at a bunt single and throwing him out at first.

With the score still 2–1 in the top of the sixth, the Dodgers had a great chance to add to their lead when Garvey laid down a beautiful bunt single toward third and then took off on a pitch that Glen Burke poked in to right field for a single. Because it took some time for centerfielder Mickey Rivers to get to the slowly hit ball, Garvey kept going all the way to the plate. He clearly beat Rivers' throw to Thurman Munson, but home plate umpire Nestor Chylack somehow got himself out of position by wandering up the first base line. He called Garvey out, costing L.A. a run.

Sometimes that one break is all you need. The first Yankee hitter in the bottom of the sixth was Willie Randolph. With the crowd still buzzing over the play at the plate, Randolph swung hard at a 2–2 pitch from Sutton and hit a scorching line drive into the first row of the left field seats. Yankee Stadium exploded. Tie game.

The score was still 2–2 in the bottom of the eighth when Randolph again came up to lead off the inning. Sutton promptly jumped ahead of him 0–2 and then unleashed an assortment of pitches just out of the strike zone, hoping to get the youngster to chase. But Randolph held up on a couple of close pitches as he worked the count full and then fouled off a tough fastball before taking ball four to get aboard. It was Sutton's first walk of the night. When Munson followed with a double into the left field corner, Randolph came all the way to the plate to give the Yankees a 3–2 lead.

In a sure sign that this game was played in the 1970s, Gullett was still in there to begin the ninth despite having thrown more than 120 pitches. But when he allowed a single and a walk around one out, Martin finally replaced him with relief ace Sparky Lyle, who gave up a seeing-eye single to pinch hitter Lee Lacy that drove in the tying run. Lyle remained in the game through the 12th inning, hitting for himself twice in the process, until Willie Randolph led off the bottom of the 12th. With Rick Rhoden now on the mound for the Dodgers, Randolph jumped on a first-pitch, outside fastball and drove a double to right field. After an intentional walk to Munson, Paul Blair, in the game because he'd replaced Reggie Jackson for defense in the ninth, failed on a couple of bunt attempts before drilling a single to left to score Randolph with the winning run. Your final: 4–3, Yanks.

A home run to tie the game in the sixth. A leadoff walk and scoring the go-ahead run in the eighth. And then a double and scoring the winning run in the 12th. It was Willie Randolph's night all the way in the game that gave the Yankees the jump on the Dodgers in the 1977 World Series.

The Dodgers hammered Catfish Hunter the following night to tie the series. But then out in L.A. a pair of impressive complete games by Mike Torrez and Ron Guidry gave the Yankees a 3–1 series lead. Gullett got knocked out early in a Game 5 loss, but that only set up the dramatics of Reggie Jackson's historic Game 6 back at Yankee Stadium, when he pounded three home runs on three consecutive pitches in 10–4 win that clinched the series and gave the Yankees their first title since 1962.

Everyone remembers Reggie winning Game 6. Hardly anyone, in all likelihood, remembers Randolph winning Game 1. And that's pretty much the way it went for Randolph for the rest of his career. His game was a quiet, steady excellence, particularly at getting on base and fielding his position. Skills that were always appreciated but never had people perceiving him as elite, exactly. He didn't win any batting titles and he certainly didn't hit a lot of home runs. But by the time he moved on after the 1988 season, he most definitely stood as the best second baseman in Yankee history.

Of all the New York players in this book, none are as New York as Willie Randolph. He was the city kid who made it from the Brooklyn projects to Yankee Stadium. And eventually, to Shea Stadium too. Randolph played and coached for the Yankees. He played for and managed the Mets. It would add up to 29 summers in New York baseball uniforms, most prominently, of course, as the Yankees' second baseman from 1976 to 1988.

Growing up a Mets fan in Brooklyn's tough Brownsville section, he honed his fielding skills fighting all the bad hops at the neighborhood's roughshod playing fields.[2] Later he made it to the Brooklyn Parade Grounds as a star at Tilden High, so much of a star that he was drafted in the seventh round by the Pittsburgh Pirates in 1972. Randolph dealt with his violent surroundings growing up by doing his best to tune it all out and concentrate on baseball. His style became steely and focused, traits that Yankee fans would come to notice during his years of steady performance while others in the organization made most of the noise and drew most of the attention.

Randolph hit the ground running in the Pirates' organization, hitting over .300 with a .400 on-base percentage in his first year of Rookie ball in the Gulf Coast League. He rose a level each season over the next three years to reach Triple-A Charleston in 1975. With his batting average sitting at .339 in late July, the Pirates called him up. Randolph debuted in the big leagues at Pittsburgh's Three Rivers Stadium on July 29, 1975, three weeks after turning 21. He got his first hit that night off of Phillies left-hander Tom Underwood, a third-inning single in what became a 1-for-4 night.

But ultimately Randolph didn't do much during the rest of the 1975 season in Pittsburgh, starting just 12 games and hitting .164. The Pirates had another young second baseman, Rennie Stennett, whom they also liked. That winter they made their choice. Looking to bulk up their starting rotation, which was solid and deep in 1975 but which included only one 200-inning starter (Jerry Reuss), the Pirates set their sights on native son George (Doc) Medich, the New York Yankee right-hander who hailed from nearby Aliquippa, Pennsylvania, and who had graduated from the University of Pittsburgh. Medich had been a major workhorse for the Yankees during his first three major league seasons, tossing at least 235 innings each year from 1973 to 1975. And he was still only 26. To get him, the Pirates gave up Dock Ellis, their flamboyant right-hander with a solid eight-year history but also coming off his worst season at age 30, and lefty swingman Ken Brett, a six-year veteran with four teams who was about to become primarily known for being George Brett's older brother. And, because they had Rennie Stennett, the Pirates also kicked in a promising 21-year-old second baseman—Willie Randolph. Just like Doc Medich, he was headed home.

For Yankee G.M. Gabe Paul, who had stolen Chris Chambliss and Lou Piniella in one-sided trades with Cleveland and Kansas City in 1974 and parlayed fan favorite Bobby Murcer into a one-year flirtation with Bobby Bonds that yielded Ed Figueroa and Mickey Rivers in 1976, the three-for-one he pulled off with Pittsburgh proved to be his best heist yet. Ellis had a terrific rebound year in 1976, going 17–8 with a 3.19 ERA in helping the Yankees to the pennant. A year later he was swapped to Oakland for Mike Torrez, who did the same thing for them in 1977 with a huge second half and a big postseason as the team won it all. Meantime Brett wasn't used much by manager Billy Martin during the early part of 1976, but a May 18 trade for him with the White Sox brought Carlos May, a solid lefty bat who became the Yankees' primary designated hitter during their run to the American League flag. Really, the combined contributions of Ellis, May, and Torrez across 1976 and '77 were worth the price of Medich, who went on to an average career with several teams after the trade before retiring in 1982. But the key to the trade hadn't even scratched the surface in the big leagues yet. Most fans and reporters had no idea what to expect from Willie Randolph. People were vaguely aware that he was a good prospect, but baseball is always filled with good prospects that don't pan out.

Marty Appel remembers: "The media often ignored him, they called it the Dock Ellis trade. But again, these were Gabe Paul's scouting reports," he says. "They weren't sure he would do so well as a young player, but Willie was very mature for his age, he was ready." Being young and unproven did have an upside—Randolph had no initial pressure to be a star. Thurman Munson was the team leader. Other veterans like Nettles, Chambliss and Roy White hit in the key spots in the lineup. Rivers, the more heralded acquisition that winter, would have a lot of eyes on him as the new leadoff hitter. Randolph wasn't going to be the center of attention that first year. He would hit low in the order, usually eighth. If he played a solid second base and hit .260 or so, that would do just fine.

It also helped that he didn't exactly have big shoes to fill. The Yankees really had nothing resembling a star at second base since Gil McDougald in the 1950s (and even McDougald wound up playing almost as much third base as he did second as his career moved along). The team's incumbent second baseman for the previous two years, Sandy Alomar, was a decent glove man who had no real punch at the plate. Before Alomar, second base had been manned for seven years by Horace Clarke, a .256 career hitter with 27 lifetime homers. Some fans may remember the way Clarke's name became synonymous with the perceived Yankee futility of the late '60s and early '70s ("the Horace Clarke Years" is how the period became branded). All of that was actually quite unfair to Clarke, who was a perfectly decent major league ballplayer with Yankee teams that were mostly average, not terrible. But in the context of franchise history, fans viewed the postseason draught between 1964 and 1976 as a dark period. And somehow it was Horace Clarke—perhaps because he was the leadoff hitter who came to the plate more than 600 times for seven of those Yankee teams—who became the face of the era.

What it all meant for Willie Randolph in 1976 was that he faced no pressure in replacing any legends. That's probably why no one panicked when he went hitless in his first three games. Randolph got his first Yankee hit in style—a fourth inning homer in Baltimore off of Orioles ace Jim Palmer in a 7–1 win. He added a walk and a single later in the game and then banged out two more hits the next day against the Twins in the home opener of the "new" Yankee Stadium, the team's first game back in the Bronx after a two-year hiatus to Shea Stadium during a major renovation.

Six days later, on April 21, the Yankees faced the Chicago White Sox at The stadium. Against Chicago pitchers Dave Hamilton and Jack Kucek, Randolph singled in the second, doubled in the fourth, singled and scored in the sixth, and then singled, stole second and scored in the seventh. A 4-for-4 day. The Yankees won 10–7 for their seventh win in nine games to open the season. After starting his Yankee career 0-for-9, Randolph was 10 for his last 19. He and the team continued to cruise through the next few weeks. On June 2, Randolph banged out a pair of singles at Fenway Park in a 7–2 win over the Red Sox. His average stood at .313; the Yankees already led the A.L. East by five games. Of course there was also the defense. It was clear to anyone watching that the Yankees had a natural at second base. It wasn't just Randolph's ability cover ground and hang tough turning double plays, it was the take-charge attitude out there—not an easy role for a rookie on a veteran team, particularly the New York Yankees. He didn't hesitate to wave off veteran outfielders on short popups to right or right-center. Positioning himself perfectly on relays and unleashing quick, accurate throws was routine. He was young and quiet, but out in the middle of the diamond, he was in charge. That his defense proved to be more about consistency than the highlight reel was great for the team, although it was probably a cause of under appreciation as well. Fans are generally used to seeing major leaguers make some great plays but also have their lapses once in a while. Randolph was generally the opposite. Remembers Marty Appel: "He was so consistent you didn't see the lapses; that would get lost. When you never see a lapse you start taking him for granted."

On Sunday afternoon July 11, in front of 53,000 fans at Yankee Stadium, Ed Figueroa shut out the White Sox 5–0, sending the Yankees to the All-Star break with a 50–31 record and a 9½ game lead over Boston in the American League East. Randolph, hitting .273 with a .373 on-base percentage, was selected for the game by American League manager Darrell Johnson, but because of an injury he had to pass his spot to Oakland's Phil Garner.

As the 1976 season played out, the Yankees took the division title easily before beating Kansas City in the A.L.C.S. and losing the World Series to the Reds. Randolph finished with a .267 batting average but with a .356 on-base percentage that was second on the team and 11 percent better than league average. He struck just 39 times, second-lowest on the team to Munson's 38 among those playing more than 110 games.

In the field, Randolph's 2.7 defensive WAR was third in the American League behind Mark Belanger and Randolph's infield teammate, Graig Nettles. Overall, his 5.0 WAR placed him just outside the league's top ten and second among second baseman to Baltimore's Bobby Grich. Yet when it came to the MVP race, Randolph's name didn't appear anywhere among the 29 players who received votes. The voting for Gold Gloves and for MVP that year really encapsulated the old-school approach of the day. Grich beat out Randolph for the Gold Glove at second base despite a 0.7 defensive WAR that didn't touch Randolph's 2.7. Why? Because just as with Graig Nettles and Aurelio Rodriguez the same year, WAR didn't exist yet, and Grich made only 12 errors to Randolph's 19. Among those receiving MVP votes in 1976 were Ed Figueroa (19 wins), Sparky Lyle (23 saves—a lot in that era) and John Mayberry (95 RBI). None of the three had a WAR higher than 2.1, but wins, saves and RBI went a long way in the 1970s. The awakening to on-base percentage and defensive range—FanGraphs says that Randolph was worth 19 defensive runs in 1976, close to the league lead and way ahead of Grich's one— came too late to help Randolph in the 1970s and '80s.

Randolph had almost as good a year in 1977, hitting .274 with a .347 OBP, numbers that were dragged down a bit by a slump over the final two weeks. Randolph turned in 12 defensive runs saved and a 1.9 defensive WAR that was down a bit from 1976 but still among the league's top 10. His 4.6 overall WAR gave him a second straight All-Star-type season. Aside from his big night in the World Series opener, Randolph didn't hit a whole lot during the 1977 postseason. But the decisive Game 5 of the A.L.C.S. against the Royals brought out another case of Willie Randolph being the best player on the field that no one remembered.

The Yankees-Royals showdown that night is remembered for two things—the Graig Nettles-George Brett fight in the first inning and Billy Martin's gutsy and controversial decision to bench Reggie Jackson against tough Kansas City left-hander Paul Splittorff. Martin's reasoning: Reggie hadn't hit Splittorff well during his career, and with the game being played on artificial turf in spacious Royals Stadium, outfield defense would be at a premium. So Martin made the call to start Paul Blair, the better defender, in right field and big Cliff Johnson, the righty-hitting backup catcher, as the D.H. The plan made sense, but this was Reggie Jackson. Benching a healthy Reggie in the biggest game of the year seemed unfathomable. Naturally it became the lead story line, the latest twist in the Billy-Reggie drama.

But on to the game. Most people remember Brett's big first inning triple that scored the game's first run and ended with a hard slide into Nettles and the subsequent bench-clearing fisticuffs that followed. What got no mention at all was that the best baseball play of the whole sequence came from Willie Randolph. Brett didn't actually hit the ball that well. He got under it a bit, lifting what was no more than a deep fly ball to right-center that should have been caught. But Mickey Rivers took a bad route to the ball and then watched it sail over his head when his late burst of speed didn't quite get him there on time. Blair alertly backed up the play and made a strong throw to Randolph, the cutoff man in short right field. Randolph made a quick turn and unleashed a picture-perfect relay to third, a pea that reached Nettles on the fly and just missed getting Brett. With Brett safe and all the attention turning to the fight a moment later, the play proved to be inconsequential. But Randolph's execution of the relay was a thing of beauty to watch.[3]

Randolph wasn't done. With the Royals leading 3–1 in the top of the eighth and Splittorff pitching a gem, he led off with a line single to center. It was the hit that chased Splittorff from the game just six outs from ending the Yankees' season. Righty Doug Bird came in and struck out Munson, but then gave up a single to Lou Piniella and another to Jackson, pinch hitting for Cliff Johnson with a right-hander now in the game, to drive in Randolph with a big run to get the Yankees to within 3–2. Still down by that score in the top of the ninth, they immediately rallied to tie it on a Blair single, a Roy White walk, and a Rivers single that scored Blair. Hard-throwing right-hander Mark Littell then came in to face Randolph, who worked the count to 3-and-1 and then launched a 400-foot fly ball that was caught by Amos Otis on the center field warning track. The sacrifice fly not only drove in the lead run, it was deep enough to allow Rivers to tag and move from first to second. He'd wind up scoring on a Brett throwing error to make the score 5–3.

The Royals got the tying run to the plate in the bottom of the ninth when Frank White touched Sparky Lyle for a one-out single. But then Fred Patek, Kansas City's diminutive shortstop, hit a grounder to third that Nettles scooped up and threw to Randolph at second. Randolph squared up against White's hard slide and fired a strike across his body to first to just nip Patek and end the game and the series. The Yankees were American League champs for the second straight year. As the culmination of a hard-fought series with the Royals, the win was one of the biggest and most memorable in Yankee history. And there's little chance it happens without Willie Randolph on the field.

Things continued to roll for Randolph and the Yankees. The 1978 season proved to be a near carbon-copy of 1977, as the club pulled out another close race over Boston in the A.L. East (this time even more dramatically in the one-game tiebreaker) and defeated the Royals and Dodgers again to win it all. For Willie Randolph in 1978: a .381 on-base percentage that ranked fourth in league, 11 runs better than average on defense, and a 5.8 WAR that was first on the Yankees and sixth in the league among position players. Randolph finished 29th in the American League MVP voting, with teammates Munson, Jackson, Rivers, Piniella and Goose Gossage all placing ahead of him.

The Yankees slipped a bit in 1979 with an 89–71 record that was only good enough for fourth place in the tough A.L. East. Lyle had been traded to Texas before the season. Gossage was lost for three months with a thumb injury after punching out Cliff Johnson in a shower room scuffle in April. Rivers joined Lyle in Texas in a July trade. And on August 2 came the devastating news of Munson's fatal plane crash, effectively relegating the grieving club to playing out the string the rest of the way. Randolph, though, just kept quietly doing his thing: .374 on-base percentage (12 percent better than average), 18 fielding runs above average at second base, and a 5.2 WAR that led all Yankee regulars and that was significantly higher than that of A.L. MVP Don Baylor (3.7). Randolph didn't get any MVP votes, and he was passed over for the All-Star Game.

Then came the 1980 season. For the first time in a few years, the Yankees took on a bit of a different look. They replaced Munson by dealing Chris Chambliss for catcher Rick Cerone. Bob Watson was signed as a free agent to replace Chambliss at first. Center fielder Ruppert Jones was acquired from Seattle to replace Rivers. The season opened in somewhat bizarre fashion in Texas in a New York reunion-type game in which Ron Guidry and former Met favorite Jon Matlack both tossed nine scoreless innings. With the score still 0–0 in the 11th, an even more popular former Met, Rusty Staub, grounded out with the winning run on second. The Rangers eventually won 1–0 in the bottom of the 12th on a Gossage wild pitch that scored Rivers from third. The winning pitcher: Sparky Lyle, who shut his old teammates down from the 10th inning through the 12th.

But the Yankees didn't lose very often in 1980. With Cerone doing an excellent job in Munson's old spot and Jackson blasting a career high 41 homers, they took the American League East crown with 103 wins, their highest total of the era. The year ended in disappointment when they lost the A.L.C.S. to the Royals in a three-game sweep, but it was a terrific rebound season. The biggest key to the Yankee resurgence in 1980: Willie Randolph, who put up his best season yet. In the year in which he turned 26, Randolph hit a career high .294 and, more importantly, decorated that average with 119 walks for a .427 on-base percentage that placed him second in the league to George Brett, the man who fans fixated on all year as he flirted with a .400 batting average (Brett finished at .390 with a .454 OBP). Now hitting in the leadoff spot in place of Rivers, Randolph stole 30 bases in 35 attempts. He even outslugged the league by a bit for the only time in his career thanks to 23 doubles and seven triples to go with his seven homers. The numbers say that Randolph's fielding dipped that year to two runs above average and a 0.8 defensive WAR, but it all added up to a career-high 6.6 WAR, seventh-best in the league.

The 1981 season essentially wrapped up an era—a crazy split season driven by a 50-day player strike in which the Yankees won the A.L. flag and lost the World Series to the Dodgers. It would be Reggie Jackson's last year in pinstripes and the team's last appearance in the postseason for 14 years. Randolph's 2.4 WAR equated to about a 3.6 over a full season, perfectly solid, but for the first time in his career a bit below All-Star level. For Willie Randolph at that point in his career: six major league seasons, five of them All-Star level, five division titles, four American League pennants and two world championship rings. He'd go one to have five more seasons of a 4.0 WAR or better, outperforming the American League in on-base percentage by at least 17 percent in all five of them. Basically, 10 All-Star caliber years. From the Jackson-Munson years of the late '70s through the Don Mattingly-Dave Winfield-Rickey

Henderson years of the mid to late '80s, there was rarely a season that went by in which Randolph wasn't one of the Yankees' top players. Through a slew of double-play partners—from Fred Stanley and Bucky Dent to Roy Smalley, Bobby Meacham and Wayne Tolleson—he persisted. "The shortstops came and went, but Willie was the rock," says Appel.

It's easy to miss the fact that Willie Randolph was about the best second baseman of his time, because marking his "time" can get a bit murky. His career partly overlapped with other Hall of Famers with bigger names and bigger offensive numbers, especially power-wise. When Randolph was just breaking in in 1975 and '76, Joe Morgan was right at his peak winning back-to-back National League MVP awards and Rod Carew was just switching from second base to first. By the time Randolph hung up his cleats in 1992, Ryne Sandberg had made nine All-Star games and taken an N.L. MVP. But if you take a look you'll see that most of Morgan's big seasons came before Randolph's prime (or even his time), and most of Sandberg's came after. The only pure peer of Randolph's who could have been a little bit better was Lou Whitaker, another snubbed Hall of Famer with a 75 career WAR who also seemed to get sandwiched between Morgan and Sandberg. Whitaker debuted full time with Detroit in 1978, two years after Randolph broke in with the Yankees. The two would play to a virtual tie over the next decade. Ultimately, Randolph would show more speed, a slight advantage in on-base percentage (.373 to .363) and a pretty decisive edge in defense (114 runs above average to 70). Whitaker countered with a lot more power, belting 244 homers in his career to Randolph's 54 that led to an OPS-plus advantage of 117 to 104.

When you get sandwiched between a couple of legends, it's easy to get pigeonholed into that second tier "very good" level in people's minds. Says *New York Post* baseball columnist Ken Davidoff: "He was one of the more underappreciated Yankees. He didn't have that MVP, Joe Morgan–type of career. That's not his narrative." Of course Joe Morgan, by most any objective measure, is one of the 25 greatest players of all time. You don't have to be Joe Morgan to be a Hall of Famer. Nolan Ryan isn't Tom Seaver, but you'll have a hard time finding anyone to claim that he shouldn't be in Cooperstown.

Quick, who is the greatest infielder in Yankee history? Ok, that's an easy one. It's Lou Gehrig. But what about after that? Most definitely it's Derek Jeter. The Yankee shortstop from 1996 to 2014, he of the .310

career batting average, 3,465 hits, five rings and golden boy pedigree during a glorious time in Yankee history. Everyone knows that Jeter deserved the Hall of Fame honor he collected in 2020.

But here's the thing: Derek Jeter wasn't that much better than Willie Randolph, who saw his name on a Hall of Fame ballot exactly once, when he got 1.1 percent of the vote in 1998, a year in which he was coaching on the Yankees' 114-win juggernaut for which Jeter hit .324 with 19 home runs. On the face of it, Jeter's offensive numbers look quite a bit better than Randolph's. His .310 average beats Randolph by 34 points. He rapped out 1,400 more hits. With good power for a middle infielder, Jeter's 260 homers and .440 slugging percentage easily dwarf Randolph's 54 and .351. Even the on-base percentage is slightly in Jeter's favor—.377 to .373. But remember, Jeter played in a far more hitter-friendly era than Randolph did. Setting each player's stats within the context of the time that he played, Randolph was the slightly better on-base guy by outdoing the American League average by 14 percent to Jeter's 12.6 percent. As you might expect, slugging is still in Jeter's favor by a good margin even after adjusting for each era—he outdid the league average by 3.3 percent while Randolph slugged 10 percent under the league average. There's no getting around the fact that Randolph just didn't hit home runs, a weakness that became a big part of his narrative.

But there's another whole part of the game—defense. On that side of the field it isn't even close. Randolph was an outstanding second baseman, Jeter was not a very good shortstop. Baseball-reference.com gives Randolph a 20.2 defensive WAR while giving Jeter -8.3, below replacement level. The advanced metrics on FanGraphs generally back those numbers up. Featured defensive metrics reported on FanGraphs made a switch from "Total Zone Rating" (TZ) to "Ultimate Zone Rating" (UZR) in 2002, right in the middle of Jeter's career. Superior technology gives UZR the nod as the more accurate fielding measure, but the FanGraphs library says that the difference is fairly minimal—both are good measures of a fielder's range and of the number of runs he saves compared to an average player at his position (FanGraphs also began reporting "Defensive Runs Saved" along with UZR in 2002, though it's calculated with less data by limiting comparisons between players at the same position to that year only, omitting historical comparisons).

To be consistent, the fairest comparison is Randolph's TZ from 1975 to 1992 to the combination of Jeter's TZ from 1995 to 2001 and his UZR from 2002 to 2014. Here's how the numbers add up: Randolph plus

114, Jeter minus 137. That's a swing of 251 runs in Randolph's favor (the Defensive Runs Saved compilation, which we're omitting here, is even less favorable to Jeter). These numbers can't be absolutely accurate, but they're largely accepted as general indicators of a fielder's range—how many plays does he make out of all the plays he could make based on balls hit to his area? The gap wouldn't be as wide if Jeter, like Randolph, had spent his career at second instead of short. But as far as who was the better middle infielder, there's really no contest.

Randolph's superior defense would explain why his career WAR of 65.9 in 18 seasons ranks close to Jeter's 72.4 in 20 seasons. Their respective peaks were quite close, with Jeter averaging half a run better than Randolph over the course of each player's 10 best seasons. Jeter did have a slightly bigger edge in the shorter peak—his five best years being better than Randolph's five best by about one win per year. In particular, Jeter's two best seasons in 1998 and 1999 outdid any season Randolph had. But as far as those All-Star caliber four-win seasons go, Jeter had eight of them, Randolph had 10.

But as so often happens, the narratives don't match the production. Jeter obviously had the more powerful bat, with 435 more extra base hits than Randolph. And as an offensive star you generally get more slack when it comes to defense, especially when you're defensive weakness is tied to range and not to bad hands or inaccurate throws, which are more apparent to the average observer. Jeter was fine by the eye test, but the numbers show that he didn't get to as many grounders as other short-stops did. His defensive shortcomings were partly masked by things like his trademark "jump and throw" maneuver that made up for a poor arm and sometimes allowed him to throw out runners from deep in the hole, and by a couple of memorable moments like the "flip play" against the A's in the 2001 playoffs and diving into the stands after a catch against the Red Sox in 2004. Lord knows that Jeter derived a ton of narrative from those plays. He was even awarded five Gold Gloves, for Pete's sake.

Add it all up, offense and defense, and Jeter's career still tops Randolph's. But barely. Yet one has his number on the Yankee Stadium wall, and the other doesn't. One became a near-unanimous Hall of Famer, the other was a one and done with a handful of votes. Once again, narratives and facts don't always align.

Let's jump back further into Yankee history to Tony Lazzeri, the second baseman from the "Murderers' Row" Yankees of the 1920s and early '30s. Lazzeri was a mainstay for the club from 1926 to 1937 before finishing his final two years with the Cubs, Dodgers and Giants. During his 12 years in the Bronx, Lazzeri hit 169 home runs, a lot for the era (he finished in the league's top 10 four times). He hit .293 with a .380 on-base percentage and 121 OPS-plus. Lazzeri was clearly a top offensive player in the American League for much of the Ruth-Gehrig era, particularly for a three-year run from 1927 to 1929 and again in 1932.

Most Hall of Fame voters weren't particularly keen on Lazzeri's candidacy after he retired. He continually got enough votes to stay on the ballot each year from 1945 to 1962, but maxed out at 33 percent, less than half the 75 percent needed. But 29 years later, Lazzeri got the nod from the Veteran Committee. He was inducted into the Hall in 1991 along with BBWAA choices Rod Carew, Gaylord Perry and Ferguson Jenkins.

Regardless of how Lazzeri got in, he's in. And as good as his career was, it wasn't as good as Willie Randolph's. The comparison is similar to the one with Jeter—a superior power bat vs. more balanced skills. Lazzeri outslugged the American League by 15 percent in his day compared to Randolph's 10 percent underperformance. That accounts for Lazzeri's sizeable OPS-plus advantage of 121 to 104. But that's where the Lazzeri edge ends. Playing in an era of higher batting averages and on-base percentages than Randolph did, Lazzeri's .380 OBP only outdid the league average by 8.3 percent, good but quite a bit lower than Randolph's 14 percent. And again, there's defense. The zone metrics show Lazzeri to be an average second baseman at five runs below average for his career (or a fraction of a run per season, about neutral), with a 5.2 lifetime defensive WAR. Randolph, again, had the 114 runs above average and a defensive WAR nearly four times higher.

Led by his defense and his ability to get on base, Randolph's 65.9 career WAR beats Lazzeri's 50 pretty handily. It's true that Lazzeri's career was a few years shorter, but his best ten seasons of 4.6 WAR per year still fall a bit behind Randolph's 4.9 per year. And Lazzeri's five seasons of 4.0 or better were half the number Randolph had.

Given that Lazzeri's career numbers run nearly identical to a couple of other old-time Hall of Fame second basemen, Bobby Doerr and Billy Herman, it's clear that they come up short of Randolph too.

"You could make a case that he's the best second baseman in Yankee history," says Marty Appel of Randolph. Perhaps he's since been eclipsed by Robinson Cano, but even that's a close call. Cano obviously had a lot more power than Randolph, to an even greater degree than Lazzeri and

Jeter did. But his .355 on-base percentage in his nine years in pinstripes before leaving for Seattle doesn't catch Randolph's .374 (league OBP averages were almost identical in their respective eras), and, like the others, his defense (negative UZR, 6.8 defensive WAR) doesn't come close. Cano averaged a hair over a 5.0 WAR as a Yankee (and just about the same in Seattle), higher than Randolph's 4.2 per year across four more seasons. Cano does have a PED issue, having been suspended from the Mariners in 2018. Whether he was playing with any kind of illegal boost during his Yankee years, no one knows. So make of that what you will. By the numbers, you've got Randolph with a higher Yankee career WAR (54 to 45) but Cano with the higher annual average. Flip a coin, or go ahead and take Cano for an amazing 2010 to 2013 Yankee peak, when he was at least 5.8 wins over replacement each year. But whether Randolph ranks first or second on the all-time Yankee second base list, he's done plenty to merit the Hall of Fame.

His case looks even stronger when venturing beyond Yankee history to other, more recent notable second basemen who have reached Cooperstown. Let's take Craig Biggio, a New York guy himself who went from Kings Park, Long Island, and then Seton Hall University in New Jersey to a stellar 20-year career with the Houston Astros from 1988 to 2007.

First and foremost—Biggio is a member of the esteemed 3,000 club, assuring himself a reservation for the Hall of Fame. He got 68 percent in his first year on the ballot in 2013, missed by literally a couple of votes in his second year, and then broke through with 82 percent in 2015. But despite voters' fascination with round numbers, Biggio's career was really no better than Randolph's. First the career WARs: Randolph 65.9 in 18 years, Biggio 65.5 in 20 years. The 10-year peak goes to Biggio 53.7 to 48.5, a difference of half a win per year. Biggio had his monster year in 1997, hitting .309 with a .415 OBP, 22 homers, 143 OPS-plus and a 9.4 WAR. But otherwise, very close. Biggio hit the four-win plateau nine times, one fewer than Randolph.

Playing in a high-powered offensive era, Biggio hit .281 with a .363 on-base percentage for his career. The OBP beat his peers by 10 percent, less than Randolph's 14 percent during his time. Once again, there's the power issue, with Biggio launching 291 homers and outslugging the league by 6 percent during his career (he was at least 10 percent better eight times) to easily outdo Randolph in that department. But yet again, we have a wide gulf on defense.

Originally a catcher, Biggio started playing some outfield in his second season, and then was ultimately converted to second base by his fifth year in 1992, where he became a mainstay for the next 16 years. What the Astros got was a very good hitting second baseman. Defensively, the numbers say he was 34 runs below average for his position, or a couple of runs per year. That's 148 runs in arrears of Randolph. Yes, we all love power, but defense counts, especially in the middle infield.

How important were the 3,000 hits to Biggio? Apparently enough that he stayed around for a subpar season to reach the plateau, hitting .251 with a 71 OPS-plus and -2.1 WAR at age 41 in 2007. In getting his 130 hits to boost his career total to 3,060, Biggio subtracted from his overall career body of work. It kind of shows the folly of a plateau for its own sake—Biggio was as much (or more) a Hall of Famer at 2,930 hits as he was at 3,060. Hopefully the voters would have elected him anyway. And they should have elected Randolph, who was just about as good.

One more comparison. Let's take a look at Ryne Sandberg, the Cubs' superstar second baseman during the mid '80s to the early '90s. Sandberg broke in full time with Chicago in 1982 after a trade from the Phillies, and broke through for his first big year in 1984 when he led the team to its first-ever division title with a .314 average, 19 home runs and a 140 OPS-plus. Sandberg became the darling of Chicago fans over the next several years, largely a Cubs version of what Derek Jeter became with the Yankees a bit later. Not that it wasn't deserved. Sandberg obviously went on to a big career, hitting 282 homers from the second base position (leading the league with 40 one year), with a .344 on-base percentage, 114 OPS-plus, and strong defense. Driving his career wasn't so much lifetime totals but a stellar peak—four separate times he put up a season with minimums of a 140 OPS-plus and a 7.0 WAR. He made it into the Hall of Fame on his third try in 2005.

Randolph never had such a peak. But his overall career wasn't far off Sandberg's at all. First, the superior defense—Randolph's 114 runs above average easily eclipsed Sandberg's 60, a good-sized gap even with Randolph playing three more seasons. The numbers show that Sandberg was a solid defender, but that his nine Gold Gloves were overkill, probably a result of low error totals used in the absence of advanced defensive metrics. Sandberg's on-base percentage beat the league average by 6.5 percent, less than half of Randolph's spread. But once again, it's the power that swings things the other way, with Sandberg outslugging the league by 18 percent and outpointing Randolph in OPS-plus, 114 to 104.

Overall, Sandberg's edge over Randolph is pretty minuscule. His 68 career WAR barely beats Randolph's 65.5. Sandberg's 10 best years of 5.8 wins a year top Randolph's 10 best of 4.9 per year, an edge driven by Sandberg's four monster years. Randolph had more quality seasons beyond that, his 10 four-win seasons topping Sandberg's seven. Sandberg has to get the final nod for that great peak, but Randolph's career was certainly almost as good.

Better than Tony Lazzeri, Bobby Doer and Billy Herman. Just a shade off the likes of Craig Biggio, Ryne Sandberg and Derek Jeter. Yes, Willie Randolph was dismissed way too quickly by Cooperstown voters.

Randolph wrapped up his final Yankee season in 1988, an injury-plagued year that saw him hit .230 (but still a .322 OBP and 1.5 defensive WAR). He signed with the Dodgers as a free agent and had an All-Star season in 1989 with a .366 on-base percentage and 4.1 WAR at age 34. On Sunday afternoon August 20 of that year, he stepped to the plate at Shea Stadium with two out and two on in the top of the ninth, the Dodgers trailing the Mets 4–1, and drove a pitch from reliever Don Aase into the right-field bullpen to tie the game. The Dodgers would score another run before the inning ended to win 5–4. It was Randolph's last big New York moment as a player.

After bouncing around to Oakland and Milwaukee and then taking a final bow close to home with the 1992 Mets, Willie Randolph called it quits at age 37. But he wasn't nearly done in New York. Two years later he'd be coaching with the Yankees, the start of an 11-year run that saw him win four World Series rings to go with the two he got as a player. In 2005 he was named the 18th manager of the New York Mets. He went 302–253 in three-plus seasons in Flushing, just missing a World Series in 2006. But all those extra years under the bright lights didn't exactly propel him into the spotlight. "You might think that his career as a coach and manager would help him, but it hasn't," says Ken Davidoff.

That's probably because Randolph managed as he played—steady and focused, day in and day out, leaving the spotlight to others.

4

Bernie Williams

The afternoon of October 5, 1996, was a warm, sunny day in Arlington, Texas. The Yankees were in town for Game 4 of the American League Division Series against the Texas Rangers. It was a series that the Yankees wanted badly, and one that would prove quite pivotal toward the mini dynasty that was about to take off. The club was already into its fourth season of recovery from a tough period in the early 1990s, but still had little to show for it. The 1993 season had brought a second-place finish and 88 wins, the team's first winning mark in five years. The following year came a league-best 70–43 record in August before it all went to waste when a player strike wiped out the rest of the season. A breakthrough of sorts came in 1995, when the Yankees took the A.L. Wild Card for their first postseason appearance in 14 years. But that first A.L.D.S. ended in disappointment when the Seattle Mariners erased a 0–2 series hole with a three-game sweep at the Kingdome to send the Yankees home.

As a sense of urgency to take the next step took hold in 1996, the team shook things up with a number of changes. Manager Buck Showalter, who had a reputation for working better with younger, up and coming players than with veterans, was replaced by the low-key Joe Torre. Iconic first baseman Don Mattingly retired and was replaced by Tino Martinez, a strong hitter from the Mariners whom the Yankees acquired in a trade that also bolstered the bullpen with right-hander Jeff Nelson. Good hitting catcher Mike Stanley was replaced by the more defensive oriented Joe Girardi. Starters Kenny Rogers and Dwight Gooden were signed to add depth to the rotation. A trade with the White Sox added veteran Tim Raines to the outfield. A couple of other veteran righty bats, Cecil Fielder and Charlie Hayes, would be added during the season. And a pair of youngsters who had just gotten their big-league feet wet in 1995—their names were Derek Jeter and Mariano Rivera—were in the fold for their first full Yankee seasons. The changes worked. The '96 Yankees weren't a team you'd call dominant, finishing in the middle of the A.L. in scoring and slightly better than average in staff ERA. But their 92 wins were good enough to take the division by four games over Baltimore, the Yankees' first division title since 1981.

Now here they were in the Division Series against Texas, and it was a dogfight. At Yankee Stadium, the Rangers had roughed up David Cone for a 6–2 win in the first game, and then jumped out to an early 4–1 lead against Andy Pettitte in Game 2. But six-plus scoreless innings from the bullpen gave the Yankees time to chip away and tie the game in the eighth and then win it 5–4 on an error in the bottom of the 12th. In Game 3 in Arlington, the Rangers got a terrific start from young left-hander Darren Oliver, who took a 2–1 lead into the ninth inning. But just three outs

Bernie Williams was the only center fielder in the major leagues to register a .900 or better OPS in every season from 1996 to 2002.

away from falling behind in the series, the Yankees rallied for two in the top of the ninth to pull out a 3–2 win.

So that's where the Yankees sat on this beautiful Saturday afternoon, with a precarious two-games-to-one lead thanks to a pair of razor-thin come-from-behind wins. A loss today would send the series to a sudden death Game 5. Things didn't begin well. Rogers started for the Yankees and was pulled after allowing four hits and two runs in the bottom of the second. Reliever Brian Boehringer started the third and immediately gave up a homer to Juan Gonzalez. Texas added one more in the inning on an error, walk and single for a 4–0 lead.

There was still time but the Yankees needed base runners, needed to get something going. Their first hitter in the top of the fourth, the guy who had been their best player all season, center fielder Bernie Williams, led off against Rangers' starter Bobby Witt with a line single to center field. With Tino Martinez at the plate, Williams got a good jump on Witt and stole second. He got to third on a wild pitch as Martinez walked and then scored on a Cecil Fielder single. The rally continued with three more singles and two more runs as Witt was knocked out of the game. The Yankees were right back in it, 4–3.

In the next inning, with right-hander Roger Pavlik pitching for the Rangers, the switch-hitting Williams led off hitting lefty and launched a deep blast over the right-center field fence. Tie game, 4–4. Meantime the Yankee bullpen began to clamp down. David Weathers retired nine of 10 batters through three scoreless innings as the Yankees took the lead in the seventh on a Fielder RBI single. After Mariano Rivera followed with two more scoreless innings, Williams padded the Yankee lead when, hitting right-handed against lefty Mike Stanton in the top of the ninth, he pulled a long home run into the left field seats to make the score 6–4. It was Williams' third homer in two games. Closer John Wetteland walked two in the bottom of the ninth but hung on, striking out Dean Palmer to end it. The Yankees had taken the series with a third consecutive comeback win.

For Bernie Williams in the finale: 3-for-5 including a homer from each side of the plate, three runs scored and two driven in. For the series: 7-for-15 with a pair of walks, three home runs and five RBI in the four games. For the first time in 15 years, the Yankees had won a postseason series, the one that would launch 14 postseason series wins in 15 tries.

Williams wasn't nearly done as the Yankees move on to the American League Championship Series against the Orioles. In Game 1 at

Yankee Stadium, with the Orioles ahead 4–2 in the bottom of the seventh, he pulled a double into right field to move Wade Boggs to third base. Boggs would eventually score on a bases loaded walk to pull the Yankees to within a run. The bottom of the eighth brought a memorable tying home run by Derek Jeter, the one on which no interference was called after the ball was famously plucked by a 12-year-old fan reaching over the right field wall. The Yankees had a chance to take the lead later in the inning, but the Orioles intentionally walked Williams with two down and a runner on second. They got out of the inning when Tino Martinez lined out.

The game moved into extra innings tied 4–4. In the bottom of the 11th, Williams led off against Randy Myers, who was working his third inning of relief. Batting right-handed for the first time in the game, he drilled a shot down the left field line that just stayed fair for a home run. Game over. As the Yankees went on to spank the Orioles in five games, Williams added another homer in Game 4 and finished the series 9-for-19 with five walks for a .474 batting average, .583 on-base percentage and a 1.567 OPS. He was the team's one-man wrecking crew on its march to the World Series, finishing the nine games against Texas and Baltimore 16-for-34 with five homers and 11 RBI.

Williams didn't hit much against the Braves in the 1996 World Series. Few of his teammates did either—the team hit .216 against an Atlanta pitching staff led by three future Hall of Famers in John Smoltz, Greg Maddux and Tom Glavine. Williams finished the six-game series 4-for-24, but he did make a couple of his hits count. After the Yankees dropped the first two games at home, he stepped up in the top of the first inning of Game 3 and delivered an RBI single off Glavine to put the Yankees ahead for the first time in the series. Later, with the Yankees holding on to a 2–1 lead in the eighth, Williams ripped a big two-run homer off Greg McMichael to boost the lead to 4–1. The Yankees took the must-win third game 5–2. The next night brought the memorable three-run homer by reserve catcher Jim Leyritz off Mark Wohlers to tie the fourth game 6–6 in the eighth inning. In the top of the 10th, Williams came up against Steve Avery with runners on first and second and two down. Despite no open base, Braves manager Bobby Cox had Avery walk Williams intentionally, much to the astonishment of Tim McCarver in the Fox TV booth.[1] That set up a bases loaded walk to Wade Boggs to drive in the lead run. After another run came in on an error, the Yankees had an 8–6 win to tie the series. They completed the four-game comeback by pulling out tight wins of 1–0 and 3–2 in the next two games. The Yankees were on top of the baseball world for the first time since 1978. And make no mistake, Bernie Williams, who had preceded his big '96 playoff run with a .305 batting average, .391 on-base percentage, 26 homers and 131 OPS-plus regular season, was their biggest weapon.

Williams had always been considered a good prospect since the Yankees signed out of his native Puerto Rico as a 17-year-old 1986. He had success moving up the chain over the next few years, but it was sporadic. At age 19 in 1988 he hit .335 for the Class-A Prince William Yankees but slumped to .235 the following year against the tougher competition of Double-A and Triple-A. But Williams, who had filled out to 6-foot-2 and about 200 pounds, was beginning to flash some power, hitting 13 homers. And he showed a good eye at the plate by drawing 85 walks in his 578 plate appearances. By 1991, when Williams was hitting .294 with a .372 on-base percentage at Triple-A Columbus, the Yankees called him up in early July.

The early 1990s were a rough time for the Yankees. Stump Merrill was the manager. Lineup regulars included Jesse Barfield, Steve Sax, Matt Nokes and Alvaro Espinosa. The team hadn't produced a top-notch homegrown player since Don Mattingly almost a decade earlier. But the Yankees did have a pretty talented guy who played Williams's position—fleet center fielder Roberto Kelly, who had hit .285 with 42 steals and 15 homers as a rare bright spot in the Yankees' last place 1990 season. It was an injury to Kelly that got Williams the call in July of '91. But with the team going nowhere, management seemed determined to give the 22-year old Williams a chance to win the center field job. With Kelly shifted to left upon his return in mid–August, Williams wound up starting nearly every day during the second half of the season. But he didn't do well, finishing the 1991 season at .236 with three home runs. He would spend most of the first half of the 1992 season back in Columbus. But after hitting over .300 for the Clippers, he was back in Yankee pinstripes by August 1. Aside from a couple of injury rehab assignments years later, Williams would never wear a minor league uniform again. Not because he went gangbusters right away—he didn't. Over the next two years, from his August 1992 recall to the August 1994 players' strike, Williams hit .279 with 29 homers. Promising, but nothing special.

But the Yankees still loved the tools. Williams had a fluid stroke and great bat speed. And he could run. He was clearly on the upswing as the

'94 strike approached, finishing his 108-game season with a .384 OBP, solid defensive metrics and a 3.2 WAR. A natural right-handed hitter, he wasn't hitting as well from the left side just yet. No doubt the club figured that if that part of his game came around, the homers over Yankee Stadium's short right field porch might start coming in bunches. In fact they were high enough on him to make a big 1993 trade, shipping Kelly to the Cincinnati Reds for right fielder Paul O'Neill. No one could have predicted it at the time, but the Yankees now had a pair of players who would stand side-by-side in their outfield for the next nine years, both of them foundation pieces for a run of championships.

It all started to click in 1995. The start of the abbreviated 144-game season was pushed into late April as the 1994 strike was finally settled. It was Don Mattingly's final year. Andy Pettitte debuted in the starting rotation. A pair of prominent former Mets came aboard when Darryl Strawberry signed as a free agent in June and David Cone arrived in a trade from Toronto in July. O'Neill hit .300 with 22 homers as the regular right fielder. And Bernie Williams, who turned 27 in September, broke out into a star. He homered on opening day in an 8–6 win over Texas, then slumped through much of May before accelerating to raise his average 50 points in June on the way to his first .300-plus season. Most of Williams's power still came from the right side, but he hit over .300 from both sides as he set career highs across the board with a .307 batting average, .392 on-base percentage, 18 home runs and a 129 OPS-plus. The advanced defensive metrics, which were not very kind to Williams later in his career, were kind to him in 1995 with 14 runs above average in center field and a 1.7 defensive WAR. It added up to a 6.4 WAR for the season, easily the best on the Yankees and sixth among everyday players in the American League. His name appeared nowhere in the MVP voting among 21 players that received votes. Boston's big first baseman Mo Vaughn, who outslugged Williams by a good margin but whose all-around game was certainly in arrears of him, took the hardware with a 4.3 WAR. Williams followed the '95 regular season with a stellar Division Series against Seattle, going 9-for-21 with a pair of homers, though the team lost in five games.

The 1995 season kicked off an eight-year run during which Bernie Williams very much dominated, yet managed to keep himself relatively below the radar. Not *un*appreciated, mind you, just *under* appreciated. This despite all the trappings of sports celebrity—the big market, the Yankee brand, the multiple championships. Williams even had the added distinction of filling the much-noted role of patrolling center field at Yankee Stadium, the guy walking in the footsteps of DiMaggio and Mantle. But Williams' style didn't scream "look at me!" He beat opponents with his all-around game as opposed to dominating in any particular phase. He was cool, casual and consistent in that way that gets people taking you for granted after a while. During one five-year stretch from 1997 to 2001, Williams's annual home run total never wavered beyond a range of 21 to 30. His OPS-plus stayed between 140 and 160 and his WAR between 5.2 and 5.5. Bernie Williams was so consistent he was boring.

Williams's style on the field seemed to reflect his personality off it. You may know that he's an accomplished musician. He always said that his time away from the field was important to him, that relaxing with his guitar was his way of recharging his batteries during the day-to-day baseball grind. He seemed to play the game like jazz musician he was, with a sweet swing, fluid strides and an understated manner. Day after day, he was just in the groove. In other words, not your typical jock. The *Post*'s Ken Davidoff, who wrote for *The Record* and *Newsday* during most of Williams's career, remembers: "He was an artist, always, in the way he approached life. He was extremely intelligent, not a style we associate with athletics. He was a different bird."

Basically, Williams was a bit "out there," people thought. He wasn't particularly absorbed in baseball 24/7. Sometimes such things can be interpreted as less than fully committed. Maybe that's why he never got the fan or press love enjoyed by Derek Jeter, his co-star on the powerhouse Yankee teams of the mid–1990s to the early 2000s. That may seem a bit strange considering how close they were in performance for a long time. Starting with the 1996 season, the year Jeter joined Williams as a lineup regular, and going through 2002, Williams's final season as a star the year he turned 34, there was little to choose between them. Says Brian Kenny, lover of numbers: "The best player on those Yankee championship teams was Bernie Williams." That's debatable, but it's certainly reasonable. Over that seven-year stretch, Williams outdid Jeter in on-base percentage .408 to .390 and outslugged him .539 to .464. Jeter had the edge in WAR, 37.3 to 34.8, thanks mainly to his pair of truly dominant seasons of 1998 and 1999 when both he and the club were right at their peaks. Jeter also had a couple of his better defensive seasons in those years, avoiding the pitfall of defense dragging down the overall WAR the way it would for him in many future seasons.

Beyond 2002, Jeter went on to put up six more seasons of All-Star or borderline All-Star level. His long-term career ultimately outdid that of Williams, who was limited by injury to 119 games in 2003 and then followed with three average to lackluster seasons before playing his last game in 2006, the year he turned 37. Williams still hit decently as his career wound down, but the defensive metrics plummeted, an indication that he wasn't getting to nearly as many balls in the outfield.

As Hall of Fame credentials go, there's no arguing that career length makes Jeter the more slam dunk case. But even for all of those years they were so close, you wouldn't know it by the coverage. Bernie was a nice player, but Jeter was the golden boy. While Jeter was always accessible and affable with the press, Williams liked to keep to himself and get home quickly. "A bit spacey," is how Davidoff puts it. "He would blow off the media." Davidoff acknowledges that he didn't vote for Williams for the Hall, mainly because the combination of the annual voting limit of ten players along with Williams's less than slam dunk case made it difficult to find a spot for him on the ballot. "What a peak, though," Davidoff said. "If you could vote for more than ten I probably would have voted for him."

Williams followed up his big 1996 regular season and postseason by hitting .328, fourth in the American League, with a .408 on-base percentage and 147 OPS-plus in 1997. He hit 21 homers and drove in an even 100 runs. Williams's 5.5 WAR ranked seventh in the league among everyday players; in the MVP voting he finished 17th. He struggled in the A.L. Division Series against Cleveland, going 2-for-17 as the Yankees dropped the series, their only postseason blemish between 1996 and 2000.

But then Williams just continued to blister the baseball as the Yankees rolled to their three straight championships beginning in 1998. He took his only A.L. batting crown that year with a .339 average, a career-high 160 OPS-plus and 26 homers as the Yanks smashed their way to a historic 114-win season and then rolled through the playoffs by going 11–2 against Texas, Cleveland and San Diego. And yet, there was never quite that full appreciation. Williams was a free agent following the 1998 season. Despite a batting a title, a .422 on-base percentage, power, and another world championship, the club hesitated to bring him back. Yankee brass sat back and watched Williams come very close to signing with the Red Sox as they flirted with Albert Belle, a monster power hitter but also known to be contentious and one dimensional, as a free agent replacement. Only after Boston offered Williams seven years did the Yankees, who had seemed to be firm on no more than a five-year deal, capitulate. They signed Williams for seven years and $87.5 million. Belle wound up signing with Baltimore.

Good thing. Williams's numbers were similar across the board during the next two years, including career highs of a .342 average and .435 OBP in 1999 and 30 homers and 121 RBI in 2000 as the Yankees took two more World Series titles, giving them four in five seasons.

Williams wasn't always statistically the best player in the Yankee lineup during the championship run, but he was always in the top three and always comfortably at All-Star level. As players like O'Neill and catcher Jorge Posada took turns popping into the top one or two in their best seasons, Williams and Jeter were the constants. Jeter at or near the top of the order, Williams in the middle. It's hard to even calculate the inherent value of having a productive switch hitter like Williams in the middle of the lineup day in and day out, balancing against the right-handed hitters like Jeter and Chuck Knoblauch and lefties O'Neill and Martinez. Williams was the center of gravity for a balanced lineup that dominated the American League for the better part of eight years.

You've heard the expression "Core Four," applied to Jeter, Rivera, Pettitte and Posada as the foundation of those Yankee teams? It's a nice moniker, but it's not accurate. It's a term that only began in more recent years because that quartet happened to make up the last four Yankees of that era who were still with the team years later (Pettitte actually left for Houston for three years and came back, but it's the same idea). All four lasted until at least 2011, and it's true that they were all part of the Yankees' 2009 championship team, which Williams wasn't. But as far as the dynasty that played in six World Series and won four of them over eight seasons, Williams was as "core" as anyone.

The Yankees didn't win another title during the Williams era, though they just about got number five in 2001 when the Arizona Diamondbacks grabbed two runs in the bottom of the ninth inning off Rivera to win Game 7 of the World Series 3–2 and end the Yankees' run. For Bernie Williams in 2001, it was another (ho-hum) five-plus win season with a .307 average, .392 OBP, 26 homers and a 139 OPS-plus. He followed with three home runs in the Yankees' six-game victory over the 116-win Seattle Mariners in the A.L.C.S., including a dramatic solo shot in the bottom of the eighth inning to tie the fourth game 1–1 and set up Alfonso Soriano's game winning homer in the ninth for a pivotal win that put the Yankee up three games to one. Williams's blast came off Seattle's lefty reliever Arthur Rhodes, who was summoned for the eighth inning because two of the three scheduled hitters in that inning, David Justice and Tino Martinez, were left-handed. Rhodes got both of them out, but, unfortunately for him, he had to face the switch-hitting Williams in between.

The 2002 season saw the Yankees fail to make it to the World Series for the first time in five years. The look of the team was changing a bit—it was the first year with the club for Jason Giambi and Robin Ventura and the second for Mike Mussina as the team spent to replace worn parts with new ones. Soriano, in his second year as the regular second baseman, led the league with 209 hits and blasted 39 homers. The team had an excellent season with 103 wins and a first-place finish in the A.L. East, but didn't pitch well in a Division Series loss to the eventual champion Anaheim Angels. Bernie Williams put up his eighth All-Star caliber year in a row—really the ninth if you count the strike-shortened 1994 season—by hitting .333 with a .415 on-base percentage, 19 home runs and a 141 OPS-plus. There were those signs, though that he was beginning to slow down in center field at age 33. FanGraphs pegged him at 17 runs below average at his position and Baseball Reference at -1.7 defensive WAR, both career worsts.

As to the defensive part of Williams's game, he was one of those players whose eye test was always better than his advanced metrics. While he never had a strong throwing arm, there were the smooth strides, the athleticism, that look of consistently having things under control. Williams always seemed to be making the plays, both coming in to take away potential shallow base hits and going back to rob those potential extra base hits by the wall. The metrics told a different story, that of an outfielder who didn't always get the best jump off the bat, the result being a lot of balls finding landing spots in his general vicinity that other center fielders would have tracked down. Says Davidoff: "[Joe] Torre could see that he didn't have the gut instincts out there."

To be consistent across this book, we're going with the metrics over the eye test. But in Williams's case, even the metrics aren't altogether unkind until the tail end of his career. They paint a picture of a perfectly capable center fielder who began to slow down as he neared his mid–30s. Williams's career -9.5 defensive WAR was lowlighted by a -9.1 during his last five years. His zone numbers on FanGraphs show a total of 44 runs below average from 1991 through 2001, or a modest 4.4 per year, with three seasons in positive territory. Then they plummet to 111 below average from 2002 to 2006, over 20 per year. You've heard of a player losing a step as he ages? Clearly Williams was losing a couple of them after age 33. But for most of his career he was a premium offensive player whose defense dragged down his overall value by just a tad. Take away the late career defense, and Williams's overall 49.6 career WAR—including eight seasons of a 4.0 or better and six of a 5.0 or better—would be several points higher.

In the end, Hall of Fame voters weren't impressed. Williams got 9.6 percent of the vote in his first year of eligibility in 2012, barely enough to stay on the ballot. By the next year he dropped to 3.3 percent, below the 5 percent threshold. That was it—Williams was two and done. He can only hope that a future Veterans Committee takes up his cause at some point.

You may believe that the voters may have essentially had it right on Williams. That a player with a great peak but also a minimal number of "tack on" seasons to boost the career totals is simply not a Hall of Famer. Very good, sure, but to make it all the way to Cooperstown you need to show more than 287 homers and 2,300 hits. And it's a perfectly legitimate argument. Fans will always have honest differences when it comes to balancing dominance and longevity. "A lot of Hall of Fame careers are built after the age of 34, as they hit milestones that make it easy to reflect back on their careers," says Brian Kenny. A good example is Dave Winfield, whose career through his age 34 season was statistically even with Williams's. But Winfield went on to play for another nine years beyond that as he bounced around among the Yankees, Angels, Blue Jays, Twins and Indians. Only two of those seasons were All-Star caliber (with the 1988 Yankees and 1992 Jays), but he managed to accumulate enough to push through the 3,000 hit and 400 home run plateaus. Basing an All-Star season on a 4.0 WAR or higher, even those extra years gave Winfield just seven such seasons, while Williams had eight, with a ninth interrupted by the 1994 strike (Winfield was not on such a pace in the 1981 strike year).

It's certainly true that Winfield's added production after age 34 has to count for something. That nine-year stretch added 11.9 WAR to push his career total to 64.2, almost 15 points beyond Williams, whose career WAR dropped by 1.1 after age 34. Ultimately, Winfield's career has to rate ahead of Williams's. But by how much? Does going along as a mostly average player for those additional years to tack on a milestone or two make the fundamental difference as to whether you're a Hall of Fame player, as opposed to the number of seasons in which you performed like a star?

Even acknowledging that Williams's career falls in arrears of Winfield's doesn't mean he's not a Hall of Famer. We're not talking about a four- or five-year peak here, à la Roger Maris or Don Mattingly, we're talking about nine years. There's plenty of precedent for such players making it to the Hall of Fame.

Let's start with Yankee centerfield history. There's no comparing Williams to Mantle or DiMaggio, but another pinstriped center fielder who made it to Cooperstown was Earle Combs, a Kentuckian who played from 1924 to 1935 and won four World Series rings. Combs was the leadoff man for the "Murderers' Row" Yankees of Babe Ruth and Lou Gehrig. He set the table for the big boys in the lineup about as well as anyone could, hitting over .300 in nine of his 11 full seasons. Combs hit .325 lifetime with a .397 OBP. For the definitive Murderers' Row team of 1927, the club that won 110 games as Ruth smashed 60 home runs and Gehrig took the American League MVP with 47 homers and a .373 average, Combs came to the plate 726 times and batted .356 with a .414 on-base percentage. He led the league with 231 hits and 23 triples, the first of three times he would lead the A.L. in three-baggers.

Combs's major league career got off to a relatively late start. He was a college graduate—rare for that era of baseball. He broke in with the Yankees a month before his 25th birthday and became a regular the following year. His career largely mirrored Williams's in that regard—shining brightly from age 26 to 34 and then slowing to part time duty for a couple of years before retiring. There is very little to choose between the two of them. The OPS-plus was identical—both finished at 125. Combs was a below average home run hitter, but his penchant for triples pushed his slugging percentage to 13.6 percent above league average, better than Williams's 10.1 percent. Combs also had a slight on-base advantage, 13.1 percent better than average to Williams's 11.6 percent. Combs was mostly average defensively, according to the metrics, coming out a bit better than Williams.

What differs is the breakdown of each career, which generally shows Combs doing a bit more during the early and later years but Williams enjoying the better peak. While it seems surprising to see that Combs outperformed the league average in slugging percentage by a bit more than Williams did despite hitting far fewer homers, it makes more sense when you realize that Williams's overall .477 mark was dragged down by five below average seasons at the beginning and end of his career. During his prime, Williams outslugged the American League by 20 percent or more six times, something Combs did only twice. The numbers are similar for on-base percentage—Williams coming in 20 percent or more above league average four times, Combs once.

As for WAR, Williams beats Combs 49.6 to 42.5, thanks mainly to his best seasons being better than Combs's best seasons. Combs had seven seasons of a 4.0 or better—one fewer than Williams—and never fell below a 2.0 until his last year. But in only two of those seven seasons did he reach a 5.0, which Williams did six times.

Earle Combs wound up making it to the Hall of Fame the hard way, passed over by the writers but ultimately getting the call from the Veterans Committee in 1970, six years before he passed away. Talk about the lore of playing center field for the Yankees. For more than four decades, pretty much uninterrupted aside from World War II, the position was held down by just three players: Combs, DiMaggio and Mantle. We know that Bernie Williams was at least as good as one of them.

There was another old-time center fielder whose career largely overlapped with Combs's, another player with big numbers who was passed over for the Hall of Fame by the baseball writers before the Veterans Committee gave him the nod years later. That would be Earl Averill, who did a lot more in his career than hit Dizzy Dean with a line drive in an All-Star Game. Playing from 1929 to 1941, mostly with the Indians, Averill batted .318 with a .395 on-base percentage, both about 12.5 percent above league average during that hitter-friendly time, and both slightly better than Williams's numbers against his peers. He also surpassed 30 home runs three times, finishing with 238 for his career. Averill led the American League with 232 hits and 15 triples in 1936. His career 133 OPS-plus beats out Williams's 125. No doubt it was Williams's edge in speed that kept his WAR about even with Averill—ultimately edging him 49.6 to 48.0.

Like both Williams and Combs, Averill bloomed late, debuting in the big leagues at age 26 and killing it for eight years before his production faded significantly in his last five. He averaged 4.8 wins in his ten best seasons (netting out at zero the rest of the way), essentially equal to Williams's 4.7 per year. If you took every centerfielder in major league history and had them form a line in order of career production, Bernie Williams and Earl Averill would be standing right beside each other, jostling over who gets to cut in front of who, with Combs observing from just a spot or two further back. Here's hoping that Williams eventually gets the same Veterans Committee consideration that Averill and Combs did.

How about some more contemporary outfielders? Kirby Puckett was one of baseball's brightest stars from the mid–1980s to the mid–1990s. A perennial All-Star centerfielder who led the Minnesota Twins to two World Series championships, Puckett was an established star when Williams debuted in 1991, their careers eventually overlapping for five seasons. Puckett hit better than .300 eight times while hitting 207 homers, good power for a central position player in a relatively dead ball era (baseball's more offensively fueled period took off near the tail end of Puckett's career). And he did it all with an infectious enthusiasm and likeability that made him one of the game's top faces just as the modern television era was launching. A Puckett highlight or two seemed to be almost a nightly occurrence during the early days of ESPN's *SportsCenter.* In 1990, he became the first player in MLB history to sign for $3 million per season, back when you could still earn the highest salary in the sport in a small market.

Kirby Puckett's career and life would end sadly, of course. A bout with glaucoma that cost Puckett his vision in his right eye ended his playing days at age 35 just before the start of the 1996 season. A decade later he passed away from a cerebral hemorrhage. But his 12-year career was brilliant. After hitting .318 for his career with six Gold Gloves, he was voted into the Hall of Fame in 2001, his first year on the ballot. The vote evoked no real controversy, with few if any people inclined to dispute Puckett's qualifications.

But was Kirby Puckett any better than Bernie Williams? In short, no, not really.

First the defense. Puckett was known for his highlight reel plays, which no doubt was the reason, along with the name recognition from his offense, for the six Gold Gloves he was awarded. But the advanced numbers show he was pretty much an average outfielder—close to neutral on runs saved with a slightly negative defensive WAR. That's still better than Williams, but below the defensive rep.

Offensively, Williams rate of getting on base was better than Puckett's, with a .381 on-base percentage that was 11.6 percent better than league average compared to Puckett's .360 OBP that was 8.9 percent better. The two had identical slugging percentages, which favors Puckett in his more pitcher-friendly era—18 percent better than league average to Williams's 10 percent with most of the difference attributable to Williams's dropoff late in his career. During each player's 10 best seasons, Puckett outslugged the league by just a bit more than Williams did. The career OPS-plus is virtually a draw—125 to 124 for Williams. The same goes for career WAR: Puckett 51.1, Williams 49.6. Both averaged a 4.7 in his 10 best years, with Williams hitting the 4.0 mark eight times to Puckett's seven.

Basically we've got two identical ballplayers here. For one to hit 82 percent of the Hall of Fame ballots and the other failing to reach 10 percent is a bit out of whack, to say the least.

How about an outfielder who reigned as an offensive force in the American League for a good chunk of the 1970s and '80s—Boston Red Sox slugger Jim Rice? After a 15-year career that ended in 1989, Rice was initially met with a tepid welcome from Hall of Fame voters, hitting 29.8 percent of ballots in his first year of eligibility in 1995. Not tremendous support, but still easily enough votes to remain planted on the ballot for several years to come. Sure enough, he climbed steadily and finally reached the Promised Land in 2009, his final year on the ballot.

Rice was slowed by vision problems toward the end of his career that hurt his production during his final couple of years and left him with 382 career homers, not a tremendous number for a corner outfielder who was seen as fairly one dimensional and who played in a ballpark that was friendly to right-handed power hitters. That would probably explain the hesitation on the part of many writers to vote for him initially. In the end though, the voters decided that they couldn't ignore the offensive resume: eight 100-plus RBI seasons, seven .300-plus seasons, top 10 in slugging percentage eight times, top 10 in total bases nine times, top 10 in homers seven times, and a memorable MVP season in 1978 when he hit .315 with 46 home runs and 139 RBI, along with league-leading figures of 213 hits, 15 triples and a .600 slugging percentage.

Bernie Williams didn't have a single year that matched Rice's 1978 MVP season, though he came quite close in 1995 with a 6.4 WAR in a slightly shortened season that projected to 7.2 over a full season, not far off Rice's 7.5 in 1978. Career wise, Rice was obviously the superior power hitter—outslugging the league by 26 percent for his career including by 35 percent or more five times. But his on-base numbers (7.7 percent better than league average) don't match Williams, and he certainly didn't get Williams's added WAR points from speed. Rice grounded into almost 100 more double plays than Williams did during his career, a big part of the speed factor in scoring WAR.

There's also that subtle factor at work, that one definitive characteristic that a player is known for. It's called being *positioned in the marketplace*. Whether it's Procter & Gamble selling laundry detergent, a political consultant running a campaign to get someone elected to office, or a baseball player being considered for the Hall of Fame, it helps tremendously to have a particular focus on which people can hang their hats. Something simple that defines him without having to think about it much. They call it the elevator pitch—a way to define someone in the tiny amount of time it takes to ascend from the lobby to the 12th floor. Says Rob Neyer: "Rice had that elevator pitch, because a few writers kept saying over and over that he was the most feared hitter in the game." That's how Jim Rice was positioned in the marketplace—"most feared hitter in the game," even though there's really no way to measure such a thing.

Can you think of a Bernie Williams elevator pitch? Probably not, right? This is why all-around players tend to get short shrift compared to those who stand out in a certain way. Guys like Jim Edmonds and Reggie Smith could commiserate with Williams.

As feared a hitter as Rice was, his career production was more choppy than consistent. There was the great three-year run from 1977 to 1979 when he averaged better than a 150 OPS-plus and a 6.3 WAR. Next came three good-but-not-great seasons when he hit a little below .300 and averaged 22 homers and just a 2.4 WAR. Rice then banged out a terrific year in 1983 with 39 homers, 141 OPS-plus and a 5.6 WAR. After that—two more so-so years before his final big year in 1986, when he led Boston to the American League pennant with another 5.6 WAR season highlighted by a .324 average, .384 OBP, and 110 RBI.

It all adds up to five All-Star caliber seasons for Rice, three fewer than Williams. Rice does have a small advantage in OPS-plus, 128 to 125, though those numbers certainly favor Williams as a centerfielder relative to Rice's corner outfield standard. Ultimately, Rice's 47.7 career WAR falls a tad short of Williams. As for peak—Rice amassed 30 WAR, about two-thirds of his total, in those five sparkling seasons. That's only a bit better than 27 WAR that Williams registered in his best five. Williams had the slightly better 10-year peak, 4.7 wins to 4.4.

Defense is a bit tougher to compare—a leftfielder vs. a centerfielder. Rice didn't have a great defensive reputation in his day, generally seen as slow and lumbering in the field. There's truth to that, but the numbers show that he was better with the glove than people tend to remember, sure-handed enough to score a bit above average in defensive runs saved (a little more than one per year). That's better than Williams did in center, but of course it's apples and oranges. Can anyone envision Jim Rice playing centerfield day in and day out at Williams's level? Common sense says there is no way it happens. As Brian Kenny puts it: "Rice was a station to station corner player. Williams was an athletic player playing a central position."

As advanced stats go, Williams's stature as a central player gave him an easier offensive standard and a tougher defensive standard to meet compared to Rice, which is why offensive WAR tilts so heavily toward Williams and defensive metrics to Rice. It all nets out pretty close, but with an edge to Williams given his longer peak.

You might think this is all a better argument for saying that the voters made more of a mistake putting Rice into the Hall of Fame than they did in keeping Williams out. You could look at it that way if you're Cooperstown standard is particularly high, but it's a tough sell when you consider that Rice still clearly stands above several Hall of Fame outfielders including Chuck Klein, Edd Roush, Hack Wilson and even a 3,000-hit man, Lou Brock. The easiest solution is to acknowledge that Bernie Williams stands with or above a lot outfielders whose plaques now hang in Cooperstown. So why not hang his plaque, too?

And while we're speaking of Lou Brock, let's take a moment to explain why he's the perfect example of why two old-school stats that Bernie Williams didn't compile a ton of—career hits and stolen bases—ought not to be automatic tickets to Cooperstown. This isn't to knock the man, who obviously had a very good career. But we now know there are better ways to measure a player's production. Brock is a member of the 3,000-hit club. Ok, it's a great accomplishment, but it's only one more than 2,999, just with many more bells and whistles attached. Most everyone on the 3,000-hit list is indeed a deserving Hall of Famer—not because of the 3,000 hits per se, but rather because they were deserving anyway. Accumulating that many hits is derivative of a player's greatness, not the cause. No player in the 3,000-hit club other than Brock had a career WAR lower than 64. The only eligible player from the club passed over for the Hall was PED suspect Rafael Palmeiro.

Then there's Brock, whose career WAR was 45.3 in 18 seasons. That's almost 20 points lower than anyone else. He had three outstanding seasons for the Cardinals in the 1960s, but only one or two others that could be considered All-Star level. His 149 homers and 109 OPS-plus were weak for a corner outfielder, and his defensive metrics were below average. Of course there is also Brock's other big claim to fame—the thing that truly positions him in the marketplace—which was retiring in 1979 as the game's all-time stolen base king. His record 938 steals have been surpassed only by Rickey Henderson over the past four decades. The problem, we know now in the enlightened age, is that stolen bases don't mean that much. A team's chances of scoring increase with a stolen base by far less than its chances decrease when you're caught and get erased from the bases. The risk-reward requires at least a 70 percent success rate to break even, according to various studies. Brock led the league in steals eight times; he also led in getting caught seven times. He finished with a 75 percent success rate for his career, which translates to a marginal contribution of runs for his teams. If you've wondered why Brock's prestigious feats on the base paths didn't particularly show up on the advanced stats meter, that's the reason.

Brock is probably a borderline Hall of Famer at best, yet he was inducted on his first try in 1985. Add him to the list of outfielders in Cooperstown who weren't as good as Bernie Williams.

Williams got his last chance to play in the World Series in 2003. This was the Yankee team that snatched victory from the jaws of defeat in the seventh game of the A.L.C.S. against the Red Sox, the game in which they erased a 5–2, eighth-inning deficit when Sox manager Grady Little infamously left a tiring Pedro Martinez in the game and then watched the Yankees score three times to tie it up. The game ended when Aaron Boone—now the Yankee manager—led off the bottom of the 11th and blasted a flat Tim Wakefield knuckleball into the left field seats.

It hadn't been an easy season for Williams. He was getting older. Torn cartilage in his left knee cost him several weeks on the disabled list during the middle of the season. He finished with a .263 batting average and 107 OPS-plus, his lowest marks since his rookie year. Still, he soldiered on through the challenges just fine—Williams managed 15 homers and a .367 OBP in his 445 at-bats. And he wound up celebrating his 35th birthday in grand style in a September 13 doubleheader sweep of Tampa Bay at Yankee Stadium. In the first game, he swatted a pair of home runs off of Devil Rays right-hander Rob Bell in a 6–5 win. He added a pair of singles in the nightcap, which the Yankees took 6–3 for their eighth win in a row. Williams finished his birthday doubleheader

5-for-7 to help push the club to a 5½ game lead in the American League East. They would clinch the division by September 24 and then defeat the Twins in the A.L.D.S. to set up the dramatic win against Boston a round later.

Maybe the Yankees were a bit spent from the Red Sox series, or maybe they just ran into some really good Florida Marlins pitching, mainly from Josh Beckett, Brad Penny and future Yankee flop Carl Pavano, but they lost the 2003 World Series in six games. Beckett won the clincher at Yankee Stadium on three days' rest with a five-hit shutout and nine strikeouts.

Even in defeat, Bernie Williams had a big series. He homered in a 3–2 loss in the first game and again in a 6–1 victory in the third game. In Game 4, he banged out four hits including a ninth inning single that sparked a two-run rally that tied the game 3–3. He led off the top of the 11th with a big double to right field that could have gone down as the biggest hit of the night had he come around to score the go-ahead run. But he was ultimately left stranded at third, and the Marlins went on to win in 12 innings to tie the series. They'd win the next two behind Penny and Beckett to take the title. Williams finished his World Series swansong 10-for-25 (.400) with a pair of homers. Those numbers helped pad a resume that currently shows Bernie Williams number two all-time in postseason hits (128), home runs (22) and total bases (223). Sure, it's apples and oranges to compare players from the expanded playoff era to older players who played fewer postseason rounds, but the numbers still say something.

In fact, the 121 postseason games that Bernie Williams put under his belt almost add up to another full season, one that also includes a .371 on-base percentage and .850 OPS. So make it 10 years as a star. Plenty for the Hall of Fame.

5

Keith Hernandez

Keith Hernandez woke up to his 29th birthday on the morning of October 20, 1982. But he knew that any celebration plans would have to wait until quite late that night, perhaps even until after midnight. There would be important business at hand first—the seventh game of the World Series.

Hernandez's team, the St. Louis Cardinals, had the town buzzing by reaching its first Series in 14 years. They were battling the Milwaukee Brewers, who had made it for the first time ever in their 13-year existence. The 1982 World Series showcased quite the contrast: a pair of also-ran clubs of the 1970s suddenly reaching the pinnacle through completely different styles. The Brew Crew had bashed its way through the season with 216 home runs, the most in the American League by a comfortable margin. The fearsome lineup that included Cecil Cooper, Paul Molitor, Ben Oglivie, Gorman Thomas and league MVP Robin Yount went by the nickname "Harvey's Wall Bangers," as it outslugged the league under manager Harvey Kuenn, who had taken over for Buck Rodgers at the beginning of June after a 23–24 start. The Brewers didn't exactly cruise to the World Series—they needed a victory in Baltimore on the final day of the regular season to hold off the hard-charging Orioles and then had to rally from a 0–2 deficit in the best-of-five A.L.C.S. to defeat the California Angels. But they'd made it.

The 1982 Cardinals hit 67 home runs. Yes, as a team, for the entire season. That's three fewer than Mark McGwire would hit for them 16 years later. Even in the dead ball era of the early 1980s, it was a shockingly low total for a club that had mustered 101 homers in the most recent full season of 1980. Playing in cavernous Busch Stadium, the Cards had made their way through the 1970s trying to compete with standard lineups—balancing power with defense and speed—that looked fine in a generic sense but didn't work well at Busch. That all changed when Whitey Herzog took over as both manager and G.M. at the tail end of the 1980 season and wasted little time in radically remaking the team. Stationary players were out, athletes were in. Offensive stars at defensive positions—catcher Ted Simmons and shortstop Gary Templeton—were replaced by Darrell Porter and Ozzie Smith, respectively. Simmons was dealt to—of all teams—the Brewers, giving Harvey Kuenn yet another Wall Banger and adding an interesting subplot to the '82 World Series as the Cardinals competed against one of their all-time great players and fan favorites. By 1982, St. Louis injected the outfield with a double dose of speed by trading for Phillies left fielder Lonnie Smith, and, by early May, calling up center fielder Willie McGee, acquired the previous winter as a minor leaguer from the Yankees.

One of the few positions that didn't need a makeover: first base. Keith Hernandez had been the incumbent at first since 1976. Herzog didn't feel compelled to make a change because in Hernandez he already had that unorthodox first baseman that fit his style and fit the ballpark. Hernandez wasn't a big bopper who belonged in a bandbox park to max-

Defensive whiz Keith Hernandez put up offensive numbers right on par with Hall of Fame first basemen Eddie Murray and Tony Perez.

imize home runs, he was an athlete playing first base. Hernandez didn't need to hit a lot of homers to drive in a lot of runs. He hit to all fields. He drove balls up the spacious outfield gaps. He had a great eye, made contact, and got on base. He was quick and agile in the field, equally adept at handling throws and covering ground on the right side of the infield.

The Cards got an early indication that things would work out in 1982 when they scored five runs in their first inning of the season in Houston, with Lonnie Smith inducing a throwing error as he stole second base and Porter homering off Nolan Ryan. They won the opener 14–3. They'd hit only 66 more home runs the rest of the way but managed to finish fifth in the N.L. in scoring by leading the league in on-base percentage. Defensively, they covered Busch Stadium's fast track with 53 fielding runs above average, second best in the league, while making the third-fewest errors. St. Louis spent the bulk of the season in first place, ultimately beating out the Phillies by three games with a 92–70 record. They made quick work of the Atlanta Braves with a three-game sweep in the N.L.C.S. to reach their first World Series since Bob Gibson, Curt Flood & company blew a three-games-to-one lead against the Detroit Tigers in 1968.

Now here they were in a topsy-turvy World Series against the Brewers. By the time Game 7 arrived, the series lead had already changed hands three times, with the Cardinals the latest to tie things up with a 13–1 blowout the previous night in which Hernandez homered and drove in four runs.

It was a classic Game 7 that matched the teams' respective aces, the talented and mercurial Joaquin Andujar for St. Louis against the big, hulking righty Pete Vuckovich—a former Cardinal who'd been included in the Simmons trade to Milwaukee two years earlier (Vuckovich would earn additional fame shortly after his playing career ended with his portrayal of Clu Haywood, the tough Yankee first baseman in the movie *Major League* who swung through three high-octane fastballs from Ricky "Wild Thing" Vaughn in the last inning of a one-game playoff).

Through three innings Andujar was perfect while the Cards pecked away with a few singles and walks against Vuckovich but failed to score, leaving five men on base. Hernandez reached on an infield hit in the first and walked in the third but was left stranded both times.

After St. Louis right fielder George Hendrick helped to short circuit a potential Brewer rally in the top of the fourth by gunning down Robin Yount at third base, the Cards broke through for a 1–0 lead in the bottom of the inning on a Lonnie Smith RBI single. Hernandez missed a chance to help the Cardinals to a big inning when with two out he swung over a low breaking pitch from Vuckovich to strike out and strand two runners. That proved costly when Ben Oglivie smoked Andujar's first pitch of the top of the fifth into the right field bleachers to tie the game. Milwaukee then shot into the lead with two in the sixth as Andujar allowed three hits and hurt himself with an error on a forced, off balance throw after fielding a Paul Molitor bunt.

Now trailing 3–1, it was crunch time for the Cardinals. And in the bottom of the sixth, they got something going. Vuckovich, who had been flirting with danger all night, allowed a one out base hit to Ozzie Smith. Lonnie Smith followed by ripping a double into the left field corner to put runners on second and third. With two left-handed hitters due up, Kuenn finally pulled Vuckovich in favor of lefty Bob McClure. Herzog countered by sending up veteran right-handed hitter Gene Tenace to hit for third baseman Ken Oberkfell. Tenace wasn't exactly new to big moments. Exactly 10 years earlier—October 20, 1972—he had connected for his fourth homer of the 1972 World Series for the Oakland A's on his way to becoming Series MVP in Oakland's seven-game victory over the Cincinnati Reds. Now, at age 36, he was a part-time player near the end of the line. In his final World Series plate appearance, he worked McClure for a five-pitch walk, loading the based with one out to set up the game's biggest moment.

Bob McClure and Keith Hernandez went back a long way together in the Bay Area, competing in Little League and briefly playing together at Terra Nova High School. They had debuted in the majors a year apart, Hernandez in August of 1974 and McClure in August 1975. McClure never became a star like Hernandez did, but he certainly had a productive career as a lefty specialist for 19 years and over 1,100 innings.

With the crowd on its feet and the decibel level rising, Hernandez took a deep breath as he stepped in and out of the box a couple of times. He took the first pitch an inch off the outside corner for ball one. McClure's second pitch was a big curve that broke over the plate for a called strike. Then came another one just a smidge off the outside black that Hernandez didn't bite at. Clearly, he wasn't allowing the big moment to make him overanxious. Next came a fastball that missed inside—the count was three and one. With the crowd now in a frenzy and nowhere to put the hitter, McClure did exactly what Hernandez undoubtedly expected—he grooved one right over the plate. Hernandez jumped on it and lifted a base hit to right field to score two runs. The game was tied, with the go-ahead run on third. When Hendrick followed with another single, the Cardinals had the lead.

With St. Louis still holding that 4–3 edge in the bottom of the eighth, Hernandez came up with a runner on second and one out. The Brewers intentionally walked him to put two men on. After Hendrick flied out, consecutive singles by Darrell Porter and Steve Braun brought in two more runs. Hernandez celebrated his birthday by scoring the final run of the series and then watching Bruce Sutter complete his two perfect relief innings by striking out Gorman Thomas to end it. The final was 6–3. The Cardinals were World Series champions for the first time in 15 years.

After starting the 1982 World Series 0-for-15, Hernandez closed on a 7-for-12 tear with three walks and eight RBI over the final three games. His bad start most likely cost him the series MVP, which went to Porter, though he probably had the better case. The championship completed Hernandez's fourth All-Star caliber season in a row, one that saw him hit .299 with 100 walks for a .397 on-base percentage and drive in 94 runs despite just seven homers. Hernandez reached base 275 times during the 1982 season, more than anyone else in the league. And there was the usual Gold Glove defense. Who would have guessed, as he celebrated his first World Series trophy and his 29th birthday that Keith Hernandez would play only 55 more games in Cardinal red?

He was a bit of a sleeper from the beginning. The Cardinals had drafted Hernandez out of high school in the 42nd round of the 1971 June draft—the 785th player taken. But talk about a baseball draft being an inexact science: peruse through the list of 784 players taken ahead of Hernandez and by any objective measure you will find two who went on to have better careers—second rounders George Brett and Mike Schmidt.

Hernandez moved through the Cardinal chain quickly, getting a taste of Triple-A before his first season ended. As his third minor league season drew to a close in 1974, Hernandez's batting average for the Triple-A Tulsa Oilers sat at .351, his on-base percentage at .425. On August 30, the Cardinals, in the midst of a tight pennant race in the National League East, called him up. The club's incumbent first baseman, a 34-year-old veteran named Joe Torre, was nursing a minor injury for a few days. Hernandez, not yet 21 years old, was thrust into the starting lineup in his hometown for a weekend series at San Francisco. He finished the three games 3-for-10 though the Cards dropped two of three.

With Torre back in the lineup after the weekend, Hernandez didn't play for the next several days. His next chance came as a pinch hitter in his first home game at Busch Stadium on September 8 against the Mets. It was a memorable home debut. With two out in the bottom of the ninth and St. Louis trailing by two, he got the call against Tom Seaver and lined a triple to right field. The big hit brought the tying run to the plate, though Seaver got the final out to nail down a 5–3 win. Hernandez wound up 10-for-34 with seven walks (.415 OBP) in his call up season as the Cardinals went down to the wire before losing out to Pittsburgh for the division title.

Less than two weeks after the 1974 season ended, the Cardinals traded Joe Torre to the Mets for a pair of pitchers, veteran Ray Sadecki and youngster Tommy Moore. Torre, the Brooklyn-born former star at St. Francis Prep High School, would finish up his playing career (and, as it turned out, launch his managing career) back home. Hernandez, still a week shy of his 21st birthday at the time of the trade, was the St. Louis Cardinals' first baseman.

It didn't go well right away. Hernandez went 0-for-4 on opening day 1975 in a loss to Montreal and wound up hitting .189 in April. Things didn't get much better in May, and with his average sitting at .203 with nine extra base hits on June 3, the Cardinals sent him back to Tulsa. The team had acquired veteran Ron Fairly the previous winter, essentially to pinch hit but also no doubt to serve as a hedge against Hernandez, the young starter at first base. But the rest of the season showed that it wasn't a matter of Hernandez not being capable, just that he wasn't quite ready. As Fairly took the reins at first for most of the next three months, Hernandez tore up the American Association. In 85 games at Tulsa, he batted .330 with a .440 on-base percentage and 10 homers while slugging .531. He kept the hitting stroke going upon his recall to the Cardinals on September 2. Over the season's final month, Hernandez went 22-for-59 (.373) with a pair of homers, raising his batting average 47 points to finish at .250 with a .309 OBP. The Cards figured they had their future starter after all.

Or so it seemed. Hernandez's start to the 1976 season was no better than his start in '75. For the first two months he struggled mightily, hitting under .200 with just a handful of extra base hits and no homers. With the Cards having acquired outfielder Willie Crawford from the Dodgers before the season, incumbent right fielder Reggie Smith started seeing a good amount of time at first base in place of the slumping Her-

nandez, who was often becoming relegated to late inning defensive replacement duty. But clearly the team wasn't close to giving up on him.
And he had nothing left to prove at Triple-A. The Cardinals were going
nowhere in the N.L. East standings—by the June 15 trade deadline they
were 25–35 and already 16 games behind the first place Phillies. Looking
ahead, the Cards needed to find out whether Hernandez was their future
at first base. That day, they dealt Smith to the Dodgers in exchange for
catcher-outfielder Joe Ferguson. In the game that night against Atlanta,
Hernandez started at first base and went 3-for-4. The playing time was
still sporadic over the next few weeks as Ferguson took on a chunk of the
catching duties and Ted Simmons took over Smith's role of converted
first baseman.

But on Sunday July 11, the last game before the All-Star break,
Hernandez hit his first homer of the year off Burt Hooton in a loss to
the Dodgers (a game that included the return to St. Louis of Reggie
Smith, who tortured them with a 3-for-5 day including a three-run
homer).

After the break, in a July 17 game at San Diego, Hernandez started
at first base with his batting average still at .190. He knocked in a run
in the second inning on a groundout to second. After that, he singled
and scored in the fourth, singled again in the sixth, and then drilled a
two-run double in the ninth. It was just his third multi-hit game of the
season. The Cardinals won 7–1.

Suddenly, multi-hit games became the norm. Hernandez had nine
more of them over the next month, raising his average to .267 and his
on-base percentage to .367. Once again, he had found the groove. Playing virtually every day down the stretch, Hernandez banged out 15 more
multi-hit games between August 31 and October 3 to finish with a .289
batting average and .376 OBP, both about 100 points higher than where
he sat in mid–July. With a 127 OPS-plus and a 3.2 WAR, Hernandez's
1976 season was just a bit shy of All-Star level, almost astounding when
you consider where he was in July.

Hernandez had clearly displayed the talent. The one thing that was
left was to put it all together for a full major league season. And in 1977
Hernandez, still just 23, did just that. As the Cardinals muddled along
to a third-place finish with an 83–79 record, Hernandez finally got off
to a good start and kept his average above .300 for a good chunk of
the season before finishing at .291 with a .379 on-base percentage, 125
OPS-plus, 15 homers and 41 doubles. His 91 RBI were second on the

team to Ted Simmons. The 4.1 WAR was also second to Simmons on the Cardinals and second among National League first baseman to Houston's Bob Watson. Hernandez didn't see the All-Star Game, passed over by the voters as the starter in favor of the more established Steve Garvey and then passed over as a reserve by N.L. manager Sparky Anderson for Willie Montanez, who was picked as the lone representative of the Atlanta Braves (rules mandated—and still mandate—that every club have a player in the All-Star Game).

Speaking of Garvey—he's a good starting point for our first Hernandez comparison, even though he's not in the Hall of Fame himself. Garvey's presence in the National League certainly cast a big shadow during much of Hernandez's career. It shouldn't have, since Hernandez proved to be a far better player, but this is another case of perception and reality not aligning. Garvey broke in to the big leagues a few years before Hernandez and saw his star rise to National League M.V.P. in 1974, the year Hernandez broke in. By the time Hernandez became a regular a couple of years later, Garvey was a household name working on his third .300-plus season and third All-Star Game.

Nothing against Steve Garvey, who was certainly very good, but he was also one of the more overrated players of his time. The reasons are easy enough to grasp—Garvey was handsome, media savvy, and he played for a big market team that won a lot. It was also the statistical dark ages. The emphasis placed on batting average and RBI back in the day–Garvey hit over .300 seven times and topped 100 RBI five times—helped to mask the fact that his paucity of walks produced mostly average on-base percentages. In his 1974 M.V.P. season, Garvey's .312 batting average was seventh-highest in the National League, but his .342 OBP was sixth-highest among the Dodger regulars. He took the award with a 4.4 WAR—certainly All-Star level. But for perspective, Mike Schmidt put up a 9.7 WAR that year, Joe Morgan an 8.6, Johnny Bench a 7.9, and Garvey's L.A. teammate Jim Wynn a 7.7.

Defensively, Garvey passed the eye test very well and was ultimately voted four Gold Gloves. But in hindsight, the zone rating numbers show that he was mostly an average first baseman, saving a handful of runs above average in most of his early years before regressing to negative numbers later to ultimately finish five runs below average for his career (Hernandez finished at plus-120 runs, a different stratosphere altogether).

Check the seven-year run of 1977 to 1983, the period when you would say that Garvey's and Hernandez's primes crossed over. Garvey hit more home runs, something that fans and press like to see from first basemen. But driven by on-base percentage, OPS-plus and defense, Hernandez outpointed Garvey by WAR in six of the seven seasons, usually by a good margin. For the full period, he rang up a 35.4 to Garvey's 19.9. Throw in Garvey's three prime years before Hernandez hit his prime (1974–76) and compare them to Hernandez's three prime years after Garvey's prime (1984–86) and that edge also goes to Hernandez, 16.9 WAR to 14.2. Garvey may not be in the Hall of Fame, but he got a lot more support than Hernandez did, peaking at 42 percent of ballots while Hernandez never got more than 10.8 percent. The point here isn't to disparage Steve Garvey, who had a fine career. But we often hear that a big criterion for the Hall of Fame is how a player stacks up against the competition during his era—was he the best at his position during his time? Keith Hernandez had that—he was certainly the top first baseman in the National League and neck and neck with Eddie Murray as the best in the game between the mid–'70s and mid–'80s. But the perception of Steve Garvey as a bigger star than he actually was made it difficult to perceive Hernandez as the top dog.

Hernandez followed up his first All-Star level season of 1977 by slumping a bit in 1978—.255 average, .351 OBP, 11 homers, 108 OPS-plus, 2.6 WAR. He managed to turn the tables on his early career by getting off to a great start but fading in the second half. But in 1979, Hernandez hit his age 25 season by showing that he was ready to dominate. If there were still doubts about him possessing superstar ability, Hernandez dispelled them in '79.

Not that it happened right away. Hernandez once again reverted to his slow-stating ways. After collecting six hits in his first four games, he slumped badly over the next three weeks. On May 2 his average stood at .213 with one homer. But the next night against Houston knuckleballer Joe Niekro, Hernandez banged out two singles and a double. A few days later in the Astrodome he went 4-for-4 against Ken Forsch. Hernandez was on his way, heating up with the weather, as usual. But in this case, even more than usual. From May 3 to June 20 he batted .392, bringing his season average to .331 and his OBP to .387. During one stretch from May 27 to June 3 he had eight multiple hit games in a row.

By the end of the season, Hernandez had taken his first N.L. batting crown with a .344 average. His .417 OBP was one point behind league leader Pete Rose, his 210 hits one behind his league-leading teammate

Gary Templeton. Hernandez led the league with 48 doubles and finished in the top five in OPS-plus and RBI. All the while, the advanced defensive metrics said he saved 13 runs above average at his position, a pretty rare number for a first baseman. It added up to a 7.6 WAR, third-highest in the league behind Dave Winfield and Mike Schmidt. At the end of the season, the writers voted him co-M.V.P. in the National League along with Pittsburgh's Willie Stargell, who put up just a 2.5 WAR in 126 games but whose 32 homers and veteran leadership, voters believed, led the Pirates to the N.L. East title (and ultimately, after the voting was completed, to a World Series championship).

As big as Hernandez's 1979 season was, there were still many who couldn't help thinking it was a bit of a fluke. The following spring, *Sports Illustrated* put him on the cover with the words "Who is Keith Hernandez and what is he doing hitting .344?" But make no mistake, Hernandez was now a star. His big 1979 season ignited a run of eight All-Star caliber years in a row, and nine in 10 years.

He followed his co-MVP run with a 1980 season that was almost as good. In another also-ran year for the Cardinals, who finished fourth, Hernandez scorched the ball to the tune of a .321 batting average, missing a second straight batting crown by three points, with a league-leading .408 on-base percentage. He finished in the top three in the N.L. in hits and total bases while adding a career high 16 homers, 99 RBI, and a 147 OPS-plus. His 6.7 WAR was third in the league among everyday players. In the M.V.P voting he finished 11th, five spots behind Garvey and his 3.1 WAR, 125 OPS-plus and far inferior defense (Fangraphs says that Garvey was two runs below average at first base in 1980 while Hernandez was 12 runs above average).

Hernandez's roll continued through the strike-shortened 1981 season: .306 average, .401 on-base percentage (his third straight year over .400), a 142 OPS-plus and 4.2 WAR that ranked third in the league for the third straight year and that projected to over a 6.0 had the player strike not short-circuited the season. Once again, the M.V.P. voters just didn't get it—Hernandez placed 20th in the balloting. He finished third on the Cardinals, behind George Hendrick, who outslugged Hernandez slightly but trailed him everywhere else, and reliever Bruce Sutter, who wasn't even having one of his particularly dominant years (2.62 ERA, 57 Ks in 82 innings, and seven blown saves in 32 chances, not a great conversion rate).

It all led up to the championship season of 1982, when Hernandez put up his fifth four-plus win season in six years and culminated it with the biggest hit of the World Series.

But behind the scenes, things were souring in St. Louis. Whitey Herzog didn't like Hernandez's habits, particularly the way he retreated to the clubhouse between batting practice and the game to sit back and work his crossword puzzles. For Hernandez, it was a way to relax and calm the nerves before the game. For Herzog, it was a blasé attitude. It wasn't until a few years later that the world learned there had been something else going on—drugs. Cocaine was a big part of the 1980s, and baseball players were no exception. The infamous Pittsburgh drug trials of 1985 that resulted in the conviction of a drug dealer with a sizable baseball clientele brought Hernandez, among a host of other big-name players, to the Grand Jury room to tell the tale of heavy cocaine use in the early '80s.

Whatever the combination of reasons, the Cardinals figured the time was right to part ways with Keith Hernandez, who would be a free agent after the 1983 season. On June 14 at Busch, he tripled and singled and knocked in two runs in a 5–4 win over the Phillies. The next day he was a New York Met, swapped for a pair of talented but underachieving pitchers, Neil Allen and Rick Ownbey. Two nights later in Montreal, Hernandez went 2-for-4 in his Mets debut, though the team, as it did on most nights, lost the game. Afterward, he sobbed in the shower. The Mets were 22–37, on their way to a seventh straight season of 90-plus losses. In just over seven months, Hernandez had gone from World Series heroics to baseball wasteland.

That's what Shea Stadium was during most of the late 1970s and early '80s—a wasteland. The 1969 Miracle Mets and the 1973 "Ya Gotta Believe" pennant winners were distant memories. So were the big crowds that led all of baseball in attendance for four straight years of that era and made New York a Mets town. Back then, it was the Yankees who were the afterthought. But of course the tide turned as the 1970s moved along. The Yankees shot back to the top just as the Mets were sinking. Reggie Jackson arrived in the Bronx while Tom Seaver was leaving Queens. By 1979, an average of 9,740 people per game were coming to watch the team hit 74 home runs, use 15 different starting pitchers, and lose 99 games.

And yet the 1983 Mets club that Hernandez joined had a better vibe going for it than its immediate predecessors did. New owners Nelson Doubleday and Fred Wilpon bought the club in 1980 and hired veteran executive Frank Cashen, who had led baseball operations for the great Baltimore teams of the late '60s and early '70s, to run the club. Cashen made his first real noise by trading for Cincinnati slugger George Foster in 1982, a deal that came complete with a lucrative contract extension. Foster wound up generally disappointing with the bat, but his mere presence told the fans that the new regime was open to making moves and spending money. The '83 season kicked off with a 38-year-old Seaver making his emotional return after five and a half years in Cincinnati and throwing six shutout innings at the Phillies in front of a packed house on opening day. Top overall 1980 draft pick Darryl Strawberry was up in early May, on his way to 26 homers and the N.L. Rookie of the Year Award. He'd followed other young players like Hubie Brooks and Mookie Wilson who had come up through the Mets' system and made their way into the starting lineup. Chatter abounded around the impressive group of pitchers the team was assembling in the minors—Dwight Gooden, Ron Darling, Walt Terrell—that was close to bearing fruit. The Mets were still losing in 1983, but with a sense that things were moving forward, finally. And now, to the shock of almost everyone, they had Keith Hernandez.

Hernandez generally won praise from teammates and press for his effort during that latter half of the 1983 season. Despite his apparent unhappiness over the trade, despite all the losing, people lauded his professionalism—the consistent daily preparation, the concentration during every at-bat, the verbal encouragement to the pitchers from his first base perch. The shock of being tossed into such a drastically different situation didn't change his approach. Hernandez wound up hitting .306 with a .424 on-base percentage and a 140 OPS-plus in his 95 games with the Mets. For the full season with the Mets and Cardinals: .297 with a .396 OBP and his best defensive season yet at 17 runs above average. It added up to a 5.6 WAR, number seven in the National League. Pro rating his strike-shortened 1981 season, it was the fourth time in five years he scored five and a half wins or better.

And the best news of all for Mets fans came that winter. Hernandez, the pending free agent, bought into the front office's pitch of a brighter future just around the corner. He signed for five years and $8.4 million, a very big contract at the time. Hernandez had turned the page—he was all in as a Met. And the club had itself a cornerstone for what was to come.

Mets fans of the era remember the 1984 season very well. It was the year of the renaissance—from 68 wins to 90, from last place to second. Davey Johnson took over as manager. Attendance shot up more than 50 percent to almost two million, practically transforming Shea Stadium from a mausoleum into a nightly rock concert. The biggest source of buzz and excitement: Dwight Gooden, the 19-year-old phenom who blew away National League hitters with a power fastball and devastating curve that racked up a rookie record 276 strikeouts and inspired Shea's first-ever K-corner.

The Mets' best player and leader, the guy more responsible than Dwight Gooden or anyone else for the '84 turnaround: Keith Hernandez. He was the player who gave an otherwise so-so lineup its heft. The Mets strong season came despite finishing right around league average in most every offensive category—batting average, on-base percentage, homers and OPS. George Foster was past his prime, Darryl Strawberry hadn't yet reached his. Mookie Wilson and Hubie Brooks were pretty good, but they weren't All-Stars. The rock, the guy hitting third in the order and producing every day, the guy running the infield from first base while the team played youngsters like Jose Oquendo and Wally Backman in the middle of the diamond, was Keith Hernandez. He finished the '84 season with a .409 on-base percentage that missed leading the N.L. by one point. He finished in the top ten in batting average, RBI, and OPS-plus. Defensively, Fangraphs gives him nine runs above average, a so-so year by Hernandez standards but still easily the best in the league at first base. Hernandez's 6.3 WAR was his best in four years and the third six-win season of his career.

And while it's hard to quantify leadership, don't ignore Hernandez's presence on an '84 club that was largely young, especially on the mound and behind the plate. George Foster, quiet by nature, wasn't going to lead. Howie Rose is a New York sports institution who has covered the Mets as a reporter and broadcaster for years. What he remembers about Hernandez above and beyond the stats was the way he filled a needed veteran role.

"When the Mets had those young pitchers in 1984, before they got Gary Carter, they had a young catcher in Mike Fitzgerald," said Rose. "Keith took it upon himself to help them. He knew the hitters, knew the strengths and weaknesses."

The following winter, the Mets decided go for it all with a big trade that brought Carter from Montreal for four players, including Hubie

Brooks. Essentially it worked in 1985, with Carter enjoying his last superstar season at age 31 and Dwight Gooden taking the big step from super rookie to nearly unbeatable superstar by going 24–4 with a 1.53 ERA, 268 strikeouts and a .965 WHIP. Strawberry had a big year, Darling blossomed into an All-Star, and youngsters Lenny Dykstra and Roger McDowell joined the fold to add to the talent-laded roster. The Mets were basically a juggernaut in 1985 with 98 wins; unfortunately Hernandez's former team, the Cardinals, won 101 playing in the same division. Hernandez continued as the rock in the three-hole of the lineup, hitting .309 with a .384 OBP, 129 OPS-plus and 94 RBI on just 10 homers. Defensively he was worth 14 runs for yet another Gold Glove at first base. Among everyday players, his 5.1 WAR was second on the club to Carter's 6.9 and 11th overall in the National League.

You probably know all about the 1986 Mets. Everything that had been building for the previous two years came to a head. Davey Johnson predicted dominance in spring training and then watched it unfold as the Mets won 20 of their first 24, built a 13½ game lead by the All-Star break and ultimately swashbuckled their way to 108 wins to claim the N.L. East by 21½ games. Then they fought off tough postseason challenges from the Astros and Red Sox to claim the second World Series title in franchise history. It was one of the great teams of all time.

All this despite a regression from Carter, whose saw his average drop from .280 to .255, his OPS-plus from 138 to 115 and his WAR from 6.9 to 3.6. But with 105 RBI and all that pedigree, Carter was pretty much perceived as the Mets' main man, placing third in the National League M.V.P. voting.

Hernandez got his share of attention, too, finishing just one spot behind Carter in the voting after hitting .310 with a .413 OBP (tied for the league lead) and 140 OPS-plus (third in the league). His 5.5 WAR led the Mets and tied for fourth in the N.L. among everyday players. And he capped the big season in vintage fashion with a virtual repeat of his 1982 World Series heroics. With the Mets trailing the Red Sox 3–0 in the sixth inning of Game 7, Hernandez stepped in with the bases loaded against Boston lefty Bruce Hurst, who had stifled the Mets all series (two runs in 22 innings up to that point). Hernandez took a deep breath and stepped in and out of the box a couple of times, just as he'd done against Bob McClure four years earlier. Then after looking at a curve break in for strike one, Hernandez jumped on a high fastball and drilled it into left-center for a two-run single that brought the Mets within 3–2 and sent Shea Stadium into bedlam. Carter followed with a sacrifice fly to tie the game, and the Mets went on to win 8–5.

It was an appropriate way, one week after his 33rd birthday, to wrap up what would prove to be Keith Hernandez's final year as a star. He'd go on to have a perfectly solid year in 1987 before injuries and age began taking their toll over his final three seasons, the last of which consisted of 43 games with the 1990 Cleveland Indians. The 1986 season was the ninth in 10 years in which he'd turned in an All-Star caliber four-win season or better. Five of those were a 5.0 or better, and had it not been for the '81 strike it would have been six.

How good was Keith Hernandez during the '77 to '86 peak? Good enough to hit .305 with a .395 OBP and 134 OPS-plus, save 105 runs above average in the field, and average more than five wins a year. By WAR, Hernandez was the fourth-best everyday player in the game over those 10 years, behind only Mike Schmidt, Gary Carter and George Brett. The only first baseman who came close to him was Eddie Murray, who averaged 4.9 wins over the same period. Murray of course did go on to have several more good seasons after 1986, tacking on enough production over 21 years to outpoint Hernandez in career WAR 68.7 to 60.4. By and large, though, there is little difference between the two. Both had nine seasons of 4.0 WAR or better. Hernandez averaged a fraction of a win more than Murray in their respective 10 best seasons (and the same for each player's five best seasons, if you want to check the peak of the peak). He saved twice as many runs in the field, say the advanced defensive stats. Murray slugged more, Hernandez got on base more, leading to a virtual draw in career OPS-plus: Murray 129, Hernandez 128.

In 2003, Eddie Murray made it into the Hall of Fame easily on his first try with 423 votes (85.3 percent). Keith Hernandez, in his second-to-last year on the ballot, got 30 votes (even Garvey got 138). Why such a discrepancy? Murray had reached a pair of magical plateaus, 500 home runs and 3,000 hits. That's incredibly impressive, of course, but Murray would have been just as deserving had he retired three years earlier and missed those juicy round numbers that so enthrall voters. Those last three seasons—one decent, two poor—didn't add any production to speak of. As to who you would take given the choice—Murray or Hernandez—it's pretty much a coin flip.

What have you mostly heard about Keith Hernandez over the years? No doubt it's the defense, right? This is a guy who won 11 Gold Gloves and has been labeled many times by many people as the greatest defensive first baseman ever. The question is, is it real or is it hype? We know that Gold Glove voting can be very subjective, with the award often going to undeserving players. And in this age of advanced stats we're constantly reminded that when it comes to fielding, the eye test can be deceiving. That a guy can look great on the balls he gets to but that his hard-to-detect range factor is lacking.

But in Hernandez's case—no hype necessary. Yes, he was the best. The splendid eye test is backed up by the numbers. And by the numbers, we mean zone rating that estimates runs saved compared to an average player at the same position, not defensive WAR, which doesn't work as a great metric for first base. A quick explanation: the dWAR calculation is broken down by position, with a built-in assumption that first base is generally less valuable than other positions on the field. The positional adjustment in the formula won't put a first baseman on par with a shortstop or a center fielder. Check the dWAR leaders over the years and you will never see a first baseman among them. Then check Hernandez and see a career 1.3 dWAR that's so tiny it makes you do a double take. That is, until you remember that it's a discounted number—that it's positive at all means that Hernandez rates as an above average fielder generally, a very difficult thing to do from first base under the dWAR formula.

More telling is the FanGraphs zone rating, which, again, directly estimates the number of runs a player is worth at his position compared to an average player. Hernandez, says the formula, was 120 runs better than average during his career. How do other notable first baseman compare? Hernandez's New York counterpart, Don Mattingly, who won nine Gold Gloves and who some in the New York press have argued (apparently with straight faces) was the better fielder, was 33 runs above average by the same formula. Gil Hodges, the former Brooklyn Dodger who won three Gold Gloves and who would have undoubtedly won more had he not been in the majors for 10 years before the award began, was worth 53 runs. Go all the way back to Hall of Famer Frank Chance, the early 20th century star with the Cubs who became noted for "Tinker-to-Evers-to-Chance" fame (an ode penned by Franklin Pierce Adams in 1910 as a tribute to the slick-fielding Chicago infield of the day). The estimate on Chance: 51 runs better than average, quite good but not in Keith Hernandez's league.

One guy who was pretty close: John Olerud, a three-year Met in the 1990s and an outstanding first baseman who scored 98 runs above average. Olerud won three Gold Gloves in his career and probably should have won more. But he's still in arrears of Hernandez by a decent amount.

Brian Kenny, a numbers devotee who is inclined to nearly always place the stats above the eye test, was so impressed watching Hernandez play that he pretty much flips the formula in his case. "He does great on the runs saved but he should be even higher. I saw Hernandez play many times, I saw the plays he made," says Kenny. "Teams called off bunts because of him, he changed the defense. He is number one all time at the position." As for offense: "He was top three in on-base in seven of eight years. Where are the New York sportswriters to make his plea?" Adds Howie Rose: "To appreciate him you had to see him every day, his brilliance was a game-by-game, really inning-to-inning type thing."

Rose argues that "if Ozzie Smith is in the Hall of Fame for defense, Keith Hernandez is the equivalent at his position." Of course it's true that Hernandez's position isn't as defensively valuable as Smith's, so it's not a dead-on comparison. But while the distinction of being the best fielding first baseman of all time isn't the same as being the best fielding shortstop of all time, it's still worth a lot, no? Is it much of a surprise that in the one full season in which Smith and Hernandez played together in the same infield, their team won the Word Series?

To put Hernandez's career into further historical perspective: there are currently 22 former first baseman in the Hall of Fame (or 21 if you want to place Rod Carew at second base, where he played a handful fewer games but where he had more of his bigger seasons), at least eight or nine of which had less compelling cases than Hernandez. We won't go through all of them, but there are a few noteworthy comparisons. Start with a guy who came up a decade earlier but whose career wound up overlapping with Hernandez for a dozen years—Tony Perez. A terrific hitter and perfectly solid defender who spent the bulk of his career with Cincinnati, Perez was a noted RBI machine who drove in 90 or more runs 12 times while hitting 379 homers, more than twice as many as Hernandez. He averaged a 4.6 WAR in his ten best seasons, a peak stretch to solidify Cooperstown range. He notched 50 percent of the vote in his first year of eligibility in 1992 and climbed past the 75 percent hurdle by 2000.

The numbers say that Tony Perez was a solid Hall of Fame choice. Was he a better player than Keith Hernandez? Not a chance. Put aside RBI, a derivative stat which doesn't truly measure performance and one in which Tony Perez benefited greatly from Pete Rose and Joe Morgan getting on base in front of him for several years, and Hernandez's offensive career looks more productive.

Despite many more home runs, Perez outslugged the league average during his career by just a tad more than Hernandez did during his—20 percent to 18 percent. The on-base numbers are much more heavily in Hernandez's favor—21 percent better than league average to Perez's 5 percent. It adds up to an edge for Hernandez in OPS-plus, 128 to 122. Looking at some of the true peak seasons for each, Perez hit a 140 or better OPS-plus four times, Hernandez did it five times. The defense, as with almost anyone you might compare to Hernandez, isn't close. Perez, after a few years as a mediocre third baseman early in his career, wound up saving 16 runs above average during his many years at first. In short, he was a guy you were perfectly comfortable putting out there at first base every day, but not someone who was going to impact the game in the field the way Hernandez did. It all explains why Perez's 54 career WAR falls a bit short of Hernandez's 60, including a ten-best season advantage for Hernandez of 53.1 to 45.6.

The success of players like Perez and Murray—and the failure of Hernandez—to win over Hall of Fame voters speaks to the perception bias of first base. It's a corner position that's supposed to provide power, or so the thinking goes. The image of the star first baseman is that of a slugger, a big guy who drives the ball over the fence. Look at so many of the first basemen elected to Cooperstown—from Lou Gehrig and Jimmy Foxx to Harmon Killebrew and Willie McCovey and on to Frank Thomas and Jeff Bagwell. They were boppers, all of them. They were strong. They were intimidating at the plate. Hernandez was a different cat, a guy who put up Hall of Fame production in a different way. As Kenny puts it: "He doesn't look the part. People see a skinny guy with a mustache, which is not what we look for in a Hall of Famer." At least not in a Hall of Fame first baseman.

Let's look at a couple of more first base comparisons to big-time names in baseball history—you might be surprised at how well Hernandez stacks up. The first is Bill Terry, a major star with the New York Giants in the 1920s and '30s. He's perhaps best known for being the last National League player to hit .400 thanks to a league leading .401 average in 1930. Terry hit a robust .341 for his 13-year career with a .393 OBP and six straight 100-RBI seasons from 1927 to 1932. But remember, this was a hitter-friendly era. Terry's .401 season, in which he also drove in 129 runs and led the league with 254 hits, got him a 7.6 WAR, the same that Hernandez got in his 1979 co–MVP season. Why? Because the National League as a whole hit .303 in 1930, not .261 like it did in 1979. For his career, Terry's on-base percentage beat the N.L. average of the day by 15.8 percent, not as much as the 20 percent Hernandez got in his day. That's countered by Terry's advantage in slugging, 26 percent above league average to Hernandez's 18 percent. By all accounts Terry was a very good first baseman, rating at 73 runs better than average, according to FanGraphs. But again, that's not Keith Hernandez territory. By WAR, Hernandez's 60.4 beat Terry's 54.2, and his ten best seasons edge Terry's 54.6 to 51.5.

And how about the aforementioned Harmon Killebrew? A top slugger of his day with the Minnesota Twins who divided his career among first base, third base and the outfield (he wound up with more games at first than at the other positions). Killebrew led all of baseball in home runs in the 1960s, hitting 393. For his full career, Killebrew blasted 573 homers, no. 12 on the all-time list. He hit .256 for his career but because he walked a lot (over 100 walks in seven different seasons) wound up with a very good .376 on-base percentage. In his M.V.P. season of 1969, Killebrew not only led the American League with 49 homers and 140 RBI but also with 145 walks and a .427 OBP.

Despite a big gap in power—Killebrew outslugged the league by 33 percent during his career compared to Hernandez's 18 percent and outdid him in OPS-plus 143 to 128—the two players wound up dead even in WAR at 60.4, which Killebrew compiled in two more full seasons. Killebrew did nine seasons at 4.0 or better, the same as Hernandez, and four seasons of a 5.0 or better, one fewer than Hernandez. The obvious reason: defense. Killebrew was not what you'd call a slick fielder, finishing six runs below average at first base during his career. Not even counting his far worse numbers during his stints at third and in the outfield, he falls 126 runs behind Hernandez in a direct first base comparison. Along with Hernandez's slight on-base advantage, it's enough to make up for the power gap at the plate. Yes, games are won in different ways. But voters dig the long ball, especially at first base.

Speaking of Killebrew, let's sneak a quick look at one of his Hall of Fame peers, Orlando Cepeda, a slugging first baseman for the Giants and Cardinals in the 1960s. A terrific player, but not someone who matches up that well against Hernandez. Despite 379 homers, Cepeda outpoints Hernandez in OPS-plus by just a small margin, 133 to 128.

With Hernandez's far better defense—Cepeda has a slightly negative zone rating compared to an average player at his position—it's easy enough to see why he beats Cepeda in WAR 60 to 50, with nine four-win seasons to Cepeda's five. Cepeda had to wait for the Veterans Committee for his Hall of Fame plaque, but even during his BBWAA period he got a lot more support than Hernandez did. He topped 40 percent of the vote several times and then ultimately missed by seven votes (73.5 percent) on his 15th and final try in 1994. When he got the good news from the Veterans Committee in 1999, Hernandez was compiling 6.8 percent from the BBWAA. He never did much better during his five remaining years on the ballot.

How little respect does Keith Hernandez get? A special election in 2018 on what the baseball Hall of Fame called the "Modern Baseball Era" ballot meant for players from the 1970s and '80s didn't even include him as a candidate even as it included Don Mattingly and Steve Garvey. Is it the notoriety of the Pittsburgh drug trials of the mid–'80s? Howie Rose, among others, figures that publicity might have hurt Hernandez a bit, but it's hard to fathom that as a difference maker. The hoopla around cocaine in the 1980s faded quite a while ago. And one of Hernandez's fellow offenders, Tim Raines, got his Cooperstown plaque in 2017.

It's not as if Hernandez has lacked a public profile since he stopped playing. He's been a popular analyst on Mets games for SNY for years. He's authored three books. He even got a famous guest gig on a special hour-long *Seinfeld* episode back in 1991 in which he nearly got Jerry to help him move and managed to score a couple of dates with Elaine. Actually, that may have been his undoing. After bragging on his 11 Gold Gloves to Elaine, she responds with "You played first base, isn't that where they put the worst player?" She must have made quite an impression. Five years later, Hernandez debuted on the Hall of Fame ballot and got 5.1 percent of the vote.

6

Jerry Koosman

On Monday night September 8, 1969, the New York Mets prepared for the biggest game of the franchise's eight-year history. The first place Chicago Cubs, leading the Mets by 2½ games in the National League East, were in town for a two-game set. The Mets couldn't move into first place during this series, but they could get themselves razor close.

Shea Stadium, according to radio broadcaster Bob Murphy, was a complete sellout.[1] This despite a light rain coming and going throughout the night that had the fans opening and closing their umbrellas during the game. Getting the start was Jerry Koosman, the Mets' 26-year-old lefty who came in with a 12–9 record and a 2.50 ERA across 191 innings. It was a tough matchup against Chicago workhorse Bill Hands, a right-hander who was on his way to 300 innings and 20 wins for the season.

What was amazing was how the Mets had gotten here. Until now, playing a big game in September had been a pipe dream. These were the New York Mets, the National League's laughingstock since their 1962 expansion days of Casey Stengel, Choo Choo Coleman and Marvelous Marv Throneberry. They'd gotten a little bit better over the following few years but hadn't ever come close to contention. The Mets had finished ninth or tenth in the 10-team National League in all seven of their seasons through 1968. Then the 1969 expansion that added two teams to each league, including San Diego and Montreal in the N.L., split the leagues into two divisions for the first time. And the Mets were suddenly looking respectable. No nonsense Gil Hodges had taken over as manager. A good pitching staff built around Tom Seaver, Koosman, Gary Gentry and Tug McGraw (along with a pre-peak Nolan Ryan) was coming together. Good hitting outfielder Cleon Jones and slick fielding shortstop

Bud Harrelson had come up through the system. Tommie Agee, Jerry Grote and Donn Clendenon arrived in key trades.

The '69 Mets surprised everyone by playing well during the first half, pulling to within 3½ games of the division lead on July 9 when Seaver shut out the Cubs with his famous "Imperfect Game" in which

Jerry Koosman tossed more than 200 innings in 12 seasons with a 3.36 career ERA.

he retired the first 25 batters before a single by young outfielder Jimmy Qualls spoiled the perfecto with one out in the ninth. A short time later, though, order was restore to the baseball universe—or so it seemed— when the Mets hit a slump during the early dog days. A three-game sweep at the hands of the Astros left them in third place and 10 games behind the Cubs on August 13.

But little did anyone know that the Mets were just getting started. Right after the Houston series they won six in a row, lost one in extra innings, and then won another six in a row. Koosman won three games during the streak, including a two-hitter over the Padres on August 27. The Mets were two games out. It would essentially stay that way into early September. They rolled into the Chicago series on September 8 as winners of 18 of their last 24.

So Koosman was the center of attention in what was not only the biggest Mets game ever, but probably the biggest baseball game in New York in nearly five years, since the Yankees' loss to the St. Louis Cardinals in the seventh game of the 1964 World Series. With the Yankees descending into mediocrity right after that, meaningful September baseball had become a memory in the city. Few would have expected the Mets to be the team to bring it back, but here they were.

With the house buzzing, Koosman started strong, retiring the Cubs in order in the top of the first, including strikeouts of Glen Beckert and Billy Williams on curve balls. Tommie Agee led off the bottom of the first against Bill Hands. At this point, let's pause for a moment for some quick perspective. The Cubs were a veteran team with a number of accomplished players—Williams, Ron Santo, Ernie Banks, Randy Hundley, Ferguson Jenkins, among a few others. They had been leading the N.L East all season, which surprised few people. But they'd come into this series on the heels of four straight losses as the young Mets nipped at their heels. Things were starting to slip away, but it wasn't too late to do something about it. And when your team is managed by Leo Durocher, one of the feistiest competitors in the game, you pretty much knew what that might be. Hands wound up for his first pitch and fired a fastball up around Agee's head, knocking him to the dirt. The message was clear: *you guys (Mets) may be hot lately, but are you sure you're ready to knock off the big boys?* Agee wound up grounding out as part of a one-two-three first inning for Hands.

In the top of the second, cleanup hitter and National League RBI leader Ron Santo led off for the Cubs. Koosman's first pitch was an inside fastball that drilled Santo on the right wrist as he backed away from the plate. Koosman's clear response message to Hands and the Cubs: *yes, we're ready, and we won't be intimated.* It's not overly dramatic to say that it was a moment of passage for Koosman and the Mets. We're here, and we're for real, they were saying. We aren't content to make a little noise, we're in this to win. Forget the old lovable loser Mets. After Santo got some treatment from the trainer and then took his base, Koosman reared back and struck out Ernie Banks, Jim Hickman and Randy Hundley in succession, all of them swinging. After two innings he had five strikeouts.

It was classic Koosman. A pretty mellow guy on the surface, but a bulldog on the mound when he wanted to be. While Seaver liked to paint the corners and pitch to hitters' weak spots, Koosman liked to go right after guys. "If Seaver was van Gogh, Koosman was Patton," remembers their teammate Art Shamsky.

In the bottom of the third, Agee came up with a man aboard and responded to Hands' first inning knockdown by drilling a 1–0 pitch over the left-centerfield wall to give the Mets a 2–0 lead. Koosman cruised through the next two innings, retiring six of seven with two more strikeouts. Through five shutout innings, he'd allowed one hit while striking out seven. He ran into his first trouble in the sixth, when Don Kessinger, Glen Beckert and Billy Williams opened with three consecutive singles to score a run and leaver runners on first and third. This was the type of development—third time through the order, opposition starting to get to you—that would have gotten Koosman yanked from the game in 2019. But in 1969, a little mid-game hiccup didn't necessarily bring the hook. Hodges stuck with Koosman, who allowed a sacrifice fly to Santo that tied the game and then, after getting Banks on a fly ball for the second out, continued to struggle with a wild pitch and a walk to put runners on first and third again. But he escaped further damage when Hundley flied to right.

The Mets took the lead right back in the bottom of the sixth as Agee continued his big night by ripping a double to left and then scored on a Wayne Garret single. Koosman's cue was to make the 3–2 lead stand up for nine more outs, and clearly Hodges was going to give him every chance to do it. In the seventh: strikeout, strikeout, groundout. In the eighth: not so easy, as Beckert and Williams opened with singles. But again, Hodges stayed with Koosman, who got Santo to ground into a double play and then whiffed Banks for his 10th strikeout. When he came to bat to lead off the bottom of the eighth, the Shea crowd greeted him with a standing ovation. Hands couldn't resist one last parting shot as he knocked Koosman down the same way he'd done it to Agee to start the game. But the crowd merely gave Koosman another big hand after he struck out and then looked ahead to closing things out in the ninth inning.

First up in the top of the ninth was Jim Hickman, who swung through a 2–2 pitch for the first out. But Hundley followed with a ground single to give the Cubs a base runner. Koosman faced pinch hitter Ken Rudolph, who also whiffed at a 2–2 pitch. One out to go. Up stepped young Randy Bobb, a September call up making his first big-league appearance of the season, to pinch hit for Hands. With the crowd now on its feet and hanging on every pitch, Koosman threw nothing but fastballs to Bobb, who fouled back the first one and swung through the second. With the count 0–2, Koosman wasted one outside for a ball. Next pitch: swing and a miss. Game over. Koosman's 13th strikeout of the night. He'd won the biggest game in Mets history to date. The Mets trailed the Cubs by just a game and a half in the N.L. East.

In what looked to be a bit of desperation, Durocher scratched his scheduled starter for the next night, Ken Holtzman, in favor of ace Ferguson Jenkins on two days' rest. It didn't work. The Mets jumped on Jenkins for two in the first inning and later extended the lead on homers from Clendenon and Shamsky. Seaver went all the way on a five-hitter for his 21st victory as the Mets cruised, 7–1. They were half a game out.

Things kept snowballing as September continued. A doubleheader sweep of the Expos the next night vaulted the Mets into first place. Then they won their next three in a row by shutout, including Koosman's three-hitter at Pittsburgh on September 12. Seaver's win in Pittsburgh the next night was the Mets' 10th victory in a row. They led the Cubs by 3½ games, and they weren't looking back. Koosman tossed another complete game shutout on September 17 in Montreal, followed four days later with yet another complete game in a 5–3 win over the Pirates at Shea to keep the Mets four games in front. The Mets continued to run away from the Cubs, clinching the N.L. East on September 24 at Shea with a 6–0 win over St. Louis behind Gary Gentry. Just for good measure, Koosman threw one more nine inning shutout in the next game, a 5–0 blanking of the Phillies. It was his third shutout in September and sixth of the season, one more than Seaver for most on the staff and two behind league leader Juan Marichal.

The Mets ended the 1969 regular season with a record of 100–62 to finish eight games ahead of the Cubs—an 18-game swing from mid–August. Koosman won his final five decisions to finish 17–9 with a 2.28 ERA, 241 innings, 1.058 WHIP, 180 strikeouts against 68 walks, and a 5.9 WAR.

The Mets hadn't had particularly high hopes for Jerry Koosman when then signed him out of the U.S. Army in 1964. A product of farm country in Morris, Minnesota, Koosman was a fairly big guy (6-foot-2, 200 pounds) and a hard thrower who never played college ball—the Mets scouted and signed him for a small bonus after watching him pitch at Fort Bliss in El Paso, Texas.[2] But by his second full minor league season in 1966, as he developed a better curve ball and slider and began learning to change speeds, Koosman dominated the Class-A New York-Penn League with a 1.77 ERA and .916 WHIP over 214 innings.

He made it all the way to the Mets at the beginning of the next season. Koosman debuted in Philadelphia on April 14, 1967—exactly one day after Tom Seaver made his major league debut at Shea Stadium against the Pirates—with 2⅔ scoreless relief innings against the Phillies. But Koosman got knocked around a bit in his next few relief outings and wound up back in Triple-A Jackson in May. Over the next four months he mostly toyed with International League hitters with 183 strikeouts in 178 innings, a 1.028 WHIP and a 2.43 ERA. His September call up to the Mets was unremarkable, with one decent start and two poor ones. But his big year at Triple-A had him well positioned to make the Mets—still a struggling franchise that didn't exactly have a bottomless pit of top starters yet—in 1968.

And it happened for him even more quickly than anyone expected. The Mets' dugout was under new management in 1968 with Hodges taking over as manager and his old Brooklyn Dodger teammate Rube Walker as pitching coach. Koosman's spring was good enough not only to make the big-league roster, but to start the second game of the season. After the Mets' bullpen blew a potential win for Seaver in a 5–4 opening day loss to the Giants, Koosman got the ball the next day in Los Angeles. For the first time ever, it was Seaver and Koosman as the one-two punch. Koosman went right after it, keeping the Dodgers hitless into the fifth inning and finishing with a four-hit shutout in a 4–0 win.

Six days later, Koosman was on the mound for the Mets home opener against the Giants in front of 52,000 fans at Shea. Many of them had just barely found their seats before Koosman put them on edge.

Ron Hunt singled, Jim Davenport reached on error by shortstop Al Weiss, Willie McCovey walked. This is how the home season began— bases loaded, no one out, Willie Mays at the plate. But if Koosman was nervous, he didn't show it. Mays took a called third strike, Jim Ray Hart popped out, and Jim Davenport struck out swinging. Right on the cusp of being yanked in the first inning, Koosman wound up going the full nine, striking out 10 in a 3–0 win. He had opened the 1968 season with back-to-back complete game shutouts of the Dodgers and Giants. He nearly made it three-for-three in his next start against Houston, but the Astros managed one run in a 4–1 Mets win in which Koosman allowed four hits and struck out 11 (the only Astro Koosman didn't whiff that day was his future teammate Rusty Staub, who got two hits and scored his team's only run).

By June 19, Koosman's record sat at 11–2, his ERA at 1.51. He had completed eight of his fourteen starts. In late July he shut out the Cardinals and Reds in back-to-back starts, totaling 20 strikeouts and allowing eight hits over the 18 innings. He continued to roll along and keep his ERA under 2.00 for almost the entire season until he allowed five runs to the Braves in his next-to-last start.

Koosman finished the 1968 season 19–12 (for a 73–89 club), with a 2.08 ERA in 264 innings. Even in the "Year of the Pitcher" in which Bob Gibson led the N.L. with 1.12 ERA, Koosman's 2.08 was still fourth in the league and way below the 2.99 league average. He completed 17 of his 34 starts with seven shutouts, tied for fourth-most in the league (Gibson tossed an astounding 13 shutouts in 1968). Koosman's 6.3 WAR was third in the N.L. among pitchers behind Gibson and Seaver. In the Rookie of the Year balloting, he finished second to Johnny Bench by one vote.

After putting up his nearly identical regular season in 1969, Koosman was ready to showcase the quality he would be mostly remembered for—that of the big-game pitcher. Though he didn't pitch well in his first playoff start against the Atlanta Braves, getting knocked out in a five-run fifth in what would be an 11–6 Mets victory. In fact, the entire 1969 N.L.C.S. turned out to be a bit strange, with the Mets rolling up a three-game sweep on the strength of their bats, not their arms (the scores were 9–5, 11–6 and 7–4).

But it was a different story in the World Series against the Orioles. Baltimore's powerful lineup led by Frank Robinson, Boog Powell, Brooks Robinson and Paul Blair had led the American League in OPS and OPS-plus and finished second in scoring behind the Twins. The O's had the pitching, too, leading the league in ERA, ERA-plus and WHIP, with 20 shutouts. Defensively, the Orioles seemed to catch everything. With Gold Gloves at third base (Brooks Robinson), shortstop (Mark Belanger), second base (Davey Johnson) and in center field (Paul Blair), they led the league in pretty much everything, from defensive efficiency and zone rating to fielding percentage and fewest errors. They buried the American League East with a 109–53 record to win by 19 games and then swept three straight from the Twins in the A.L.C.S.

So the Mets weren't given much of a chance in the World Series. The logic seemed reasonable—their strengths, pitching and defense, were also Baltimore strengths. And the Orioles' lineup was just so much better ... the Mets' magical run had to end here, right?

That it didn't go that way wasn't a miracle, much as that's how the story goes. It was pitching. The Orioles' staff may have matched (or even slightly exceeded) the Mets' staff in depth, which goes a long way over a 162-game season. But in a best-of-seven series, it's the main horses getting most of the innings. With their big front three of Mike Cuellar, Dave McNally and Jim Palmer, Baltimore had some good horses. But none of them were as good as Seaver. And none of them were as good as Koosman. That was the Mets' edge right there—they had the two best pitchers in the series. The Orioles had to face the lefty-righty duo four times in five games. To win under those conditions is a tall order, even for the powerful '69 Orioles.

Still, the series started off as most expected, with Cuellar shutting down the Mets' lineup and the Oriole bats pecking away just enough at Seaver for a 4–1 home win in Game 1. That put a big Game 2 onus on Koosman to get the Mets even against McNally the next day.

His first batter was Don Buford, the switch-hitting outfielder who had opened the first game with a home run off Seaver. Koosman essentially showcased his entire afternoon against Buford in the first—fastball, hard curve, slow curve, fastball, fastball. Buford swung through the last one for strike three. Koosman, calm and collected, kept mixing those pitches all day as he breezed through the potent Baltimore lineup as if he were on a back field in a spring training "B" game.[3] He fooled big Boog Powell on a couple of off-speed pitches to open the bottom of the second with a strikeout. After a two-out walk to Davey Johnson, Koosman retired his next 13 in a row to take a no-hitter into the seventh. He had a 1–0 lead thanks to a Clendenon home run in the fourth. Paul Blair erased the no-hitter by leading off the bottom of the seventh with a base hit and eventually came around to score on a base hit by Brooks Robinson. But those two hits were all the Orioles would get. After the Mets strung together three straight singles to take a 2–1 lead in the top of the ninth, Koosman retired the first two batters in the bottom half before getting into some trouble by walking Frank Robinson and Powell. With righty-swinging Brooks Robinson up, Hodges summoned right-handed reliever Ron Taylor for the final out. Koosman had now won the two biggest games in Met history—a key September matchup against the Cubs and now an 8⅔ inning two-hitter in the second game of the World Series after the Mets' Cy Young Award pitcher, Seaver, had lost the first game.

The Mets' pitching dominance continued to assert itself as the series moved along. Following their seventh inning run off Koosman in Game 2, the Orioles didn't score in their next 19 innings. A combined shutout by Gentry and Ryan gave the Mets Game 3, and then Seaver took a 1–0 shutout into the ninth inning the following day before yielding the tying run on a Brooks Robinson sacrifice fly—the play that featured the famous diving catch in right field by Ron Swoboda—to tie the game. But the Mets won it in the bottom of the 10th to set it up for Koosman to win the clincher.

And right on cue, despite some early trouble, he slammed the door. After breezing through the first two innings, Koosman served up a two-run homer to his fellow pitcher McNally in the third for the game's first runs. Two outs later, Frank Robinson blasted a deep home run over everything in left field to give Baltimore a 3–0 lead. After that, a peeved Koosman retired 16 of his next 17 hitters. The Orioles' only hit the rest of the way was a harmless two-out single by Powell in the sixth. The Mets rallied to win 5–3, the "miracle" was complete, and Jerry Koosman, with two series wins, was the man. After the final out, Koosman leaped into the arms of his catcher, Grote, in what became an iconic photograph in which the look of pure joy on his face seemed to sum up the story of the team's journey from national joke to world champions. Jerry Koosman was as responsible for the journey as anyone aside from Seaver, and he was almost as responsible as him.

"The biggest money pitcher in Mets history," says Howie Rose.

Koosman's next All-Star caliber season didn't come for another four years, although he continued to pitch well during the early part of the 1970s. Some nagging injuries held him back a bit at the beginning of the '70s—Koosman's innings dropped from 241 in 1969 to 212 in 1970 and then to just over 160 in both 1971 and '72. His cumulative 5.8 WAR over those three seasons didn't earn him any All-Star bids, though he still pitched to a better than average WHIP in all three seasons and a better than average ERA in two of the three. The 1972 season (0.4 WAR) was particularly challenging. The sudden death of Gil Hodges from a heart attack just days before the season started seemed to hit Koosman pretty hard. He clearly lost some rhythm at the beginning of the year and wound up spending some time in the bullpen to regain his mechanics.[4] This relative slump following the two big years to open his career probably went a long way toward the perception of Koosman as less than a Hall of Fame pitcher. Even though he'd go on to several more excellent seasons, that separation between the big years prevented a long, continuous stretch of dominance. It goes back to what Brian Kenny said about Ron Guidry—a little slump in the middle means having to piece together the player's Cooperstown value, something voters often aren't inclined to do.

The strength, mechanics and live fastball were back for the 1973 season. Koosman shot out of the gate with four straight wins, allowing four earned runs in 34 innings. He went on to make 35 starts, the most of his career, with 263 innings, a 2.84 ERA and a 5.8 WAR that tied for third in the league among pitchers. He finished 14–15, an inconsequential won-lost record compiled for the second-lowest scoring team in the National League. The Mets were hammered by the injury bug to several players in 1973, falling into the basement before the All-Star Game and still sitting there on August 30, though the mediocrity (or "balance," if you prefer a nicer word) of the N.L. East that year left them just 6½ games out of first. The Mets then went on their famous Tug McGraw-led "Ya Gotta Believe" September rally to capture an improbable division title with an 82–79 record. For Koosman, a huge part of the late surge with a 5–1 record over the final six weeks and 31 consecutive scoreless innings in late August and early September, the playoffs brought the next chapter in his "big game" legacy.

The Mets were big underdogs against the Cincinnati Reds, but managed to split the first two games of the best-of-five N.L.C.S. on the road. Koosman got the ball for the pivotal third game at Shea. Against the powerful Big Red Machine lineup of Joe Morgan, Johnny Bench, Pete Rose and Tony Perez, Koosman went all the way, scattering eight hits (six of them singles) with nine strikeouts, without walking a batter. And just for good measure, he added a couple of hits at the plate and drove in a run. The Mets battered Cincinnati starter Ross Grimsley early and cruised to a 9–2 win. Another big game in Mets history, another big performance by Jerry Koosman. Most people didn't particularly remember Koosman in this game, though. Why? This was the day of the famous Pete Rose-Bud Harrelson fight at second base, a memorable brawl that led to unruly fans throwing bottles and cans at Rose as he stood in left field during the next half inning that almost cost the Mets a forfeit. You still hear a lot about that Rose-Harrelson fight today, probably the biggest reason you don't hear a lot about Koosman's performance.

After the Mets went on to upset the Reds in five games, they faced the defending champion Oakland A's in the 1973 World Series. Koosman started Game 2 after the A's took the opener but didn't fare well, getting yanked in the third inning after giving up three runs. But the Mets managed to rally back in what became a bit of a crazy game, ultimately winning 10–7 in 12 innings. After the two teams split the next two games, Koosman's next turn came in Game 5, another pivotal postseason matchup. He tossed a scoreless game into the seventh inning to team with Tug McGraw on a three-hit shutout in a 2–0 Mets win, giving them a 3–2 series lead. Unfortunately, the Mets weren't able to capitalize as they dropped the last two in Oakland to lose in seven games. Had they been able to close it out, Koosman's pivotal (there's that word again) Game 5 win would have stood out that much more.

The 1973 season spurred a run of three All-Star caliber seasons in four years in which Koosman pitched at least 240 innings with a minimum 4.7 WAR in each year. In 1976 he had his first 20-win season, finishing 21–10 with 2.69 ERA and 1.096 WHIP in 247 innings. But Koosman wasn't actually selected for the All-Star Game in any of those seasons. In fact, after making it in his first two big years in 1968 and '69, he never made it again. Why? Probably because as good as Koosman was during these years, he seemed to get a bit lost in the shuffle of a strong Mets pitching staff. In addition to Seaver, the Mets called up talented young lefty Jon Matlack in July of 1971 and then watched him shoot to National League Rookie of the Year in 1972 with 15 wins, 244 innings and a 2.32 ERA. Matlack became a mainstay in the rotation with several strong years during the early-to-mid-'70s.

During the five-year run from 1972 to 1976, Matlack outperformed Koosman overall (25.5 to 17.9 in WAR, mainly due to the combination of Koosman's 0.4 in '72 and Matlack's amazing 9.1 in '74 when he led the league with seven shutouts and tossed 265 innings). Even though

Koosman was better than Matlack in three of the five years, a general perception took shape—and that's all it was, a perception—that Matlack was no. 2 behind Seaver in the Mets' rotation, bumping Koosman to no. 3. That perception pretty much started in the 1973 playoffs, when manager Yogi Berra, after opening with Seaver, started Matlack in Game 2 against the Reds even though Koosman had had the better year. Matlack did reward Berra's faith with a dominant two-hit shutout of the Big Red Machine, which Koosman followed with his own complete game win in the Rose-Harrelson game. Prior to the emergence of Matlack, the Seaver-Koosman duo had pretty much taken center stage with the Mets—it was basically the club's version of the Dodgers' Koufax-Drysdale tandem earlier in the 1960s. But with Matlack in the fold as part of what you might call a 2A and 2B with Koosman, the shine was off that apple. It was Matlack who was picked for three All-Star teams during that stretch while Koosman was shut out. Of course, how well Matlack pitched for the Mets shouldn't have anything to do with Koosman who, like anyone else, ought to be judged solely on his own merits. If a club has a number of strong pitchers, so be it, right? Yet to be viewed as the third pitcher on your own team for a good chunk of your prime isn't helpful when it comes to Hall of Fame votes.

As the Mets began to unravel after 1976, Koosman became one of very few remaining links to the better days of the recent past, and something of a martyr as the talent around him shriveled. Across 1977 and '78, which would be his final two seasons as a Met, Koosman mostly pitched quite well. But because the team was terrible, his reward was 11 wins and 35 losses. He followed that 20-win season in 1976 with a 20-loss season in '77, a statistical quirk that strongly worked its way into Koosman's career narrative. Of course it was meaningless, since he tossed 226 innings and outdid the league average by 11 percent in both ERA and WHIP, by 23 percent in FIP, and led the league with 7.6 strikeouts per nine innings. He wasn't as good in 1978 with a slightly below average ERA (3.75) but still did a bit better than average in WHIP, 22 percent better than the league in FIP, with 160 strikeouts that ranked eighth in the league. Take away that two-year 11–35 mark through no real fault of his own, and Koosman's career winning percentage shoots from .515 up to .548. He'd have had the 200-plus wins without the 200-plus losses. Even though wins and losses aren't true measures of a pitcher's effectiveness, Hall of Fame voters still give them a lot of weight. Would they have looked at Koosman a bit differently with a 211–174 record instead of his 222–209 mark? Probably not enough to get him elected, but it would have been interesting to see how much more support he might have gotten.

Another part of Jerry Koosman's narrative: he never won a Cy Young Award, a fact that should be inconsequential but isn't because it plays directly into the "Hall of the Very Good" perception that seeped into his career. The big problem with this view: there is nothing about a voted award that can be called a performance measurement. Winning a Cy Young or an MVP is nothing more than the result of a bunch of writers' opinions in a given year. The postseason awards are fun, and they're good marketing tools for keeping fans engaged with the sport, but they don't particularly mean anything. It's not as if the deserving player wins every time. Koosman actually could have taken the hardware a couple of times, having matched or exceeded the winner in WAR in 1976 (Randy Jones, N.L.) and 1979 (Mike Flanagan, A.L.). In the bigger picture, take a look at the pitchers who took the N.L. Cy Young during Koosman's Mets run from 1968 to 1978. Nine of the 11 were captured by Tom Seaver, Bob Gibson, Steve Carlton, Ferguson Jenkins and Gaylord Perry, all of whom are not only Hall of Famers but upper tier Hall of Famers. You don't need to beat out one of these guys for a Cy Young Award to qualify for Cooperstown.

As the 1979 season beckoned, Koosman was 36 and the Mets were deep into an abyss that showed no signs of ending anytime soon. He requested a trade and the team complied by sending him to his hometown Minnesota Twins in exchange for a young lefty reliever named Jesse Orosco. All he did that first year in Minnesota was toss 263 innings with a 3.38 ERA (20 percent better than league average), 1.33 WHIP (5 percent better than average), a 3.46 FIP (18 percent better) with a career-high 7.2 WAR that tied Boston's Dennis Eckersley for the league lead among pitchers. He went 20–13 to help the Twins stay in the A.L. West race for most of the season before they finished six games out at 82–80.

It was Koosman's last All-Star caliber season (though he was passed over for the team once again), but he soldiered on for six more years for the Twins, White Sox and Phillies to add another 62 wins and 9.4 WAR before retiring in 1985 (the White Sox, who had acquired Koosman from Minnesota in 1981, dealt him to the Phillies in February of 1984, less than a month after they had plucked an unprotected Tom Seaver from the Mets as a free agent compensation pick. Hence, Seaver and Koosman were technically reunited as teammates in Chicago without actually playing together there). In his next-to-last season with the 1984

Phillies at age 41, Koosman started 34 games and pitched 234 innings with a 3.25 ERA. His 3.0 WAR was second on the staff (incidentally, he pitched at Shea three times that season, beating the Mets once and losing to them twice).

When it was all said and done, Koosman finished his 18-year career 222–209 with a 3.36 ERA for mostly weak hitting clubs, and a 110 ERA-plus that, among some of his elite peers, was just a bit behind Ferguson Jenkins and Steve Carlton and ahead of Don Sutton and Catfish Hunter (all of these pitchers including Koosman did quite a bit better than 110 in their better seasons). Koosman's 2,556 strikeouts rank 30th all time. His 57.1 WAR is higher than 25 pitchers currently in the Hall—nearly half. He averaged just about a 5.0 WAR in his 10 best seasons, a feat that's easy to miss since they weren't particularly bunched together.

Despite all the numbers you won't find many people who would put Jerry Koosman in the Hall of Fame. Certainly not the voters. When Koosman's name came up on the ballot in 1991, he got four votes. Less than 1 percent—one, done, forgotten. Howie Rose sums up the popular opinion: "I love him, but I don't think he had enough Hall of Fame seasons."

It's a fair point. Jerry Koosman wasn't Tom Seaver or Steve Carlton, and his Cooperstown credentials aren't patently obvious. But that doesn't mean he didn't do plenty to merit the Hall of Fame. Compared to many pitchers who rate a notch below the Seavers and Carltons of the world but still made the cut, Koosman has an excellent case.

Recall the analysis that placed Ron Guidry right on par with Hall of Famers Whitey Ford, Red Ruffing, Lefty Gomez and Dizzy Dean. Koosman has to rank right with those pitchers too, because Koosman's career was certainly as good as Guidry's, perhaps a bit better. Breaking down the numbers shows a close call. Guidry's career marks against the league average in strikeouts, WHIP and ERA all beat Koosman, mainly because Guidry's top season was so frighteningly good (his ERA-plus was an absurd 208 in 1978, or more than twice as good as the average pitcher). For the full career, Guidry's ERA-plus tops Koosman 119 to 110. Year-by-year, though, both exceeded a 120 six times. The comparison is similar for WHIP, where Guidry's 14 percent above league average handily beats Koosman's 5.6 percent. But Koosman still outdid the league average by 10 percent or more five times, just one fewer than Guidry. The two pitchers were virtually identical in Fielding Independent Pitching, both at 19 percent above league average. Guidry's biggest edge is in strikeouts, where he beats the league average of Ks per inning by 36 percent, way better than Koosman's 11.5 percent.

But underlying all of it is the fact that Koosman's career had both more years and heavier annual workloads. He compiled his numbers across 3,839 career innings, a lot more than Guidry's 2,392. Koosman hit 240 innings in seven different seasons, Guidry in three. A few of Koosman's lesser years naturally served to drag down his final career numbers in WHIP and ERA, but he wound up with the same number of All-Star caliber seasons as Guidry—six. By WAR, both pitchers averaged just over six wins per year in their five respective best years and just over 4.6 per year in their respective 10 best years (Guidry squeaks out the five-year WAR edge 30.7 to 30.1, Koosman the 10-year edge 46.7 to 46.1). And for the full career, it's Koosman over Guidry 57.1 to 47.9 in six more full seasons. So the comparison is pretty clear for the two great New York lefties—all those extra years and innings made it tough for Koosman to keep pace with Guidry in WHIP in ERA, but they did boost his WAR that much higher. Much like Red Ruffing, Koosman's advantage over Guidry in career length largely counters Guidry's edge in some of the year-to-year peak seasons. Call it just about a draw.

Who is the greatest left-hander in the history of New York baseball? Most would say it's Carl Hubbell of the old Giants, whose famous screwball led to three ERA titles, six WHIP titles, five 20-win seasons, and a 68.6 career WAR. Right after Hubbell, most would name Whitey Ford. But you would have just as strong a case arguing for Jerry Koosman or Ron Guidry.

What about some of Koosman's elite peers who made it to the Hall of Fame? Some—Seaver, Carlton, Jenkins, Ryan, Palmer—were clearly better. But some weren't. How about Jim "Catfish" Hunter, who pitched for 15 years, won 20 games or more five times and took five World Series rings with the Athletics and Yankees? Hunter was widely perceived to be the ace of those great Oakland clubs that dominated the first half of the 1970s, because he won the most games. In reality, he was the staff ace on only a couple of the Athletics teams he pitched for, dating back to his rookie year in 1965 and going through 1974. In his first seven seasons, Hunter pitched at an All-Star level in one of them, when he put up a 2.81 ERA, 114 ERA-plus and 4.6 WAR in 1967. Later, he found his groove with three big seasons in four years between 1972 and 1975, the last of which came during his first season with the Yankees after he famously won an arbitration battle with Oakland owner Charlie Finley over a contract violation and became a free agent. Hunter's 1975 season in New York: 328 innings, league-leading 1.009 WHIP, 144 ERA-plus and career-best 8.1 WAR, along with a 23–14 record.

Hunter was a terrific pitcher, but he also had the advantage of playing for a slew of strong teams, which boosted his win totals and his national profile. In the 1970s the nation saw him pitch in the playoffs seven times and in the World Series and All-Star Game six times. His five 20-win seasons came bunched right in a row (1971–75), giving him that perceived "dominant period," even though the advanced stats say in hindsight that he pitched at an All-Star level in just three of the five years.

Would Jerry Koosman have had himself five or six 20-win seasons pitching for teams like the early '70s A's and late '70s Yankees? There's no way to know for sure, although common sense says yes. The one thing that is certain is that Jerry Koosman was a better pitcher than Catfish Hunter. Pitching some 400 more innings over his career, Koosman's 110 career ERA-plus edges Hunter's 104, with Koosman putting up 120 or better six times to Hunter's three. Fielding Independent Pitching isn't close, with Hunter coming in below league average for his career while Koosman finished 19 percent better than average, an indication that Hunter benefited from some nice defensive help for much of his career. Hunter's strikeout rate also fell below league average (-5 percent) while Koosman's was 11.5 percent above average. Hunter did have the advantage in WHIP, 10.4 percent better than league average compared to Koosman's 5.6 percent, thanks mainly to Hunter beating the A.L. average by 25 percent three times during his peak period of 1972 to 1975. As for WAR—again, not close. Koosman's 57.1 easily beats Hunter's 36.3. Breaking it down, Hunter's best couple of years were a bit better than Koosman's, but Koosman still winds up with the slightly better five-year peak (30.1 to 28.0) and a decidedly better 10-year peak (46.8 to 35.7).

But boy, do voters love to see championship rings and 20-win seasons, as if any pitcher can control either of those things by himself. Catfish Hunter was named on 53.7 percent of ballots in his first year of eligibility and broke through with 76.3 percent by his third year in 1987. He wound up outpolling Koosman 315–4 in Hall of Fame votes—welcome to baseball's Bizarro World.

Koosman also stacks up pretty well against another Hall of Fame pitcher of his time—Don Sutton. A durable right-hander who lasted 23 seasons and pitched more than 5,000 major league innings, Sutton had a few seasons that were great and a whole lot more that were very good or solid. It all added up to a career that landed him at number seven on the all-time strikeout list (3,574) and tied for number 14 on the all-time wins list (324). Before even going through the more advanced stats, a pitcher with that kind of pedigree is going to be voted into the Hall of Fame, and should be.

Sutton debuted in the majors a year before Koosman did, coming up to the Los Angeles Dodgers in 1966. After five solid if unspectacular years, he hit his stride with a great three-year run from 1971 to 1973 as he clearly emerged as the ace of a Dodger staff that was in the midst of adding Tommy John and Andy Messersmith and would later include the likes of Burt Hooton, Rick Sutcliffe and Jerry Reuss. Those big years in the early '70s had Sutton largely perceived as the ace of those strong Dodger pitcher staffs during the rest of his tenure there through 1980 even though he was rarely the top pitcher on the staff after 1973. Altogether, Sutton had six seasons you would call All-Star level, adding 1977 (240 innings, 121 ERA-plus, 4.5 WAR), 1980 (league-leading 2.20 ERA, 161 ERA-plus, league-leading 0.989 WHIP, 6.3 WAR) and strike-shortened 1981 (league-leading 1.015 WHIP, 2.8 WAR) to his 1971–73 run. The rest of his long career was spent piling up those good-but-not-great seasons, adding to the impressive career totals. Yes, by and large Don Sutton was more "compiler" than dominant pitcher. But when a guy compiles so much on top of a handful of seasons that were genuinely dominant, it's tough to say that he isn't roughly among the top 50 pitchers of all time, and hence Cooperstown worthy. Sutton was inducted on his fifth try in 1998.

Don Sutton is much like Jerry Koosman—a notch below the likes of Seaver, Carlton and a few others but still holding Hall of Fame pedigree. It's tough to argue that Koosman's career was superior to Sutton's. But it's not tough to argue that it was very close. Koosman had a slight ERA-plus advantage, 110 to 108, with both putting up six years of a 120 or better. Koosman also had the better FIP, 19 percent above league average to Sutton's 10.7 percent, and a better strikeout rate of 13.7 percent above average to Sutton's 11.2 percent. Sutton was an excellent control pitcher who allowed just 2.3 walks per nine innings for his career, leading to several strong seasons in WHIP (he led the league four times), where he had a clear advantage over Koosman of 13.3 percent better than average to 5.6 percent. And of course Sutton had the advantage in breadth—five more seasons and some 1,400 more innings—leading to a career 68.3 WAR to Koosman's 57.1. But Koosman had a slightly better peak, averaging 6.0 wins in his five best years to Sutton's 5.5, and 4.7 in his 10 best years to Sutton's 4.4.

So it's quite close—Koosman with the edge in FIP and strikeout rate, Sutton superior in WHIP, with ERA about even. Overall, Koosman's stronger years were a bit better than Sutton's stronger years, balanced by Sutton ultimately adding a few more quality seasons to roll up more career wins and strikeouts. In the end you're probably going to give Sutton the nod based on the extra work and higher career WAR, but there's not a lot to choose between the two. Yet we know why Don Sutton got 386 Hall of Fame votes to Koosman's four—300 wins. The magic number strikes again. Had Sutton missed the arbitrary plateau, he probably would have met the same fate as his onetime teammate Tommy John, who wound up with 288 wins and no plaque. Again, hitting that round number gives fans and voters pause to reflect back on your career and build a narrative. It also helps to pitch for strong teams—Sutton's tenure with the strong L.A. clubs of the 1970s led to eight seasons with teams that won at least 90 games, not even counting the 1982 Brewers, for whom he pitched briefly, or the champion 1988 Dodgers, where he had a final swansong at age 43 and didn't quite make it through the season before retiring. Koosman pitched for two 90-win clubs in his entire career, the '69 Mets and, much later at age 40, the 1983 A.L. West champion White Sox. Don Sutton had a great career, and few people question his Hall of Fame status. So few ought to have reason to question Jerry Koosman getting there either.

Jerry Koosman made his last appearance at Shea Stadium on Thursday afternoon August 15, 1985. He was 42 years old, pitching for the Phillies and matched up against 20-year-old Dwight Gooden, who had just started kindergarten the night Koosman plunked Ron Santo and struck out 13 Cubs. Gooden was now the phenom and staff ace of a revitalized Mets club that had seemingly moved an entire generation past the Seaver-Koosman days. And this was Gooden's signature year—he came into the game 19–3 with a 1.64 ERA and leading the universe in strikeouts, on his way to 24–4, 1.53 and a Cy Young Award.

But the sentimental matchup for Mets fans of old hero vs. new hero fizzled pretty quickly. Gooden turned in his worst outing of the season, but Koosman, who'd had some good outings earlier in the year including an eight-inning shutout at Wrigley Field and a complete game shutout in Montreal, had been showing signs of wilting in the summer heat as the

1985 season progressed. Even with Gooden showing that he was human that day, Koosman couldn't take advantage.

After the Phils scored one off Gooden in the top of the first, Koosman settled in for the bottom half. His first batter, Wally Backman, was a switch-hitting second baseman who was so notoriously weak from the right side (.122 average against lefties in '85) that he normally platooned. On this day he was in there, and Koosman walked him to lead off. Then Tom Paciorek, a veteran backup outfielder getting a spot start, homered. After Darryl Strawberry flied out, Gary Carter homered. Koosman walked George Foster. Ray Knight homered. In the bottom of the second, Koosman retired his first two hitters, but then walked Paciorek and yielded back to back singles to Strawberry and Carter for another run. Manager John Felske came and got him. Koosman had faced 13 hitters and retired five of them, allowing six runs. Not a happy Shea finale. The Mets would take the game 10–7 with the win going to Jesse Orosco after his two scoreless innings of relief. Fourteen months later, Orosco would be the guy celebrating on the Shea Stadium mound after the final out of the World Series, the only Met to ever do that other than Koosman, for whom he was traded in 1979.

Koosman started in Philadelphia the following week and was promptly lit up in the first inning by the Dodgers in what became a 15–6 Phillies loss. It was his last game. At the time Koosman finally called it a career, only 15 pitchers in baseball history had struck out more batters. Only 15 in the post–World War II era had pitched more innings. During his career, no left-hander in the game aside from Steve Carlton had outperformed him (Tommy John and Mickey Lolich, who both got a lot more Hall of Fame votes, came close as did Frank Tanana, who was shut out completely). Jerry Koosman wasn't Carlton, Seaver or Ryan, but there are more than 60 pitchers in the Hall of Fame. Koosman should be one of them.

7

David Cone

You could see that it was likely to be a good day for David Cone right from the start. His first pitch to young Montreal Expos leadoff hitter Wilton Guerrero was a fastball for a called strike. Next came a sharp breaking curve fouled back for strike two. Then a back-door curve that just scratched the outside black for a called strike three, sending a befuddled Guerrero back to the dugout on three pitches.

"That may be one of those pitches we see an awful lot today," proclaimed Bobby Murcer in the Yankees' TV booth.[1]

And it was. July 18, 1999, was Yogi Berra day at Yankee Stadium. Among the dignitaries on hand was Yogi's battery mate who threw a perfect game in the World Series on the same field in 1956—Don Larson. It was also a hot, humid Sunday afternoon, the temperature reaching 95 degrees at game time. A scheduling quirk coming out of the All-Star break had the Yankees opening a three-game series against Montreal on a Sunday following three against the Braves on Thursday, Friday and Saturday. The Yankees had lost two of the three against Atlanta to fall to 53–36 and a four-game lead in the A.L. East. Not exactly struggling, but not exactly replicating the previous year's 114–48 juggernaut that had crushed the competition before the All-Star Game (the Yankees led the division by 14 games on the same date in 1998).

A visit from the young, small market Montreal Expos was more than welcome. A lineup of mostly inexperienced free swingers against a veteran pitcher attuned to changing speeds, setting up hitters and throwing any one of four pitches for strikes. It had all the makings of a mismatch as long the well-rested Cone—whose last outing had been a two-inning stint in the All-Star Game five days earlier—had his good stuff. And from the first batter, it was pretty clear that he did. Cone got the next two first inning outs on fly balls and then opened the second by getting Wilton Guerrero's talented-but-still-young brother Vladimir to chase a slider way out of the strike zone for strike three. After a pair of groundouts ended the inning, the Yankees jumped on Montreal starter Javier Vasquez for five runs in the bottom of the second. The inning included a monster two-run homer into the right field upper deck by Ricky Ledee and then a two-run shot over the left field fence by Derek Jeter.

Already with a comfortable lead to begin the third inning, Cone took thorough control. Wearing his age—36—on his pinstriped back, Cone's guile was too much for the young, aggressive Expo hitters. The smooth,

David Cone's 2,668 career strikeouts rank 25th on the all-time list.

rocking motion, the multiple arm angles, widening the strike zone both inside and outside. In the third, Chris Widger put a weak half-swing on an outside breaking pitch for strike three, and then both Shane Andrews and Orlando Cabrera took full swings at the same pitch but still missed for their third strikes. Nine up, nine down, with five strikeouts.

Cone mostly stayed on the outer part of the plate or off the plate altogether as he moved through the middle innings. Occasionally he'd zip one inside to keep them honest. The hitters kept chasing. In fourth came two more fly outs around a strikeout of Terry Jones. Then three straight fly balls in the fifth and two popups and another flyout in the sixth. In the Yankee booth, Tim McCarver said: "I can see it in David Cone's body language, he's going to be very disappointed if the Expos get a base runner in this game."

McCarver was known for predicting a lot of things correctly during his long run as a broadcaster, and he did it again this time. Vasquez recovered from his rough second inning to pitch well as the game moved along, but it didn't much matter. The Expos weren't touching Cone. Not only did they not have any base runners, they hadn't hit a single ball hard. Almost everything was a strikeout, a popup, or a lazy fly ball. With nine outs to go for perfection, Cone finished his 1–2–3 seventh by whiffing both James Mouton and Rondell White on sliders way out of the strike zone that they couldn't lay off of. "Call your friends," bellowed McCarver to the TV audience. In the eighth, Vladimir Guerrero popped up before Jose Vidro gave the fans a scare with Montreal's hardest hit ball of the day, a sharp grounder to the right of second baseman Chuck Knoblauch. But Knoblauch's quick feet got him over toward second quickly enough to backhand the ball on the outfield grass and gun Vidro out at first. Cone then disposed of big lefty-hitting Brad Fullmer on three pitches, freezing him with a curve for the called third strike. He walked off to a huge ovation.

In the ninth, after the Yankees had tacked on another run on a Bernie Williams RBI single, Cone threw three pitches to Widger- curve swung and missed, another curve for a called strike, and the patented slider off the outside corner that Widger chased for strike three. Cone had 10 Ks and 25 outs in a row. Pinch hitter Ryan McGuire lofted an easy fly to left field that Ledee had a bit of trouble with in the sun but managed to corral for the second out (whew). The last batter was Orlando Cabrera. With 41,000-plus on their feet and Don Larson watching from a box upstairs, Cone went right after it. He pulled the string on

Cabrera to get him out in front on a swinging strike. After a ball outside, Cabrera popped up the next pitch in foul territory near third base. Scott Brosius squeezed it for the final out. In his 13th full season, David Cone had pitched his first career no-hitter and the 16th perfect game in major league history. He dropped to his knees, got lost under a pile teammates for a few moments, and then emerged to be carried off the field by Knoblauch and by his catcher, Joe Girardi.

Cone's perfecto helped to ignite the Yankees to seven wins in their next eight games. By July 27, they led the division by 7½ games, on their way to 98 wins and a third championship in four seasons.

David Cone's magical day at Yankee Stadium came 18 summers after his debut in the Gulf Coast League—he'd spent half his life as a professional pitcher, much of it starring for both New York teams. A product of Rockhurst High School in Kansas City, Missouri, he was drafted in the third round by his hometown Royals in 1981. Cone put up big numbers in the low rungs of the minors for two years before tearing his ACL in the spring of 1983 and missing the entire season. He found the going tougher when he hit Double-A and Triple-A in 1984 and 1985 (17–27 with an ERA over 4.00 over those two years). Cone was showing good stuff but still walking too many hitters. But then he put together an excellent season at Triple-A Omaha in 1986, going 8–4 with a 2.79 ERA the year he turned 23. The Royals called him up for a few relief appearances in June and then for a handful more in September.

But Kansas City had a few decisions to make after the 1986 season. The club was just one season removed from a World Series championship it had won largely on the back of a young, strong starting rotation that included Bret Saberhagen, Charlie Leibrandt, Mark Gubicza, Bud Black and Danny Jackson. Cone was a good prospect, but he was pretty much blocked by a deep major league rotation. Meantime, the Royals needed to address their catching situation. Veteran Jim Sundberg, an outstanding defensive catcher for years who fit perfectly with the young pitching staff during the 1985 championship season, was now 35 and approaching the end of the line.

Cone went nearly all the way through spring training with the 1987 Royals until the team pulled the trigger in late March on a deal that suddenly shipped him to the Mets for 26-year-old catcher Ed Hearn, who had performed well in limited duty during the previous season as a backup to Gary Carter. The Royals' logic was understandable: they were dealing from the strength of a deep pitching staff, and Hearn, a good hitter in the minors before doing well in spot duty for Carter, seemed to be a decent bet as a potential no. 1 catcher for a team that needed one. Of course, things don't always work out as planned. For the Mets, the deal wound up as legitimate payback for the haunting trade in which Kansas City had stolen Amos Otis from them for Joy Foy in 1969. Hearn, unfortunately, hurt his shoulder soon after arriving in Kansas City and never really made it back. He wound up playing a total of 13 more major league games before retiring. Cone, heading to New York, was about to see his career take off. For the next dozen years or so, he'd display some of the nastiest stuff in the game.

Expectations were fairly modest initially. The Mets, coming off their dominant 1986 championship club, were bringing back the same deep rotation that had just led the National League in ERA during a 108-win season. Cone figured as a swingman, a young righty with promising stuff who could work out of the bullpen and spot start when necessary. But for the Mets, the good fortune of a healthy 1986 pitching staff didn't last into 1987. The ominous tone was set before the season even started when Dwight Gooden tested positive for cocaine, costing him a two-month suspension right out of the gate. Bob Ojeda, an 18-game winner in 1986, hurt his left (pitching) elbow and made only 10 starts. Sid Fernandez suffered some nagging injuries that reduced his innings to 156 from 204. The only starter who stayed healthy most of the way, Ron Darling, wound up spraining his thumb on September 11 when he fell covering first base on a bunt single by the Cardinals' Vince Coleman and missed the final three weeks (this was the game in which Terry Pendleton homered off reliever Roger McDowell to tie the game with two out in the ninth before St. Louis went on to win in 10 innings—instead of cutting the Cards' N.L. East lead to half a game, the Mets trailed by 2½. They would go on to lose the division by three games).

All the upheaval in the rotation gave Cone a chance to start pretty quickly. After a few relief outings, he made his first major league start against the Astros at Shea and was promptly knocked around for 10 runs in five innings in an 11–1 loss. Pretty much out of necessity, manager Davey Johnson stuck with him. Two starts later he won in Cincinnati on a complete game four-hitter and then beat the Giants at home after allowing two earned runs in eight innings. But just two starts after that on May 27, facing the Giants in San Francisco, Cone squared around to bunt in the fifth inning against Atlee Hammaker and took an inside fastball smack on his pitching hand. A bone was broken—he was done for almost three months. When it rains it pours—instead of filling the gap caused by the pitching injury jinx, Cone became part of it himself.

But his August return brought the first consistent glimpse of the David Cone that fans would come to know in the future. As the Mets hung with the Cardinals down the stretch in their (ultimately) unsuccessful attempt to win the division, Cone turned in some of the best games of his young career. In his first start back against the Dodgers, he allowed a two-run first inning homer to John Shelby and then just two hits over the next five innings in a tough 3–1 loss. Right after that, he beat San Diego with a three-hitter into the eighth inning, with seven strikeouts. On Sunday September 13, after the Mets had lost two straight to St. Louis (the Terry Pendleton game followed by a Dwight Gooden stinker the following day) to fall 3½ behind, he played stopper by allowing one earned run into the seventh to beat the Cards and get a game back for the Mets. Though he finished the season at a pedestrian 5–6 with a 3.71 ERA, Cone was ever so quietly becoming one of the Mets' most reliable starters, a surge of momentum he would take into the 1988 season.

Not that he got the chance right away. With the Mets' 1986 rotation—Gooden, Darling, Ojeda, Fernandez and Rick Aguilera—healthy and intact again to begin 1988, Cone once again opened the season in the bullpen. Even when Aguilera went out with an elbow injury on April 18, the team stuck with four starters through periodic off days over the following two weeks. But the first time the Mets needed that fifth starter, they gave the ball to Cone against the Braves on May 3. He turned in the first complete game shutout of his major league career in an 8–0 win. A week later he held the Astros to one run and four hits over seven innings in a 5–2 victory. Cone was 4–0 with a 2.16 ERA, and the Mets were 22–8. What ensued was a Mets runaway in the N.L. East for the second time in three years, and Rick Aguilera getting "Wally Pipped" out of the Mets rotation by David Cone (if you don't know the reference, Pipp was the first baseman for the 1925 Yankees who suffered an injury and was replaced by Lou Gehrig, who went on to play 2,130 consecutive games). Upon his return two months later, Aguilera began pitching out of the bullpen, the first step in a forced career transition that would see him rack up 318 saves, most of them coming after he was traded to the Minnesota Twins a year later.

Cone just kept rolling through the 1988 season. He threw a seven-inning shutout with 12 strikeouts at San Diego on May 17. On June 2, he fanned 10 Cubs in 10 innings at Shea Stadium in what became a

13-inning, 2–1 loss. After going 10 innings again two starts later against the Cardinals (this time a 2–1 Mets win in 12 innings), he dominated the Phillies with a two-hit shutout on June 19. By the All-Star break, Cone was 10–2 with a 2.52 ERA and 98 strikeouts in 114 innings. National League All-Star manager Whitey Herzog picked him for the team— what began as another swingman season in the bullpen resulted in an All-Star appearance by July. Cone pitched a perfect fifth inning, retiring three future Hall of Famers—Rickey Henderson, Paul Molitor and Wade Boggs—in succession.

Cone picked up where he left off after the break, winning his next three decisions and then striking out 12 in seven innings in a loss at San Francisco on August 17. It was his third and final loss of the 1988 season. Cone started eight more games and won all of them, including four complete games, with 66 Ks in 64 innings. As the Mets finished with 100 wins to take the division by 15 games, David Cone finished his first full season as a starter 20–3 with a 2.22 ERA, 145 ERA-plus, 1.115 WHIP and four shutouts in 231 innings. His 213 strikeouts ranked second to Nolan Ryan, his 5.5 WAR second to Orel Hershiser, the 1988 N.L. Cy Young Award winner whose 23-win season for the Dodgers was highlighted by a memorable 59-inning scoreless streak late in the season that broke the record of former Dodger Don Drysdale by a third of an inning. Cone's season was such a whirlwind that he even inspired a new breed of fan at Shea Stadium—the Coneheads. Big clusters of fans were showing up dressed with the big plastic cones on their heads in their best attempts at impersonating Jane Curtain and Dan Aykroyd of *Saturday Night Live* sketch fame.

The 1988 season, successful as it was, also brought on Cone's first perception problem with the press. As the playoffs approached, one local reporter wrote that while Cone had the best season among Mets starters, Dwight Gooden was the ace of the staff. The reasoning would be that Gooden had been a rock in the Mets rotation for five years at that point, while Cone was the newbie who had pretty much come out of nowhere. Of course the reasoning was flawed. Gooden had a fine season (18–9, 3.19, 3.4 WAR), but Cone was easily the Mets' best pitcher. Since when is your best pitcher not your ace?

Manager Davey Johnson went with (and hence reinforced) the media narrative by starting Gooden in Game 1 of the N.L.C.S. against the Dodgers. He pitched very well, but it was looking like he would lose a tough 2–0 duel to Hershiser until the Mets suddenly rallied for three in the top of the ninth for a 3–2 win. Cone then got knocked around early in a 6–3 loss in Game 2. After the Mets took the third game, Gooden again pitched very well for most of Game 4, leading 4–2 in the ninth before a walk to John Shelby and a homer into the right field bullpen by Mike Scioscia shockingly tied the game. It became the most gut-wrenching postseason loss in Mets history after the Dodgers went on to win in 12 innings to tie up the series. After the Dodgers put the Mets on the brink in by winning Game 5, it was Cone's turn to shine in the playoffs with a complete game five-hitter in a 5–1 win in Game 6. But it went for naught when the Dodgers knocked Ron Darling out early in Game 7 and, despite three scoreless relief innings from Gooden, won the pennant with a 6–0 victory. They would go on to knock off the Oakland in A's in the World Series in five games.

Gooden had certainly pitched well enough in the series to justify Davey Johnson's decision to tab him No.1, while Cone mixed a good start with a bad one. But regardless of the outcome of the series or of the games started by Cone or Gooden, Johnson's choice of Gooden to open the N.L.C.S. encapsulated the perception disadvantage that would mark Cone's tenure with the Mets, and again later with the Yankees. Namely— he pitched on good staffs, surrounded by big names. Over the course of the nearly five-year run from 1988 until he was traded to Toronto late in the 1992 season, David Cone was the Mets' best pitcher. But he was also in a rotation with Gooden, Darling, Fernandez, Ojeda, and, as of mid–1989, Frank Viola. There's your perception: on all those good pitching staffs, it was easy to see Cone as one cog in the machine, not as the clear-cut main man. As much as a player ought to be judged solely by his own performance, the extraneous factors always seem to come into play.

Cone fell off a bit in 1989 with 3.52 ERA, 190 strikeouts and a 1.3 WAR while going 14–8. But in both 1990 and 1991, he topped 200 innings and led the league in strikeouts in both seasons, whiffing 233 hitters in '90 and 241 in '91. He finished well above league average in ERA, FIP and WHIP in both seasons, including an N.L. leading 2.52 FIP in 1991.

But the Mets' big run that had begun in 1984 was fizzling by the early 1990s. Keith Hernandez and Gary Carter were gone. So was Darryl Strawberry, who made a dramatic free agent departure to the Dodgers. On the pitching staff, Gooden and Darling were slipping while Viola followed his superb 1990 season with a big dropoff in '91 before the Mets let him walk as a free agent. It was the end of an era, one that had beat a lot of excitement into the hearts of Mets fans who pushed Shea Stadium attendance to the top or near-top of the league each year to watch their club finish first or second for seven straight seasons. Many were disappointed that the run only produced one championship, but everyone sure seemed to have a lot fun watching the team go for it in all those seasons. And with a bit more luck, such as avoiding those ill-timed home runs by Terry Pendleton and Mike Scioscia, they might well have wound up with more rings.

Cone was indeed the clear ace of the Mets' pitching staff by 1991, though it didn't seem to mean a whole lot with the team now dragging. But he punctuated the season with a historic performance on the final day. The 76–84 Mets were in Philadelphia on Sunday, October 6. The stakes were not high—these were two also-ran clubs playing out the final game. The Phils' lineup—much like the 1998 Expos—was loaded with youngsters who were no match for David Cone's repertoire. But it was an amazing thing to watch nonetheless. It was the kind of performance that reminded you that David Cone probably had the best stuff of any pitcher in the major leagues.

In the first inning he struck out the side. In the second inning he did it again. High fastballs, curves dropping off the table, sliders breaking out of the strike zone. The Phillies hitters were flailing at everything. Cone had to settle for one strikeout in the third inning while getting the other two hitters to pop up. But he quickly reverted to form by whiffing the side again in the fourth, the second of which saw veteran Dale Murphy lose his grip and send the bat bouncing out to shortstop, which allowed young call up Jeff Gardner to finally do something as he retrieved the bat and handed it to the bat boy. Four innings, 10 Ks. After six innings it was 15. He continued to toy with the Philly lineup into the ninth inning, when he got Mickey Morandini to swing over a sharp breaking curve that catcher Charlie O'Brien couldn't quite grab cleanly, which meant that first baseman Chris Donnels had to touch the ball for the third time all day as he took the throw from O'Brien to complete Cone's 19th strikeout. He had tied a National League record and missed the all-time record by one strikeout when Murphy grounded out to end it.

But Cone didn't get the chance to be the Mets' ace for very long. The team's attempt to rebuild on the fly in the wake of the Carter-Hernandez-Strawberry era by bringing in Eddie Murray, Bobby Bonilla, Bret Saberghagen and Vince Coleman wasn't working. Coleman simply wasn't that good. Saberhagen pitched very well at times but was limited by injuries. Murray was old. Bonilla was reasonably productive but not the major star the team thought it was getting. The team didn't seem to have much of a plan beyond throwing a bunch of players together and hoping it worked. When it didn't, the realization came that it was time to rebuild. On August 23, 1992, with the Mets in fifth place, Cone, now a pending free agent, allowed three hits to the Padres in seven innings in a 4–3 loss. It was his last Mets game (at least for the next 11 years). Four days later, he was dealt to the A.L. East-leading Toronto Blue Jays to help with their championship push. In return, the Mets got second baseman Jeff Kent and outfielder Ryan Thompson. As much as Cone had left in him, the deal actually would have been fruitful for the Mets had they not traded Kent before he fully blossomed awhile later. But such is life.

Blue Jays fans showed that they knew full well what they were getting, showing up to SkyDome with their own Coneheads. Getting David Cone was a big deal to them. And Cone did help the Jays down the stretch, starting seven games and allowing 39 hits with 47 strikeouts in 53 innings with a 2.55 ERA. He finished the full season with 249 innings, 261 strikeouts, a 2.81 ERA and 5.1 WAR, his fourth All-Star caliber season in five years. By October he would own his first championship ring. After the Blue Jays lost the first game of the A.L.C.S. at home to the Oakland A's, Cone got them a much-needed win in Game 2 with a five-hitter over eight innings in a 3–1 victory. They would take the series in six. Cone's first World Series game against the Braves wasn't very good—five walks and four runs before getting yanked in the fifth inning—though the Jays came away with a 5–4 win. In the Game 6 clincher, Cone held Atlanta to one run and four hits in six innings before leaving with a 2–1 lead. He was denied a win when the Braves scored in the ninth to tie it, but the Jays came back with two in the top of the 11th and then held on for a 4–3 win. The first World Series championship for Canada, and the first for David Cone.

But while the trade to Toronto that year gave Cone a chance to pitch for a championship, it also began what became a somewhat strange middle phase of his career, a three-year run as a nomadic hired gun. Between 1992 and 1995, he went from the Mets to the Blue Jays to the Royals, back to the Blue Jays, and then to the Yankees. He was in his late 20s and early 30s and pitching some of the best baseball of his career, yet he wasn't the favorite son of anyone in particular. "A very strong [Hall of Fame] candidate, but not having one fan base can hurt you," says Brian Kenny.

But Cone's first free agent contact said a lot about his value. Shortly after picking up his World Series ring, Cone signed back with his original team, the Kansas City Royals. This was the tail end of the era that preceded the 1994 strike, before the payroll gulfs between big market and small market teams had reached gargantuan levels. Just three years earlier, Kirby Puckett and Rickey Henderson had become baseball's first $3 million-a-year players by signing with Minnesota and Oakland, respectively. Cone's deal in 1993: three years and $19 million. The top gem of that winter's free agent class was Greg Maddux, who had been an All-Star level pitcher for five years and who was coming directly off a dominant Cy Young Award season with the Cubs. Maddux signed with Atlanta for five years and $28 million. Two years longer than Cone, but with a bit less annual money. The market didn't value Cone too far behind Maddux. "He was outstanding, and the marketplace treated him that way," says Kenny of Cone. "He was a pennant race changer."

Cone charged ahead with Royals, turning in two dominant seasons. In 1993, his 7.2 WAR and 7.3 hits allowed per nine innings were both third among American League pitchers. His 191 strikeouts ranked fourth, his 254 innings fifth. And his 3.33 ERA ranked 10th in the league and 23 percent better than average (138 ERA-plus). The 1.256 WHIP wasn't in the top 10 but rated 11.4 percent above average. Pitching for a Kansas City club that scored the fewest runs in the American League, Cone's effort was rewarded with just an 11–14 record, yet another example of the folly of won-lost records. The next year brought more of the same. In the 115-game 1994 season that ended with an August players' strike, Cone finished in the league's top three in ERA and WHIP and in the top eight in innings, strikeouts and FIP. His 6.9 WAR led American League pitchers and placed second among all pitchers behind Maddux. When the baseball writers decided to go ahead and vote for postseason awards despite the incomplete season, Cone was voted the American League Cy Young Award in a pretty close vote over Jimmy Key, his rotation mate from 1992 Blue Jays who had since moved to the Yankees.

At that point—two years in Kansas City, two seven-win seasons—David Cone was sizzling. But as the start of the 1995 season was delayed into late April by the spillover from the 1994 strike, Cone, who had been a very outspoken union man during the walkout, was entering the last season of his three-year deal. The Royals, no doubt feeling a lot more small market-ish than they did before the strike successfully prevented an industry salary cap, shipped Cone and the $8 million remaining on his contract back to the Blue Jays for three minor leaguers.

But Cone's second trip north of the border didn't last long. He pitched very well for the Jays for four months in 1995, with a 3.38 ERA (140 ERA-plus) over 131 innings, with 102 strikeouts, 1.182 WHIP and a 9–6 record. But the talented club, one that was just a year removed from a second straight world championship, never got it all together. Pretty much no one on the impressive roster that included Pat Hentgen, Al Leiter, Roberto Alomar and John Olerud had one of his better years in 1995, ultimately leaving the club in the A.L. East basement. The Jays were now on the opposite end of where they had been three years earlier—they were the also-rans looking to trade Cone, the pending free agent, to a contender. In late July they struck a deal to send him to the Yankees for a package of youngsters, none of whom turned out to be consequential.

Two years and 11 months after he'd left, David Cone was back in the Big Apple. The sight of him in Yankee pinstripes was odd at first, but it wouldn't take him very long to carve out his Yankee identity. The trade surely must have energized him—Cone finished the final two months of the 1995 season with a flourish. In 13 Yankee starts he went 9–2 with a 3.82 ERA (which translated to a 122 ERA-plus in a hitting-heavy year) with 89 strikeouts in 99 innings in helping the team to the A.L. Wild Card for the Yankees' first playoff appearance since 1981. For the full season with the Blue Jays and Yankees: 18–8, 3.57 ERA, 131 ERA-plus across a league-leading 229 innings, with a 1.236 WHIP that was 16 percent better than league average and a 4.03 FIP that was 14 percent better. His 191 strikeouts ranked fourth in the league, his 7.0 WAR ranked second among pitchers behind Randy Johnson. Cone had essentially registered three seven-win seasons in a row (that would count his 6.9 in 1994, a strike-shortened season that projected to a 9.7 over the full year). It was official—David Cone was a monster. How tough is it to do a 7 WAR three years in a row? Ask Tom Seaver, Steve Carlton or Nolan Ryan, none of whom ever did it.

That winter, the Yankees signed Cone to a three-year, $19 million contract, essentially an extension of the previous three-year deal he'd inked with Kansas City. As he turned 33 heading into the 1996 season, Cone was just getting started on his second big New York run, one that would bring three more All-Star level seasons, four World Series rings and, of course, a perfect game.

He was the Yankees' clear ace as the '96 season started, and coming out of the gate, he pitched like it. Cone allowed one earned run with 20 strikeouts in his first three starts (21 innings) and then after a couple of struggles in Milwaukee and Kansas City beat the White Sox on a complete game five-hitter on May 2. No one could have guessed what would happen next. Cone was pitching great, but behind the scenes he was experiencing periodic tingling in his fingers.[2] That brought him to a doctor to be examined. The prognosis was an aneurysm—a bulge in the artery—near the front of his right shoulder. Left to fester, an aneurysm can potentially grow and become a dangerous source of bleeding. Cone opted to have surgery immediately, which thankfully turned out to be successful. He would be fine, but his 1996 season was shut down for four months.

The Yankees hung in there and led the division by four games as Cone made his return in Oakland on September 2. All he did was toss seven no-hit innings at the A's before manager Joe Torre, more concerned with Cone's workload after a four-month absence than with a no-hitter—pulled him after 85 pitches. As the Yankees went on to take the A.L. East, Cone would make four more September starts and finish his season 7–2 with a 2.88 ERA (with a whopping 175 ERA-plus; he'd have won the ERA title had he pitched enough innings to qualify), 1.167 WHIP with 71 Ks in 72 innings across 11 starts. It was an abbreviated version of his three straight seven-win seasons that preceded 1996.

Cone didn't pitch particularly well in the 1996 American League playoffs, losing a game to Texas and getting a no-decision in the Yankees' one loss to Baltimore. But then came the World Series against the Braves, which set him up to win one of the biggest games in Yankee history. After the Braves had drubbed the Yankees twice in New York (12–1 and 4–0), Cone was up in the same must-win Game 3 situation that Ron Guidry had faced 18 years earlier.

And without any acrobatic help from his third baseman (Charlie Hayes), Cone came through to pitch the Yankees back into the series. After giving up a pair of first inning singles, he retired his next nine in a row before walking Fred McGriff with two out in the fourth. But he avoided damage by freezing Ryan Klesko on an inside fastball for a strikeout to end the inning. He continued breezing through the fifth as the Yankees built a 2–0 lead. Cone allowed his first run in the sixth when he uncharacteristically walked three batters around a bloop single. Perhaps the most interesting part of the sequence was Torre's trip to the mound and his subsequent decision to stick with Cone despite the trouble he was having in that inning as the Yankees clung to a one-run lead in a game they needed to stay in the series. In the Fox booth, Tim McCarver described Cone as having "the guts of a burglar" after he threw a 3–1 splitter to Klesko with the bases loaded that Klesko fouled off.[3] That was Cone—fearless and resilient. He was once quoted saying that if a starter goes out and gives up five runs in the first inning, the goal becomes to still be pitching in the ninth having still allowed just the five runs. No throwing up your hands and figuring, hey, I guess it's not my night.

Cone got out of that sixth inning in Atlanta by getting Javy Lopez to pop out to end the inning and strand three runners. The Yankees still led by a run. Cone's outing: six innings, four hits, one run. They'd go on to win 5–2, a victory that launched their four-game comeback to take the franchise's first title since 1978. Like Guidry back then, Cone avoided a likely Game 7 start when the Yankees wrapped it up in six.

With a second World Series ring now on his finger, Cone would go on to overwhelm the American League again in 1997, essentially his fifth dominant season in a row if you include the 1996 short version. His '97 season: third in the league behind Roger Clemens and Randy Johnson in ERA (2.82), ERA-plus (159) and strikeouts (222), and fifth in WAR (6.7) across 195 innings. All this despite missing a month late in the season due to a sore shoulder for which he'd have arthroscopic surgery after the season. As it happened a slew of no-decisions left him with a 12–6 mark for the season, which didn't register well with Cy Young Award voters. Cone got zero votes—not even of the fifth-place variety.

After Cone came back to make two starts in late September, manager Joe Torre went with him to open the A.L.D.S. against Cleveland. But when the Indians jumped on him for five runs in the first inning and knocked him out in the fourth (the Yankees won the game anyway), he was done for the season. Torre would skip him in Game 5–Cleveland would beat Andy Pettitte 4–3 to advance to the next round.

Quite the bummer to end the year in shoulder pain. But it was another great season for Cone, who was right around a seven-win player for the fourth time in five years, the exception being his aneurysm-plagued 1996 when he still put up a 2.8 in about a third of a season.

He went on to add two more All-Star caliber seasons for the Yankees in 1998 (20–7, 125 ERA-plus, 4.0 WAR) and 1999 (12–9, 136 ERA-plus, 5.1 WAR and the perfect game) as the team rolled to two more World Series titles. He culminated the '99 season with a one-hitter over seven innings in Game 2 of the World Series against the Braves, the Yankees' second win a four-game sweep.

Cone seemed to generally get his share of attention during his out-standing 1995–1999 Yankee run, during which he was the team's best pitcher. But again there was that perception issue. Much like his Mets days pitching alongside Gooden, Darling, et al, Cone's time in the Bronx teamed him in a rotation with Andy Pettitte, David Wells, Orlando Her-nandez and eventually Roger Clemens. Like the '80s Mets, the '90s Yan-kees were seen almost as a staff of aces. As good as Cone was with both clubs, people didn't always see him as the main horse.

After 1999, Cone was pretty much spent. He fell off dramatically at age 37 even as he picked up one more championship ring with the 2000 Yankees. Although his last Yankee moment was a nice one. It came at Shea Stadium in Game 4 of the 2000 Subway Series against the Mets. With the Yankees leading the series two games to one and leading the fourth game 3–2 in the sixth inning, Torre summoned Cone to relieve Denny Neagle to create a righty vs. righty matchup against Mike Piazza. Cone got Piazza to pop up to end the sixth inning. His Yankee career was over. The team hung on to win and then wrapped its fourth title in five years the following night. Cone finished out his career with a decent year for the 2001 Red Sox and, after sitting out a season, an abbreviated, sentimental comeback with the 2003 Mets that lasted five games before he retired for good at age 40.

The final numbers for David Cone: 194–126, 3.46 ERA, 121 ERA-plus, 1.256 WHIP, 3.57 FIP, 8.3 strikeouts per nine innings, 61.6 WAR. Cone's 2,668 career strikeouts rank no. 25 all time. As for the tremen-dous peak: his dozen-year run from 1988 to 1999 produced a 59.8 WAR. Exactly two pitchers did better over that stretch: Roger Clemens and Greg Maddux.

"For twelve years he was an average five-win player, that's a Hall of Famer," says Brian Kenny.

Yet when Cone's first year on the ballot came up in 2009, he got 21 votes—3.9 percent. Another one and done. And consider this for a sec-ond: Don Larsen, the man watching Cone throw his 1999 perfect game from a Yankee Stadium box, was rewarded with 15 years on the Hall of Fame ballot thanks to a single game. A mostly mediocre pitcher for 14 seasons who finished with a 12.1 career WAR, 99 ERA-plus (slightly worse than average) and an 81–91 record, Larsen received as many as 53 votes one year as he hovered between 6.4 percent and 12.3 percent from

1974 to 1988. So in addition to round numbers and career milestones, a number of voters also like to reward historic moments at the expense of far superior careers. Larsen had a big day on October 8, 1956, when he retired 27 straight Brooklyn Dodgers in a World Series game. But his outing would have been just as good if one of the 20 balls put in play against him had found a hole and left him with a one-hitter. Unless he strikes out all 27 hitters, a pitcher never gets a perfect game by himself. Yet it's probably safe to assume that one hit would have left Larsen with zero Hall of Fame votes.

David Cone certainly stacks up pretty well against some Hall of Fame pitchers of his time and against many from before his time. Cone's career largely correlated with the Atlanta Braves' famed "Big Three" of Greg Maddux, Tom Glavine and John Smoltz, all of whom are in the Hall of Fame. There's no comparing Cone (or hardly anyone) to Maddux, who by most any account is one of the top five or six pitchers of all time. But it gets a lot more interesting with Smoltz and Glavine.

John Smoltz pitched for 21 years (and essentially 18 full years) and accumulated a 66.4 career WAR and 213 wins. David Cone pitched for 17 years (and essentially 14 full years) with a 61.6 career WAR and 194 wins. Cone averaged 5.4 wins above replacement in his 10 best seasons, Smoltz 4.9 in his 10 best. Cone did a 6.7 or better four times, Smoltz once, in his 1996 Cy Young season when he led the league in innings and strikeouts while going 24–8. Career ERA-plus is almost even: Smoltz 125, Cone 121. Smoltz gets the edge in WHIP and FIP, outperforming the league average by a little bit more than Cone did. Cone was the better strikeout pitcher, beating the league average of Ks per nine by a better margin than Smoltz, who did have 400 more career strikeouts in 575 more innings (and remember Cone spent the better part of his career in the A.L., where Ks are tougher to come by).

Smoltz's career took an unusual turn when elbow trouble forced him to sit out the 2000 season and then cut back on his workload beginning early in 2001. The Braves made him a closer that year at age 34, and he handled the job with aplomb for close to four seasons, racking up over 150 saves. He was particularly unhittable in 2003, putting up a 1.12 ERA and 0.87 WHIP. Smoltz made the Hall easily with more than 80 percent of the vote on his first try. You heard a lot of writers who supported his Hall of Fame case say they loved the combination of 200 wins and 150 saves (round numbers again). It's really not a great reason—not only are wins and saves poor performance metrics, but most any good starter who shifts to the bullpen for a few years and is consistently given the ball in the ninth inning for a top team is going to pile up a lot of saves. More impressive was Smoltz's ability to rebound back into a top starter in 2005 and put up three straight All-Star caliber years from the ages of 38 to 40 before finally slowing down in his final two years.

Again it comes down the honest differences people tend to have when measuring dominance vs. longevity. Both Cone and Smoltz had eight seasons of a 4.0 WAR or above, with the bulk of Cone's big seasons clearly better. Smoltz added more solid tack-on seasons—five years between a 3.0 and a 4.0 to Cone's two. If you favor the better lengthy peak, Cone had the better career. If you like a few more quality seasons, you'll take Smoltz. They certainly stand very close to each other on baseball's all-time pitching list. Again, the huge disparity in Hall of Fame votes between two pitchers with nearly identical careers is puzzling, but somehow predictable.

Ken Davidoff, who covered Cone's Yankee career, sums it up. "The thing is, what's your narrative?" Not enough wins in Cone's case? "Yes, that's his narrative. Like Bernie [Williams], he didn't have that third act."

Says Rob Neyer: "It never made the jump into my mind to look at him analytically, he didn't have the career length."

Actually Cone's career length (17 years, 14 full ones) is right up there with plenty of Hall of Fame pitchers. It's the win total—coming up just short of 200 in that column, let alone 300, doesn't send a lot of fans and Hall of Fame voters reflecting back on your career. You're left wanting that punctuation mark that doesn't seem to be there.

The ultimate third act pitcher would be Tom Glavine, who persevered in the majors for two decades and pushed through—let's have the drum roll—the 300-win plateau. Glavine (73.9 career WAR) had an outstanding career, and he'd have easily been Hall of Fame worthy even if he'd packed it in a couple of years earlier, short of the magic 300. He sailed into Cooperstown even more easily than Smoltz did, getting 92 percent in his first try in 2014.

Was Glavine any better than David Cone? A bit, perhaps, considering the career length that resulted in more than 4,400 career innings, about 1,500 more than Cone. But Cone beats Glavine slightly in most of the major categories—ERA-plus, WHIP and FIP. Cone's 5.4 average WAR in his 10 best seasons edges Glavine's 5.1. And he was a far better strikeout pitcher, fanning 8.3 per nine innings to Glavine's 5.3 (Cone even had a handful more total strikeouts despite so many fewer innings and despite all the years in the American League). With Glavine accumulating his numbers over more seasons and innings (those last few seasons dragging down the career averages a bit), you probably have to rate him ahead of Cone. But certainly not by much.

Glavine, Smoltz, Cone ... little to choose among them, yet hundreds of Hall of Fame votes separate Cone from the Atlanta aces.

How about some aces from yesteryear? And we mean big-time aces, a pair Hall of Famers who were considered to be two of the truly dominant pitchers of the 1960s, Don Drysdale and Juan Marichal. Along with Willie Mays, Willie McCovey and Sandy Koufax, these two were headliners of the intense West Coast battles of the '60s between the Dodgers and Giants. Marichal, the undisputed San Francisco ace, made it to Cooperstown in his third try with 82 percent of the vote. Drysdale, no. 2 behind Koufax in the L.A. rotation for much of his prime, had to wait 10 years for his due as voters gradually shook of their "second banana" perception of him and focused on things like the three strikeout titles, four 300-inning seasons and 49 shutouts, among other impressive numbers.

Over the years, few have questioned Drysdale's Cooperstown cred, and you'd be hard pressed to find anyone who has questioned Marichal's. And that's good, because it's true that both deserve to be there. It's also true that neither of them was any better than David Cone.

Marichal hails from an era that saw starters typically pitch more innings and pitch to more decisions compared to more modern pitchers. In his 16 seasons (13 full seasons—a career length very close to Cone's), he won 243 games and tossed 3,500 innings, compared to Cone's 194 wins and 2,900 innings. Marichal mainly had his great run from 1963 to 1969, highlighted by his monster back-to-back years of 1965 (295 innings, 169 ERA-plus, 0.915 WHIP, 10.3 WAR) and 1966 (307 innings, 167 ERA-plus, 0.860 WHIP, 9.1 WAR). Those two seasons top Cone's very best. But overall the respective careers are razor close. Marichal's 123 ERA-plus just squeezes past Cone's 121. Marichal pitched to a career WHIP 13 percent better than league average, Cone 10 percent better. In FIP it's Cone 14 percent above average, Marichal 11 percent. In strikeouts it's not even close–Marichal was not a particularly prolific strikeout pitcher, averaging 5.9 per nine innings that topped the league average by less than 2 percent. Even if you eliminate his weaker late-career strikeout numbers and look at his 1963–69 peak, Marichal's strikeout rate of 15 percent above average still doesn't touch Cone's 34 percent. As for career WAR: Marichal 61.8, Cone 61.6. In the 10 best seasons, Marichal just edges Cone 5.7 wins per year to 5.4. Marichal turned in six seasons of a 4.0 or better, Cone eight. Could it get any closer between two pitchers?

But so often it comes down to that old-school (non) performance metric—wins. Not only career totals, but how many times a pitcher hits that nice round 20-win mark during his career. Pitching during an era when 20-win seasons were more common, Marichal did it six times, including four years in a row from 1963 to 1966. Cone hit the 20-win mark just twice, a decade apart. Even though we all know that a pitcher can't control a win or a loss, for many the "20-win season" is too tempting to ignore. Recall the earlier mention of Cone's 7.2 WAR season in 1993 that resulted in an 11–14 record pitching for the lowest scoring team in the league. Contrast that with Marichal's slightly better 7.8 WAR in 1963, when he finished 25–8 pitching for the second-highest scoring team in the league. Even with all the measurement tools showing that Marichal's season was only a little bit better (he had a decided advantage in FIP and a decent advantage in WHIP, while Cone had a better ERA-plus and about the same strikeout rate), 25–8 is going to build your Cooperstown resume much more that 11–14 is, unfortunately.

The comparisons are similar with Drysdale. The intimidating righty who led the league in hit batsman five times didn't strike out hitters at the same rate that Cone did, but otherwise finished with career numbers that look like Cone's spitting image. Career WAR: Cone 61.6, Drysdale 61.3. Ten best seasons: Drysdale 5.4 per year, Cone 5.4 per year. Four-plus win seasons: Drysdale nine, Cone eight. ERA-plus: Drysdale 121, Cone 121. WHIP: Drysdale 11 percent above league average, Cone 10 percent above league average. FIP: Drysdale 15 percent better than league average, Cone 14 percent better than league average. Did anyone ever claim to see David Cone and Don Drysdale in the same room?

Oh wait, there's one more stat. Hall of Fame votes: Drysdale 316, Cone 21. If you can explain the rationale, bless you.

The biggest debate over David Cone's career ought not to be whether he deserves a plaque at Cooperstown, but rather which New York cap his bust should be sporting. Five-plus years in both Queens and the Bronx with eerily similar results. He's taken on more of a Yankee identity since his playing days, calling games from the YES Network television booth where he sometimes goes head to head against his old teammate Keith Hernandez over on SNY. David Cone established himself as a star with the Mets and got his rings with the Yankees. So take your pick. But get him a plaque.

8

Thumbs Up
or Thumbs Down?

The list of potential Hall of Famers among former Mets and Yankees goes well beyond our seven featured players. The names of many former players and manager bring plenty of debate, borderline calls, and arguments ranging from passionate to casual. Some are long since retired and well past their initial eligibility, while some are more recent and still awaiting their eligibility. Some had the bulk of their better seasons in other towns but still played prominent roles on the Yankees or Mets for a period of time, hence their inclusion. Some are better choices than others, but they all deserve a conversation. We'll call them the best of the rest.

Andy Pettitte

What a fan favorite Andy Pettitte was, and still is. A focal point of the great Yankee championship run of 1996 to 2000 who added a fifth ring in 2009 and won 256 big-league games, the quiet lefty would seem to be a solid Hall of Fame choice. But the early indications show that things aren't shaping up that way. In his first year of eligibility in 2019, a big Hall of Fame year in which the B.B.W.A.A. elected four players—Roy Halladay, Edgar Martinez, and two of Pettitte's fellow Yankee pitchers Mariano Rivera and Mike Mussina—Pettitte amassed just 9.9 percent of the vote. That's enough to remain on the ballot but it's a low total to build on going forward. By contrast, Mussina, who was elected on his sixth try, had garnered 20 percent in his first year on the ballot in 2014, a better base of support to work from that ultimately bore fruit.

If you had to name one player in MLB history who best fits the definition a "bubble" Hall of Fame candidate, Andy Pettitte is as good a choice as anyone.

Pettitte largely epitomizes the dominance vs. longevity debate that many voters struggle with. Most want to see some of both—the lengthy career with impressive totals highlighted by at least a decent number of All-Star seasons. Pettitte has the career numbers, but the year-by-year component gets murkier. There is also the dreaded PED issue—Pettitte was cited in the 2007 Mitchell Report for using Human Growth Hormone a few years earlier. He copped to using it for the brief time for which it was cited in the report, claimed it was to help rehab an injury, and apologized. He's mostly escaped public condemnation thanks to the limited scope and his direct response. But it's hard to fathom that at least some Hall of Fame voters haven't weighed it into their decisions.

His career was certainly on the right track early on. The Baton Rouge, Louisiana, native was drafted by the Yankees in the 22nd round of the 1991 draft out of Deer Park High School in suburban Houston, Texas. He rose steadily through the system and reached the big show by April 1995, shortly before his 23rd birthday. Pettitte put together a decent rookie year (12–9, 4.17 ERA, 111 ERA-plus, 2.9 WAR) as the Yankees took the A.L. Wild Card but lost to Seattle in the opening round. Then Pettitte really hit his stride over the next two years, pitching like a star just as the team was beginning its dominance over the American League. He never had overwhelming stuff, never made you say "wow." What he had was that total package—fastball, slider, change, curve, sinker. Always cool and collected on the mound, he would flash that cold stare toward the hitter and hit his spots, throwing any pitch in his repertoire for a strike. The team had enough confidence in him to deal fellow lefty starter Sterling Hitchcock to Seattle in the Tino Martinez trade in December 1995. Pettitte rose to the occasion to become the Yankees' co-ace with David Cone as the 1996 season got going, and then the clear ace after Cone went out with his aneurysm in May. He made 34 starts in 1996, going 21–8 with a 3.87 ERA (129 ERA-plus) in 221 innings. The 1.362 WHIP was 10 percent better than league average in the hitter-friendly season, while the 4.08 FIP was 17 percent better. Pettitte's 5.6 WAR led the Yankees and placed eighth among A.L. pitchers.

His 1996 postseason had its ups and downs—a mediocre start against Texas followed by another against Baltimore, but then a big effort in the Game 5 clincher over the Orioles when he allowed three hits and two runs over eight innings. Pettitte then got blasted in the first game of the 1996 World Series against the Braves, but came back four days later to win one of the biggest games in Yankee history. With the series tied at two games apiece he went out and stifled the Braves in the crucial fifth game, tossing a five-hit shutout into ninth as the Yankees squeaked out a 1–0 win on a Cecil Fielder RBI single in the fourth inning. His big effort allowed the team to return home with both a 3–2 series lead and a well-rested bullpen. They'd wrap up the title behind Jimmy Key and four relievers in the next game.

Pettitte built on his strong '96 season with an even better year in 1997. He finished in the top four in the league in innings (240), ERA (2.88), ERA-plus (156), and FIP (2.96). His 1.24 WHIP ranked 10th. He was also the stingiest pitcher in the league allowing home runs, giving up just seven in his 240 innings. Pettitte's 8.4 WAR ranked second among A.L. pitchers to his friend and future teammate Roger Clemens, who celebrated his first season in Toronto with a Cy Young Award. Pettitte didn't do well in the '97 postseason, losing to the Indians twice as the Yankees got bounced in the Wild Card round. But his dominant season the year he turned 25 held the promise of lots more to come.

And there was much more to come, only never quite at the same level. By the time Andy Pettitte hung up his cleats in 2013, he'd accumulated 256 wins and 2,448 strikeouts, both of which make the all-time top 50. His career 60.6 WAR beats 21 starting pitchers currently in the Hall. It also beats Koosman (slightly) and Guidry, and sits virtually even with Cone. What Pettitte didn't have: a lot of All-Star type seasons. As he plugged along as a consistent Yankee starter for the next six years, he was nearly always good but never great. His name only occasionally surfaced among the league leaders in the various major pitching categories—innings, ERA, FIP, strikeouts, WHIP, etc. The WAR never retreated below 2.4 from 1998 to 2003 although it never reached 4.0 either. That was Pettitte most of the time—steady, reliable, a key part of the staff, but not dominating. His 21–8 season in 2003 included top 10 finishes in strikeouts and FIP, but not in any other categories. Basically, he was a very good pitcher winning games for a top team.

When Pettitte took off for Houston in 2004, a torn flexor tendon in his left elbow short circuited his season to 15 starts and 83 innings. But following surgery, he was back strong in 2005. So strong, in fact, that he turned in best season in eight years. Pettitte started 33 games and tossed 222 innings in 2005, finishing second in the National League in

ERA (2.39) and ERA-plus (177), third in WHIP (1.03) and sixth in FIP (3.07). The 6.8 WAR, the second-best of his career, ranked third among N.L. pitchers. Pettitte teamed with Clemens and Roy Oswalt to form an outstanding front three that led the Astros to the 2005 World Series. He didn't pitch particularly well in the 2005 postseason, giving up 12 runs in 25 innings in four starts against the Braves, Cardinals and White Sox.

Speaking of the postseason, Andy Pettitte developed something of a reputation during his career as a big-game pitcher. Was he? Not really, at least not to any degree beyond what you would expect based on all that he displayed in the regular season. Pitching for teams that regularly made the playoffs for so many years during an era of expanded playoff rounds, Pettitte got to pitch in the postseason *a lot*. Call him something of a modern version of Whitey Ford, pitching in October year after year, with the expanded format allowing twice as many starts as Ford got. Pettitte started 44 postseason games in his career, pitching 276 innings. He won some big games and lost some others. His 19–11 record was certainly good, but the measurement tools that gauge effectiveness showed him to be—like Ford—virtually the same pitcher he was during the regular season. His 3.81 playoff ERA was nearly a carbon copy of the regular season, his 1.305 WHIP a bit better. Whether regular season or postseason, Pettitte was what he was—a very good pitcher who was occasionally outstanding and who occasionally took his share of knocks. But the big postseason workload, which amounted to an additional full season and then some, has to add something in his favor. People have different opinions on just how much.

"The question is how much credit do you give for postseason pitching?" says Rob Neyer. "There has never been a consensus when it comes to how much a guy should be rewarded."

Pettitte's Houston glory didn't last beyond 2006. His third and final year there was mediocre (14–13, 106 ERA-plus, 1.426 WHIP, 1.5 WAR), after which he returned to the Yankees as a free agent at age 35. He had a solid four-year run, picked up another World Series ring along the way, ostensibly retired after the 2010 season, and then came back for two more decent years in 2012 and 2013 before calling it a career for good at age 41.

So does he make it? Pettitte did average 4.4 wins above replacement in his ten best seasons, giving him that good peak to go along with his 60 career total. The difference compared to many other such pitchers is that the peak stems mostly from his three big years in 1996, 1997 and 2005.

Those were the only seasons in which you would say he was All-Star caliber, although a couple of others were close. In that regard, Pettitte rates quite close to Red Ruffing, who is in the Hall, and also to Tommy John, who isn't. His 10-year peak comes up short of several of his contemporaries or near-contemporaries who didn't get many Cooperstown votes—Brett Saberhagen, Chuck Finley, Kevin Appier, Johan Santana, Kevin Brown, Roy Oswalt—but at the same time his dropoff beyond the peak was generally less pronounced, giving his career a bit more heft than the others (the exception being Brown, briefly a Yankee himself who was one of the nastiest pitchers in the game during the 1990s and early 2000s with a 68 career WAR, 58 peak war in his 10 best years and 127 ERA-plus over 18 years and more than 3,200 innings. That Brown went one and done with 2.1 percent of the Hall of Fame vote in 2011 is almost criminal).

As far as the PED cloud goes, the consensus seems to be that Pettitte got little help from any extra, illegal juice, if you take him at his word that the HGH phase was brief and used mainly to help rehab an injury. No one seems to believe it made the kind of difference in his stats that it did for Barry Bonds or Mark McGwire, who came to resemble Thanksgiving parade balloon characters as they bashed freakish numbers of home runs. Still, the stigma probably does hurt him, because as a borderline Hall of Famer to begin with even a little bit of extra unsavory help can be perceived as a difference maker.

The verdict: No, not quite. A terrific career, but only a few seasons where he ranked among the league's top handful of pitchers.

David Wright

Quite simply, David Wright is the best everyday player in Mets history. He gets it by a nose over Darryl Strawberry, who might have gotten the honors had he stayed a bit longer instead of bolting home to Los Angeles after his eighth season. Wright also beats out the likes of Mike Piazza, Keith Hernandez and Carlos Beltran, all of whom had several of their big years elsewhere before going to the Mets.

Wright fell to the Mets as a compensatory draft pick in 2001 right after they lost pitcher Mike Hampton as a free agent. Many Mets fans probably remember being upset when Hampton, who was instrumental in helping the team to the 2000 World Series, ended his New

York career after that one season by inking a huge deal with Colorado. But you never know how things will work out. As Hampton proceeded to flop in the Denver altitude, Wright, basically an anonymous high school third baseman from Virginia, made his way up the Mets' chain. By age 21 in in 2004, he hit .341 with 18 homers in just over half a season in the minors before the Mets called him up in late July. He pretty much never looked back, taking over as the third baseman and as the leading man on a Mets team that began to regain its mojo after a few years in the wilderness during the early 2000s.

After hitting .293 with 14 homers in 69 games in 2004, Wright turned in All-Star-type seasons over the next two years by hitting over .300 with close to .400 OBPs and 25-plus homers in 2005 and 2006. The 2006 club, armed with the likes of Jose Reyes, Carlos Beltran and Carlos Delgado along with Wright, ran away with the N.L. East and just missed the World Series when they dropped the N.L.C.S. to the Cardinals in seven games.

Wright followed with two more years that were even better, hitting .325 with a .416 OBP, 149 OPS-plus, 30 homers and an 8.3 WAR in 2007, and then a .302 average, .390 OBP, 142 OPS-plus, 33 homers and a 6.9 WAR in 2008. David Wright had opened his career with four All-Star caliber years in his first four full seasons, two of which placed him in the league's top five in WAR. He was 25. The sky was the limit, or so it seemed.

But it would be a few years before Wright would have another truly big season. He hit well in 2009 (.307 with a .390 OBP) but fell to 10 homers and slumped a bit over the final weeks after a concussion. He rebounded to 29 homers in 2010 but the average fell a bit to .283 and a .354 OBP that was good but also the lowest of his career. Then nagging injuries limited him to 102 games and 14 homers in 2011, with a .254 average. All the while, the advanced numbers said his defense at third declined during those three years from the solid levels that came before.

Wright rebounded again with two big years in 2012 and 2013, hitting over .300 and finishing in the N.L.'s top 10 in WAR in both seasons. But that was pretty much it. After a decent age 31 season in 2014 Wright was caught up in the injury bug—most seriously the unfortunate case of spinal stenosis that affected his back—that limited the rest of his career to 75 games. He will be eligible for the Hall of Fame ballot in 2024.

He finished with 14 seasons, having played 100 or more games in 10 of them. He hit .296 with a .376 OBP and a 133 OPS-plus (140 or better five times). After hitting 130 home runs by age 25, he finished his career with 242. His 50.4 career WAR breaks down this way: 47.9 in his 10 best seasons and very little otherwise. Fangraphs says his defense was a little bit below average for his position during his career, with a few above-average seasons mixed in.

As far as a Hall of Fame case, the best thing Wright has going for him is that impressive 133 OPS-plus, spearheaded by his ability to consistently get on base and supplemented by some good power seasons. Among premium third basemen, that mark edges Wade Boggs (131), Ron Santo (125), Paul Molitor (122) and Scott Rolen (122). It's also very close to George Brett (135) and pretty close to Chipper Jones (141) and Eddie Matthews (143). But of course all of those guys put up their numbers over more seasons and games than Wright did. The only non–Hall of Famer of the group, Rolen, just became eligible in the past couple of years and owns far better defensive metrics than Wright (hence his 70 WAR over 17 years, which ought to get him in eventually).

In a historical context, Wright's career production at third base puts him more on par with Ron Cey and Matt Williams than with the likes of Brett, Boggs and Jones. That's not bad company at all—those are a couple of historically underrated players with decent Cooperstown cases who should have gotten more than the paltry support they did. But they're not in the slam dunk territory of the others.

Wright's career on-base percentage and OPS-plus also beat out his contemporary Adrian Beltre, who retired after the 2018 season with a 96 career WAR that figures to make him an easy Hall of Fame call. Wright's handful of best seasons hang pretty well with Beltre's, but again there's the matter of longevity and defense. Playing for two decades, Beltre flashed an all-time glove at the hot corner—Fangraphs gives him 196 runs above average at his position while baseball-reference rates his defensive WAR at 29.3—both higher than Graig Nettles. Beltre had so many good years that even after you get past his elite 6.6 wins per year in his 10 best seasons you discover that he averaged a solid three wins per year in his *next* 10. Yes—you can remove his 10 best seasons and discover that Beltre still had a career that was pretty solid for most players.

David Wright wasn't Adrian Beltre, but he was good enough to be in the Hall of Fame conversation. As usual, the debate comes down to dominance and longevity. Andy Pettitte had the career heft but not a lot of Hall of Fame seasons. Wright is basically the opposite—more Hall of Fame seasons (six, by most counts) but without the heft. There's no set rule for breaking down the two things. How many solid years do you need to add to adequately offset a modest number of great ones? And the same in reverse—how many All-Star-type years are needed to make up for a relatively brief career? The answer is always subjective. Wright is actually similar to Ron Guidry is this regard—six seasons you would call All-Star level without a ton of tacking on. Guidry, though, really had a seventh All-Star year if you prorate the 1981 strike season, and he tacked on a bit more than Wright in those better seasons just beyond the respective peaks. The subjective opinion here is that while Guidry just did enough to make it through, Wright just missed.

The verdict: No. Wright's number 5 probably belongs on the Citi Field wall, but he needed another big season or two to reach Cooperstown.

Jorge Posada

Who would have guessed two decades ago that a 24th round draft pick from a community college would wind up in a serious Hall of Fame conversation? Jorge Posada belongs there, though, despite voters turning him down unequivocally in 2017 by giving the former Yankee catcher just 3.8 percent in his first year on the ballot. Now he's gone, with no shot unless a future committee decides to put him on one of those special ballots sometime in the future.

And let's hope they do, because Posada shouldn't have been dismissed so quickly. On the face of it, you can understand how he fits the good-but-not-great description: .273 career hitter, 275 homers, a career WAR just over 40, and a reputation as less than a stellar defensive catcher. There's also the usual perception issue: no one particularly saw him as a main man on championship teams. And usually he wasn't. Posada was a younger player during the Yankee title run of the late 1990s, making only a token appearance on the 1996 championship team and contributing fairly marginally on the 1998 and '99 teams as he shared catching duties with veteran Joe Girardi. But he then stepped up as a major force on the final championship team of that run with 28 homers, a .417 OBP and team-leading 5.5 WAR in 2000.

That season kicked off a run of six All-Star caliber seasons over eight years, a fairly rare achievement for a catcher. Posada had most of his big years between the 2000 and 2009 Yankee championships, when he was part of those powerful lineups with A-Rod, Hideki Matsui, Gary

Sheffield and Jason Giambi, along with Jeter. These were the Yankee teams that were very good but not winning championships, which may or may not have played a part in people associating Posada with the "good stats-no rings" era after his stint as mostly a supporting player on the teams that did win rings. You hope that isn't the case, since it obviously wasn't Posada's fault that the Yankee pitching declined by the mid–2000s as the team tried to replace Roger Clemens, Andy Pettitte and David Cone with 40-year-old versions of Randy Johnson and Kevin Brown and disappointing flops like Javier Vasquez and Carl Pavano. That's why the team dipped from great to very good.

Jorge Posada was clearly one of the game's elite catchers during his 15-year career. Despite a so-so .273 batting average, his ability to draw walks lifted his career OBP to .374, with four seasons over .400. He topped 20 home runs eight times, hitting 30 once. He outperformed Ivan Rodriguez in WAR in six of eight years from 2000 to 2007 (I-Rod had a few of his bigger years before Posada hit his stride but was still largely considered the standard bearer at catcher during the early-to-mid–2000s).

The big thing to remember when adding up Posada's production is this: he was a catcher. The grading scale is different than it is for the outfield or the infield. A switch-hitting catcher who gets on base and adds good power is a rare commodity. Measuring Posada against the entire Hall of Fame population, his numbers come up short. Measuring him purely against catchers, he looks much better. A 42.7 WAR doesn't normally scream Hall of Fame, but only 16 catchers in history did better. The physical demands of the position ensure that the career production of a top catcher isn't going to match that of a top infielder or outfielder. Look at any other position on the field, and see that the career WAR leader surpasses 100 at every spot, including 11 outfielders and eight pitchers. The top catcher, Johnny Bench, whose knees were never going to last as long as Mike Schmidt's or Willie Mays's, checks in at 75. For those behind the plate, you're grading on a curve.

Posada's 121 OPS-plus beats Carlton Fisk, Ivan Rodriguez and Gary Carter. It just misses Bench, Yogi Berra and Bill Dickey. It does come in a good ways behind Mike Piazza (142), certainly the best hitting catcher ever. The defensive metrics say Posada was indeed mediocre for most of his career, negative in runs saved with a career 2.6 dWAR (with little "range" factor, catcher is a tough position to evaluate. Fangraphs primarily measures a catcher's ability to block pitches in the dirt, prevent stolen bases, and execute general fielding plays such has applying tags on runners and throwing out hitters on bunts or slow rollers; pitch framing estimates were added in 2008, near the end of Posada's career).

Posada's defensive numbers come up short of Fisk, Berra and Dickey and don't even touch Bench, Carter or I-Rod. That would explain those guys' significantly higher career WARs. But remember, these are the top handful of catchers of all time—there's room for more at Cooperstown. Posada finished with six four-plus win seasons, the same number as Fisk, just one fewer than Berra and two fewer than Rodriguez, Carter and Piazza (Bench, the master, had 12). And it's more than Hall of Famers Gabby Hartnett and Ernie Lombardi.

A search for the closest comparison to Posada brings us to new Hall of Famer Ted Simmons, a similar offensive-oriented catcher who came up a generation earlier and had most of his big seasons with the Cardinals in the 1970s. Simmons was very much historically underrated for a long time, overshadowed during his career by Bench in the National League and also by the high profile Carlton Fisk-Thurman Munson rivalry in the American League. In a two-decade career, he hit .285 with a .348 OBP and 248 homers in a pitcher's park during a dead ball era, with a 118 OPS-plus. He hit .300 or better six times and put up an OPS-plus of 135 or better five times (Simmons hung around for several seasons beyond his prime as a part-time catcher and pinch hitter, pulling his career averages down a bit). Simmons' defensive metrics are a bit better than Posada's, slightly negative in runs above average and slightly positive in dWar. His 50 career WAR is 11th among catchers and includes seven seasons of a 4.0 or better.

Ted Simmons's one and only appearance on the B.B.W.A.A. Hall of Fame ballot in 1994 was virtually identical to Posada's in 2017—a whopping 3.7 percent. He seemed to be a mostly forgotten man until he finally got his due when the Modern Baseball Era committee suddenly ticketed him to Cooperstown in 2019. The careers of Simmons and Posada were very close, with Simmons holding an edge thanks to slightly better defense and for hitting almost as many home runs as Posada during a time when it was much harder to hit them. He outpoints Posada in WAR pretty modestly, about eight points higher over four more seasons and by an average of 4.5 to 4.0 in each catcher's 10 best seasons. Simmons was most definitely due for a spot Hall of Fame, and Posada is right behind him.

The verdict: Yes, especially with Simmons getting the nod. When you're one of the 20 best players of all time at the most physically demanding position on the field, you belong in Cooperstown.

Thurman Munson

After breaking down Jorge Posada's Hall of Fame case, it only makes sense to jump right to Munson, the other Yankee catcher whose career put him right on the cusp but who failed to get the nod from voters. Munson never really came close despite eking out enough votes to stay on the ballot for the full 15 years—he peaked at 15.5 percent in his first year of eligibility in 1981 and never reached 10 percent after that.

At the time of Munson's sad and untimely death in a plane crash on August 2, 1979, he had established himself as one of the top four catchers of his time along with Bench, Simmons and Fisk and, more importantly, as one of top 10 or so catchers of all time. Only a few have surpassed him over the past four decades—Carter, Rodriguez and Piazza, perhaps Joe Mauer, with Posada coming close (we'll see where Buster Posey ends up).

Thurman Munson was a highly touted prospect from the start, drafted fourth overall by the Yankees out of Kent State University in 1968, a bonanza draft year that also included Cecil Cooper, Steve Garvey, Ron Cey and Greg Luzinski. Munson made it up to the Yankees by August 8, 1969, squeezed right between the moon landing and Woodstock. His big-league debut came in the second game of a doubleheader at Yankee Stadium against the A's, when he caught a complete game shutout by Al Downing and went 2-for-3 with a walk in a 5–0 Yankees victory. He became the Yankees regular catcher the following year and took A.L. Rookie of the Year honors by hitting .302 with a .386 OBP. His 126 OPS-plus led American League catchers, and his 5.5 WAR just missed the league's top 10.

Munson caught 125 games during that big rookie year. He would drop slightly to 117 in 1971 but then launch a seven-year run of at least 121 games behind the plate, usually quite a few more. He was the workhorse, the guy with the most dirt on his uniform at the end of the game, night in and night out. His pitchers loved him and almost never shook him off.

And of course he could hit. During the dead ball 1970s, Munson was hitting .280 to .300 almost every year while the league was hitting

.250 or so. His .346 career OBP was almost 10 percent better than league average, unusual for a catcher. He'd put up six All-Star level seasons from 1970 to 1977, just missing in the other two years. The WAR would eclipse 5.0 four times, and just about five times if you sneak in his 4.9 in 1977.

By his fourth year in 1973, Munson led the team during its final season at the original (pre-renovated) Yankee Stadium by starting 147 games behind the plate, batting .301 with a .362 on-base percentage, 20 homers and a 142 OPS-plus. His 7.2 WAR was third in the league. Munson gunned down 48.5 percent of attempted base stealers that year, third-best behind Oakland's Ray Fosse and Milwaukee's Ellie Rodriguez. He never had a cannon for an arm, but he made up for it with a super-quick release and with good instincts for knowing when a runner was likely to take off. His 2.1 defensive WAR in 1973 put him in the league's top 10. For his career behind the plate, Fangraphs rates Munson 34 runs above average at his position, while baseball-reference.com gives him a 12.9 dWAR, both very solid. Munson would catch 130 games and hit .318 with 102 RBI in 1975 and then capture the American League MVP Award with a .302 average and 105 RBI in 1976, when the Yankees reached the postseason for the first time in 12 years. We've already argued that Graig Nettles should have been the MVP that year, but Munson certainly had a big season, one that he capped by batting .435 in the A.L.C.S. victory over the Royals and then .529 (9-for-17) in a World Series loss to the Reds.

You probably know that Munson was very much known for his personal rivalry with Boston's Carlton Fisk. It was a natural: Yankees-Red Sox, two star catchers, two leading men. And it was razor close. Munson already had a couple of All-Star years in his pocket when Fisk burst onto the scene with his big rookie year in 1972. During the seven years in which their primes crossed over (1972–78), Munson outpointed Fisk in WAR in four of them, with the cumulative total just tilting to Fisk 34.5 to 33.8. They were about as evenly matched as could be, with Munson the tougher out, Fisk hitting for more power, and defense almost dead even.

Of course Fisk went on to a very long career in Boston and Chicago, ultimately piling up a 68 WAR while popping 351 of his 376 career homers as a catcher, the second-most at the position in MLB history. He made it into Cooperstown on his second try in 2000. But again, how much of the Hall of Fame is about longevity compared to peak?

It's understandable why many voters couldn't pull the trigger on

Munson. Those things you like to see—the lengthy career, those solid tack-on seasons beyond the peak—just weren't there. But the thing is, those types of tack-on seasons are rare for a catcher anyway. Fisk was an exception—the bumps and bruises a player accumulates from more than 1,000 games behind the plate make it much more difficult to keep producing All-Star or near-All-Star play into the mid–30s the way an infielder or an outfielder might. Again—grading on the curve here.

Let's do a quick comparison of Munson's career to a pair of Hall of Famers who preceded him as Yankee catching greats, Bill Dickey and Yogi Berra. When Munson's plane sadly went down in Akron, Ohio, in 1979, he owned a 46.1 career WAR in just over 10 seasons, giving him 4.6 per year during his 10-year peak, which in Munson's case was just about his full career. He was 32 years old.

Bill Dickey's career WAR at age 32 was 47.2, a tiny smidge higher than Munson. He went on to play five more years, only one of which was All-Star level, to finish with a 58.4 career WAR. When considering a player for the Hall of Fame, should sticking around for a few more seasons as an average player be the difference between a thumbs-up or thumbs-down? The comparison is almost identical with Yogi: a 47.4 WAR by age 32, barely ahead of Munson, followed by six years of mostly average production (one borderline All-Star year) to push the final WAR to 59.8. Basically, aside from sticking around for a few average seasons beyond age 32, Dickey and Berra were no better than Munson.

The verdict: Yes. Munson was a hair better than Posada and a short hair behind Ted Simmons. All three are among the top 20 catchers of all time and should be in.

Darryl Strawberry

Instinctively, you say no. Inspect the numbers, and it's closer than you think.

Many Mets fans remember Darryl Strawberry as an enigma during the 1980s—exciting, often awesome, sometimes infuriating. Drafted as the first overall pick out of high school in 1980 when the club was right in the middle of its late '70s–early '80s funk, the six-foot-six, power-hitting Strawberry was hailed as the savior. Talk about pressure.

He made it up to the Mets in May of 1983 and, after a slow start, wound up with 26 homers with a .257 average and .336 on-base percentage to take the National League Rookie of the Year Award. It helped that the Mets were on the verge of turning the corner just as Strawberry arrived—Keith Hernandez would join the team a month later, with Dwight Gooden set to debut the following year. The team's growing talent base took some pressure off Strawberry to carry things. But the expectations were still sky-high, and as well as he played, he rarely seemed to meet them in many people's eyes.

Strawberry had his first All-Star caliber year in 1985 (29 homers, 164 OPS-plus, 4.7 WAR). After dropping a bit in the Mets' championship season of 1986, he went on a four-year run from 1987 to 1990 with the OPS-plus never dropping below 125 or the WAR below 4.8. Strawberry had a 30–30 season (homers and steals) in 1987 and then led the league in homers, slugging and OPS-plus in 1988, while just missing his second straight 30–30 year by swatting 39 home runs with 29 steals.

Yet there always seemed to be the distractions that people liked to focus on. Strawberry was moody. It seemed to bother some fans that he wasn't always superman, and it bothered him that it bothered them— that wasn't fair. He didn't seem to always get along with manager Davey Johnson. He once had a little scuffle with Hernandez in spring training. Basically, things that were minor but had a tendency to get blown out of proportion on the soap opera, 1980s Mets. Later would come the tales of hard partying, the booze and the drugs, which didn't help his image and which became a disproportionate piece of his narrative.

Even Strawberry's performance on the field wasn't as appreciated as much as it might have been later in the sabermetrics age. Strawberry had power and speed, but he struck out a good amount, he didn't hit for a great average, and his defense often seemed shaky. Few people appreciated his ability to draw walks, which pushed his on-base percentage way above his batting average. And the defensive metrics show his play in right field to be about neutral, as his speed and athleticism helped to counter his so-so instincts. If stats like OPS and WAR had been around when Strawberry was playing, maybe more fans would have seen his relative weaknesses from a different perspective. Perhaps Steve Somers, a likeable WFAN radio host who is still going strong today, wouldn't have bellowed "good riddance" to Strawberry upon his defection to the Dodgers following his big 1990 season (37 homers, 140 OPS-plus, 6.3 WAR). Somers liked to harp back then on things like Strawberry missing the cutoff man too often on throws from the outfield, as if that practically negated finishing in the league's top 10 in homers, slugging, OPS-plus, RBI, and WAR.

When it was all said and done, Strawberry played 17 seasons in the major leagues with the Mets, Dodgers, Giants and Yankees (all four of the clubs that originated in New York). Injuries took their toll after his first season in L.A. in 1991, leaving him with just one more 100-plus game season for the rest of his career. The final batting average was .259 but the on-base percentage was .357. His 138 OPS-plus beat Jim Rice and Dave Winfield and fell exactly one point shy of Reggie Jackson. The career home run total of 335 doesn't score Hall of Fame notice, but it's impressive coming mostly in the dead ball era (baseball's offensive surge that began in the mid–90s coincided with the tail end of Strawberry's career, when he was helping the Yankees win championships as a part-time player). Defensively, Fangraphs says he was seven runs below average for his career, or a fraction of a run per season—very close to neutral. He finished with 42.2 career WAR, averaging 4.2 in his 10 best seasons and essentially adding nothing more.

He certainly compares well to some outfielders who outpolled him by good margins in the Hall of Fame voting. The writers dismissed Strawberry very quickly—1.2 percent of the vote in his one year on the ballot in 2005. They weren't as quick to dismiss Dave Parker, a fellow right fielder who came up a decade before Strawberry and had a great run for a while in the late '70s before his star began to fade. Parker didn't come very close to being elected to the Hall, maxing out at 24.5 percent of the vote, but he did well enough to stay on the ballot for the full 15 years. Yet it's tough to say that he was as good as Strawberry, who beat him handily in OPS-plus 138 to 121 (Parker had the better batting average but Strawberry the better OBP) and edged him in WAR by a couple of points. Parker had a reputation as a big-time defensive player, thanks to a strong arm. But Fangraphs and baseball-reference.com very much shoot down that view by giving him mediocre defensive metrics that trail Strawberry's. It's easy to notice a cannon arm, it's not so easy to pick up on a lack of outfield range.

Another outfielder and Strawberry peer who didn't make it to Cooperstown but who got a lot more votes than Strawberry did was Dale Murphy. A big star for a while with the Braves during the early-to-mid–1980s, Murphy is best known for winning back-to-back National League MVP awards in 1982 and 1983. Like Parker, Murphy got enough support to remain on the Hall of fame ballot for all 15 years without actually coming close to getting in (23 percent was his top haul). Murphy's statistical career does beat Strawberry's, but only by a bit. Playing 600 more games, Murphy outhomered Strawberry 398 to 335 and just outpointed him in WAR 46.5 to 42.2. In the 10 best seasons, Murphy averaged 4.8 wins, Strawberry 4.2. Strawberry wins OPS-plus pretty easily 138 to 121 and edges Murphy in on-base percentage .357 to .346. Defensively, Murphy who came up as a catcher, played most of his career in center field where the metrics say he was well below average. The writers awarded him five straight Gold Gloves in center from 1982 to 1986, which Fangraphs now basically says was bogus hardware. Murphy did much better in right field—Strawberry's position—scoring slightly above average to beat Strawberry by just a bit.

In 2017, the Modern Baseball Committee saw fit to include both Dave Parker and Dale Murphy on its special ballot. Neither was elected by the 12-man committee, but it's curious that both were nominated while Darryl Strawberry—probably better than Parker and right there with Murphy—wasn't.

The verdict: No. He was right on track until the injuries and minimal production beyond age 29 short-circuited the Cooperstown path. But Strawberry deserves a shout out for holding up well against players who got many more Hall of Fame votes. An underrated career.

Dwight Gooden

Dwight Gooden's narrative follows Darryl Strawberry's almost to a tee. He's the other young stud who came up to the Mets in the mid–1980s, lifted the club and excited the fans by flirting with greatness for a while, but flamed out too quickly by allowing the lure of drugs and drink to swallow up his career.

Again, that's the narrative. But while there's a certain amount of truth to all that, it isn't nearly so simple. There was the injured shoulder that first appeared in 1988 that sapped some of the power from Gooden's fastball. Then the unofficial lowering and widening of the strike zone by the late 1980s and into the '90s that had hitters laying off the Gooden fastball just above the belt knowing it would be called a ball. Ultimately, Dwight Gooden didn't flame out as much as he simply failed to duplicate his early greatness as the years went along. But like his fellow prodigy Darryl Strawberry, his Hall of Fame case is more solid the narrative dictates.

After the Mets drafted Gooden out of Hillsborough High School in Florida with the fifth overall pick in 1982, he toyed with minor league hitters for two seasons—300 strikeouts in 191 innings at Class-A Lynchburg in 1983—before making his much-ballyhooed Mets debut at age 19 in 1984. To say he took the city by storm would be an understatement. His first game came at Houston—five innings, three hits and one run in a 3–2 win. The first double digit strikeout game came on May 1 when he fanned 10 Cubs in an 8–1 victory. Gooden was basically a two-pitch pitcher—fastball and curve—but both were devastating (the baseball lingo that historically referred to a curveball as an "Uncle Charlie" was upgraded to "Lord Charles" for Gooden). Particularly impressive was his ability to put the ball where he wanted to at such a young age—he wasn't just throwing. As the Mets shot back to contention in 1984 following their seven years in the wilderness, the buzz surrounding a Gooden start grew with each passing week. He was Dr. K, the biggest act in town. Shea Stadium was alive again, never more so than when Gooden was pitching. He did take his share of lumps early in 1984, mixing in a few clunkers along with the brilliance—pretty much what you'd expect from a 19-year-old who was both super talented and raw. But once Gooden put it all together—forget it.

He closed the '84 season with an 8–1 record and 1.07 ERA over his final nine starts—the one loss coming in a 2–1 game at Philadelphia in which he struck out 16 in eight innings—with 105 Ks in 76 innings. He finished the season 17–9 with 2.68 ERA and 137 ERA-plus while leading the league in strikeouts (276 in 218 innings), WHIP (1.073) and FIP (1.69). Gooden's 5.5 WAR led National League pitchers, though he finished second in the Cy Young Award voting to Rick Sutcliffe, who was acquired by the Cubs in a June trade with Cleveland and went 16–1, 2.69 the rest of the way to help push the Cubs past the Mets to the N.L. East title. The overall numbers say that Gooden should have won, but voters were not going to let 17–9 beat 16–1 in 1984 (that Sutcliffe was mostly knocked around in Cleveland during the first half wasn't a factor in the N.L. voting).

The flourish with which Dwight Gooden ended 1984 resumed without a hiccup in 1985. You probably know all about the signature Cy Young year, when a Gooden start meant you could pretty much put a win in the books. The mind-boggling numbers one more time: 24–4,

1.53 ERA, 229 ERA-plus, 2.13 FIP, 0.965 WHIP, 268 strikeouts in 276 innings, eight shutouts. The 12.2 WAR was the highest by a pitcher in a season since Walter Johnson's 15.1 in 1913. And no one has topped him since—not even the best single seasons turned in by Roger Clemens, Greg Maddux, Pedro Martinez or Randy Johnson quite top Gooden '85.

Across the final six weeks of 1984 and all of 1985, Dwight Gooden started 44 games and went 32–5 with a 1.43 ERA. He pitched 353 innings and struck out 373 hitters—and this during a contact hitting era when a typical pitcher whiffed only 5.5 per nine innings. Only nine times in the 44 starts did he give up more than two earned runs, and only twice did he give up more than three. For a season-plus, there was probably never a better pitcher.

Gooden turned in another All-Star caliber year in 1986 (17–6, 2.84, 1.108 WHIP, 200 Ks, 4.4 WAR), when the Mets dominated the National League and went on to a title, and pretty much another one in 1987 when he came back from a two-month suspension to post a 3.7 WAR in 25 starts with a 15–7 record, 3.21 ERA, 1.197 WHIP and 148 strikeouts in 179 innings. The All-Star-type seasons essentially stopped after that— good but not great in 1988, an injury that cost him half of 1989, and a subpar 1990 (despite a 19–7 record) in which he put up a 1.295 WHIP and a 3.83 ERA (98 ERA-plus, below average). Beyond that, he had two more solid years with the Mets in 1991 and 1993, but nothing resembling the old Dr. K. Then came the 1995 suspension for violating baseball's drug policy, a so-so two-year stint with the Yankees that included a no-hitter, a decent year in Cleveland in 1998, and, aside from a memorable interleague win over the Mets at Shea during a brief return to the Yankees, a couple of forgettable years before his career ended in 2000.

The won-lost record that stood at 91–35 after his first five seasons wound up at 194–112, with a 3.51 ERA (111 ERA-plus), 1.256 WHIP (a bit better than average), and 2,293 strikeouts that rank no. 58 all-time. The career WAR of 48.1 beats 10 starting pitchers currently in the Hall including the previously mentioned Lefty Gomez and Dizzy Dean and the recently inducted Jack Morris. Gooden did average the four-plus wins over his 10 best seasons (4.4 per year).

Gooden's 48. 1 WAR also edges Ron Guidry by an eyelash. What works against Gooden compared to Guidry and some others is that only four of his individual seasons could be called All-Star level. A full 12.2 of that 48.1 came in the one amazing year. Following his first four years, he averaged fewer than two wins above replacement over the next

12 seasons. In the end, Gooden's career most closely resembles those of David Wells and Vida Blue—terrific pitchers but not Hall of Famers.

The verdict: No. Gooden needed a couple of additional All-Star seasons. But like Strawberry, he's rarely credited with being the solid near-miss that he is. Gooden's career wasn't one big flameout, it was an excellent career that just comes up a little ways short of Cooperstown.

Don Mattingly

For a period of time in the mid–1980s, watching Don Mattingly hit was appointment television. If you had the Yankee game on but were paying sporadic attention while reading or chatting on the phone, you stopped what you were doing and glued your eyes to the screen when Mattingly came up. It was that stance, that lefty swing, so picture perfect.

Baseball has a way of handing you those occasional individual pleasures that go beyond the scope of the game—Ozzie Smith making a tough hop look easy and then gunning a runner out at first, David Cone buckling a hitter's knees on a ridiculous curve, and for a few prime years, watching Don Mattingly hit.

The Indiana native was very much an early sleeper, drafted by the Yankees in the 19th round out of high school in 1979. But after killing it the minors for three years, he got his first taste of the big leagues in September of 1982 and then a 91-game stint in 1983 in which he had modest success with a .283 batting average and 107 OPS-plus. The Yankees had been in a state of flux at first base since trading Chris Chambliss after the 1979 season, blowing through veterans Bob Watson, John Mayberry and Jim Spencer during the early '80s. They were also taking a good look at young Steve Balboni, a big guy with pop in his bat but who struck out a lot and struggled to keep his average above .200.

Few people, if any, predicted what would come next. Following Mattingly's decent 1983 showing, the Yankees traded Balboni to Kansas City. But manager Yogi Berra still opened the 1984 season with veteran Ken Griffey, a converted outfielder, at first base. Mattingly worked in off the bench as an outfielder-first baseman until, with his average at .348 in his first 46 at-bats, Berra started him at first against the Twins on April 25. He went 2-for-4, raising the average to .360. He remained planted on first base the rest of the way as Griffey returned to the outfield. By the time the '84 season ended, all Mattingly had done was win the

American League batting title with a .343 average, pop 23 homers, and lead the league with 207 hits and 44 doubles. His 156 OPS-plus was a close second to Eddie Murray in the American League, and his 6.3 WAR tied with Wade Boggs for fifth-highest in the league among position players. Out of almost nowhere, the Yankees had their next superstar.

Don Mattingly then spent most of the next five years creaming the baseball. He shot from batting champ in 1984 to A.L. MVP in 1985 when he hit .324 with 35 home runs, 145 RBI and another 156 OPS-plus that was third in the league behind George Brett and Yankee teammate Rickey Henderson. He had to settle for MVP runner up in 1986 (to Roger Clemens) even though his year was even better than the previous one: .352 average, .394 OBP, 31 homers and leading the A.L. in hits, doubles, OPS and OPS-plus while playing all 162 games. Mattingly's 1984 to 1986 offensive run was truly something special: over the three years he averaged .340, 30 homers, 123 RBI and a 158 OPS-plus while collecting more than 200 hits in each season. And he was still just 25.

The next three seasons were very good, too, though off a bit from the three-year zenith. In July of 1987, Mattingly homered in eight straight games to tie a 31-year-old record held by the Pirates' Dale Long (the record has since been matched by Ken Griffey, Jr., the son of the guy who Mattingly inherited first base from). He put up a 5.1 WAR in 1987 on 30 homers and a 146 OPS-plus, fell back a bit with 18 homers 128 OPS-plus and 3.7 WAR in 1988, and then 23 homers, 133 OPS-plus and 4.1 WAR in 1989. As the 1980s ended, Mattingly could look back on hitting over .300 for six straight years between 1984 and 1989, driving in more than 100 runs and topping a 4.0 WAR in five of them, with the OPS-plus never falling below 128. But the back problems that had begun popping up as early as 1987[1] were taking more and more of a toll. He still wasn't quite 30 years old, but as the 1990s arrived, Mattingly's days as a star were over.

He'd solider on for six more years, hitting for decent averages but no longer with much power. Mattingly would hit just 58 homers over those last six years to finish his career with a relatively paltry 222. The .358 career on-base percentage was solid but only about 8 percent above league average during his career—really not high enough to counter the low home run total. As for defense, Mattingly had a sparkling reputation as a first baseman, enough to earn nine Gold Gloves. The Fangraphs numbers pretty much shoot that eye test down, declaring Mattingly 33 runs above average for his 14-year career—perfectly solid, but not nearly nine-time Gold Glove territory. It's a pretty good bet that the name recognition Mattingly earned with his bat helped a lot when it came to Gold Glove votes.

Mattingly never came very close to getting elected to Cooperstown, peaking at 28 percent of the vote, but he got enough support to do the full 15-year run on the ballot. His career 42.2 WAR is low as far Hall of Fame territory goes. During his great run he put up a 4.0 or better five times (reaching as high as 7.2 once), but in only one other season did he even reach a 3.0. Emotionally, a lot of fans want to see him in the Hall of Fame, so fond are their memories of watching him shine during that mid–'80s peak. Statistically, he rates behind several first basemen who have received scant Hall of Fame support, including Fred McGriff, Will Clark, and Todd Helton. The first baseman who probably compares most closely to Mattingly is Carlos Delgado, who had better career offensive numbers but a slightly lesser peak, weaker defense and a comparable 44.4 WAR. Delgado went one and done on the Hall of Fame ballot, receiving 3.8 percent in 2015. That Mattingly was able to get many more Hall of Fame votes than Delgado, Clark and Helton speaks to his popularity, but it doesn't mesh with the numbers.

The verdict: No. The back problems were unfortunate, but Mattingly just didn't do enough beyond the few big years.

John Olerud

Speaking of first baseman who were better than Don Mattingly, there's another one who fits the bill—John Olerud. Yes, really, despite the reverence for Mattingly, and despite the way Olerud seemed to quietly glide through a 16-year career, the numbers don't lie. We're talking about one of the premium defensive first basemen in MLB history who also got on base at just about a .400 clip for his career. Even with so-so power numbers, this is a premium player.

That Olerud is included in this group of New York players is a bit of a stretch, given that he played just about 13 of his 17 big-league seasons in Toronto and Seattle. But the lefty first baseman did turn in some of his best seasons as a prominent three-year Met during the team's rise from mediocrity to contention during the late 1990s (he was also briefly a Yankee in 2004). It was the Mets who originally drafted Olerud, taking him in the 27th round out of Interlake High School in

Bellevue, Washington in 1986. But he opted to attend Washington State University, where he turned himself into a third-round pick by the Toronto Blue Jays three years later.

The Pac-10 experience helped him jump to the majors very quickly. Olerud played summer ball in Alaska as he negotiated a contract with the Blue Jays, which he ultimately completed during the tail end of the 1989 season.[2] The club gave him a six-game look in September—he never played a game in the minors. A year later he was the Jays' regular first baseman at age 21 and hit 14 homers with a .364 OBP to finish fourth in the A.L. Rookie of the Year voting. He followed with two more good if unspectacular seasons for a rising Toronto club that took the A.L. East in 1991 and then a World Series title in '92. Then came the true breakout season. On a powerhouse 1993 Blue Jays team that rolled to a second straight title with a lineup that included Roberto Alomar, Paul Molitor, Devon White and Joe Carter, 24-year-old John Olerud was their best player. Coming to the plate 679 times, Olerud captured the American League batting crown with a .363 average along with 114 walks for an almost astounding .473 on-base percentage, the second-highest OBP in the A.L. in 31 years, topped during that span only by Wade Boggs' .476 in 1988. Olerud added 24 homers and a league-leading 54 doubles to slug .599. His 1.072 OPS and 186 OPS-plus also led the league. His 7.8 WAR placed second to Ken Griffey, Jr. It was also higher than Don Mattingly's 7.2 in 1986, which tends to be remembered as the gold standard for first base during that era.

Olerud dropped off during his last three seasons in Toronto, the OPS-plus never topping 124 or the WAR topping 3.2. How much had his stock fallen with Blue Jays brass? The team dealt him to the Mets after the 1996 season for mediocre relief pitcher Robert Person *and* agreed to cover the bulk of his $6.5 million 1997 salary in the process.

The quiet Olerud may not have fit the prototype of a guy who would welcome the New York stage. But the energy seemed to rejuvenate him. Fitting into a lineup that included power hitting catcher Todd Hundley and up-and-coming third baseman Edgardo Alfonso, Olerud hit .294 with a .400 OBP, 22 home runs, 135 OPS-plus and 4.1 WAR in 1997. He and Alfonso were the main catalysts in spurring the Mets to 88 wins, a 17-game improvement from the previous year. The Mets quickly signed him to a two-year extension—a good thing. He was even better in 1998, nearly matching his monster 1993 season with a .447 on-base percentage, 22 homers and a 163 OPS-plus that beat MVP Sammy Sosa, who along with Mark McGwire was commanding the attention of the entire world with an epic home run battle in which both broke Roger Maris's single season record of 61 homers (McGwire edged Sosa 70 to 66). Olerud's 7.6 WAR in 1998 was second in the league to Barry Bonds, beating McGwire by a hair and Sosa by more than a full point. In the National League MVP voting he finished 12th—how could the quiet first baseman with the all-around game stand a chance against an entertaining long ball battle? The only thing that John Olerud seemed to get attention for was his practice of wearing a helmet in the field, which he did for protection in the wake of an aneurysm he'd had removed from his head during his college days. The '98 Mets, who swung a big trade for Mike Piazza early in the year, again won 88 games and missed the playoffs on the final day.

When they broke through with 97 wins and a playoff spot in 1999 (squeaking into the National Wild Card with a one-game tiebreaker victory over the Reds), Olerud helped lead the way with another stellar year: .298 with 125 walks for a .427 OBP, 19 home runs and a 129 OPS-plus, very much helping to set up Piazza's 124 RBI season. Just for good measure, Olerud finished the '99 season by hitting .438 in the Mets' opening round playoff win over Arizona, and then .296 with a pair of homers in the their tough six-game loss to Atlanta in the N.L.C.S., a series that saw the Mets claw back from a 0–3 deficit with two straight wins and then nearly tie it before blowing two late leads in the crushing Game 6 loss.

Then there was Olerud's defense. Fangraphs says he was worth only three runs above average in his first Mets season in 1997, but then 15 and 12, respectively in the next two years—Keith Hernandez territory. A 1999 *Sports Illustrated* cover featured Olerud along with fellow infielders Alfonso (now playing second base), Rey Ordonez and Robin Ventura under the heading "Best infield ever?" And there was a very persuasive case that the '99 Mets infield defense was just that. The quartet combined for just 27 errors the entire season and prevented, according to Fangraphs, 88 runs more than average players at their positions.

The Mets lost Olerud after that 1999 season when he decided to head home to Seattle. He was only a Met for three years, but he was All-Star caliber in all three. His acquisition was every bit as important as Piazza's in rejuvenating the Mets lineup in the late 1990s, though of course it was never as heralded. And it was easy enough for Mets fans put Olerud's departure behind them quickly when the team made it to the 2000 World Series without him. Yet it should be noted that the Mets scoring declined from 853 runs to 807 when Olerud left—they took the next step thanks mainly to improved pitching led by the acquisition of Mike Hampton and a better year from Al Leiter.

Olerud went on to enjoy a borderline All-Star year with the 2000 Mariners and then big years in 2001 and 2002 (over .400 OBP and 5.0 WAR in both seasons). Basically he was All-Star caliber in five of six years from 1997 to 2002, and really in all six if you count his borderline .392 OBP, 103 RBI, 117 OPS-plus and 3.7 WAR in 2000. He finished up with three so-so years for the Mariners, Yankees and Red Sox before hanging it up at age 36. In his first year on the Hall of Fame ballot in 2011, Olerud got four votes—less than 1 percent.

In his 16 major league seasons, Olerud put up a .398 on-base percentage, the last couple of seasons nudging it under .400. The advanced fielding metrics say he prevented 98 runs above average for his position, a stellar number at first base. His 58 career WAR and 4.8 average WAR in his ten best years place him just a hair behind Keith Hernandez and the two Hall of Famers that Hernandez compares closely to, Harmon Killebrew and Bill Terry. The six four-win seasons include five that exceeded a 5.0. And he was able to add the solid tack-on seasons: four additional years of a 3.0 or better.

The verdict: Yes. Voters may want more than 255 home runs from his position, but Olerud's defense and on-base acumen make him a top 20 all-time first baseman, even if he did it too quietly for some people to notice. Getting four votes makes him one of the most underrated players ever.

Mark Teixeira

As long as we're on a roll with first basemen, let's go to the most recent star of the bunch. Mark Teixeira was a Yankee for eight years (2009 to 2016), a big, switch-hitting first baseman who helped anchor many strong lineups both in and out of New York. He figures to be strongly in the conversation when he becomes eligible for the Hall of Fame ballot in 2022.

After a standout three-year college career at Georgia Tech, Teixeira was picked fifth overall by the Texas Rangers in the 2001 June draft. He became the Rangers' regular first baseman just two years later, hitting 26 homers with a .331 OBP as a rookie in 2003. By the next year he established himself as an offensive force in the American League, blasting 38 homers with a 131 OPS-plus and 4.6 WAR in 2004. That was the first of five straight All-Star-type years with the Rangers, Braves and Angels, highlighted by particularly big seasons in 2005 and 2008 (above a seven-win player in both of those seasons, with a 144 OPS-plus in '05 and a 152 OPS-plus in '08, which he split between Atlanta and the L.A. Angels during his pending free agency). He was a true switch hitter who produced from both sides of the plate, hitting for more power lefty and getting on base more righty.

The 2008–09 baseball offseason was one of the funkiest in modern history. This was the winter of the great recession, right after the bursting of the housing bubble had Wall Street reeling and businesses laying off people left and right. The baseball industry was feeling the pinch, too. The scuttlebutt at the Las Vegas winter meetings was how tough the free agent market was shaping up to be, with predictions (mostly accurate) that many more players than usual figured to remain available well into January. It was against this backdrop that the Yankees were faced with opening their brand-new, expensive ballpark while coming off their first playoff miss in 15 years. They were looking to reload, particularly in the starting rotation, a weak spot in 2008, and at first base, where Jason Giambi's big seven-year deal from 2002 had expired. There may have been a recession on, but the Yankees were pretty much their own breed. While many other clubs were pinching pennies, they opened the checkbook to commit $423 million over the next several years to land the top three free agent prizes of 2009: Teixeira, CC Sabathia and A.J. Burnett. The biggest cut of that loot went to Teixeira–$180 million over eight years,[3] which showed how much he was valued as he approached his 29th birthday.

The Yankees' aggressiveness paid off big time, at least in the first year. They celebrated their first season in the new Yankee Stadium with 103 wins and a world championship, with all three of the big free agents putting up All-Star level seasons. For Teixeira in 2009: league-leading totals of 39 home runs, 122 RBI and 344 total bases, along with a .383 on-base percentage, 141 OPS-plus and 5.3 WAR. It was his sixth All-Star caliber season in a row.

Teixeira followed with another All-Star season (though he wasn't selected for the team) in 2010 with 33 homers, a 124 OPS-plus and a 4.1 WAR as the Yankees finished first again with 95 wins but bowed out in six games to the Texas Rangers in the A.L.C.S. That was pretty much it for Teixeira as a major star, though he contributed solidly for most of his final six years, including two more 30-plus home run seasons and three more seasons of three-plus WAR. In the middle was a lost year in 2013 when a wrist injury cost him most of the season.

Did the Yankees get their money's worth from Teixeira? Technically, probably not, so gargantuan was his contract. For that kind of dough, you expect more than two All-Star years out of eight. But he did add a couple of near-All-Star seasons after 2010, and of course the club may not have sipped World Series champagne in 2009 without Teixeira's big year. So perhaps overpaying him on the back end of the deal was worthwhile.

But we digress. Teixeira's Hall of Fame case isn't related to the return on investment he provided the Yankees. It's about his full career, much of it filled with big seasons before he donned pinstripes. Upon his retirement after the 2016 season, he'd belted 409 home runs, hitting the 30 mark nine times, with a 126 OPS-plus and a .360 on-base percentage that was about 9 percent above league average. While his 14-year career—really 13 years with the lost 2013 season—wasn't long enough to hit the (supposedly important) 500 home run mark, here is an indication of his power: Teixeira went deep just about once every 17 times up during his career, almost twice as often as the average player from 2003 to 2016. It's true that first baseman are generally supposed to hit homers, but for further perspective Teixeira's home run rate matched Miguel Cabrera and came quite close to Albert Pujols, who homered every 15 times up during the same period. Teixeira didn't hit for the same averages or get on base as often as Cabrera or Pujols did—these are two of the greatest hitters of all time, after all—but his power was right there with them as he maintained above-average on-base numbers.

Defensively, Teixeira's range and instincts were first rate. Fangraphs shows his numbers ebbing and flowing some over the years but ultimately resulting in 59 runs better than average at first base—not Keith Hernandez or John Olerud territory but still excellent.

Teixeira's 51.8 career WAR included seven seasons of four wins or better along with near misses in two others. He scored 48.9 in his 10 best seasons, making him just about an average five-win player across those 10 years. The career production puts him in a virtual tie with McGriff, whose Cooperstown case is much stronger than his vote count, and a bit ahead of inductees Tony Perez and Orlando Cepeda.

The verdict: Yes. This is really a close one. The relative lack of tack-on seasons prevents Teixeira from being a slam dunk, but the all-around game of power, defense and on-base percentage should be enough. When you *average* five wins a year for a decade, you deserve a plaque.

CC Sabathia

On April 30, 2019, at Chase Field in Arizona, CC Sabathia whiffed his former Yankee battery mate John Ryan Murphy for his 3,000th career strikeout. Less than two months later, on June 19 at Yankee Stadium, Sabathia allowed one run in six innings to beat the Tampa Bay Rays for his 250th career win.

Presto—social media was abuzz declaring that Sabathia had cleared the hurdles—he had just pitched himself into the Hall of Fame. It was all a bit silly, the quintessential round number obsession. Sabathia is certainly a strong Cooperstown candidate based on all he's done since breaking in to the majors in 2001, regardless of something like 249 wins vs. 250. Watching him struggle through a tough 2019 at age 38 made it clear that he didn't add to his Hall of Fame case simply because he's surpassed a couple of those numbers ending in zero. Yes, he's only the 17th pitcher in major league history to record 3,000 strikeouts. But did you know that only 23 pitchers have recorded as many as 2,773 strikeouts? Of course not—who is going to notice that number? Once Sabathia becomes eligible for Cooperstown in 2025, voters will have plenty of more substantive things to consider, especially his six years of mid-career dominance that made him a top ace of his time.

Debuting with the Cleveland Indians three years after the club drafted him out of Vallejo High School in northern California, Sabathia won 17 games as a rookie while allowing the fewest hits per nine innings in the American League. He was a lefty power pitcher who could throw the ball past hitters—171 strikeouts in 180 innings. His flaw at age 21 was control—95 walks for the season, or 4.7 per nine innings. He would cut down on the walks, by a little bit at first and then, after a few years, by a lot. In his first five seasons he didn't dominate, but he impressed, winning 69 games with a slightly better than average ERA across 30 or more starts each season. By 2005, he walked just 2.8 batter per nine.

It was during Sabathia's age 25 season in 2006 that he really kicked it into gear. Career bests In ERA (3.22), WHIP (1.173), FIP (3.30), strikeouts (172) and WAR (4.6) clearly established him as Cleveland's ace.

That season ignited a six-year run during which the WAR never dropped below that 4.6 and topped 6.0 four times. The WHIP stayed below 1.2 in five of the six years while the ERA-plus never fell below 136. In his Cy Young Award season in 2007, Sabathia pitched to a 141 ERA-plus over a league-leading 241 innings, going 19–7. He was even better the next year, when he put up one of the more memorable pitching seasons in recent history. With the 2008 Indians sitting well below .500 at midseason and Sabathia a pending free agent, the team dealt him to the contending Milwaukee Brewers. Sabathia proceeded to put the Brewers on his back and carry them to the 2008 National League Wild Card by going 11–2 with a 1.65 ERA and 128 strikeouts in 17 starts and 130 innings. How dominant was Sabathia during the second half of 2008? He wound up leading the Brewers in WAR (4.9) even though he didn't join the team until July. His overall WAR with Cleveland and Milwaukee came in at 6.8, a career high.

Sabathia cashed in with the Yankees that winter and pitched like a stud for them during his first three seasons, going 59–23 with a 139 ERA-plus and 17.4 WAR (5.8 per year) while throwing at least 230 innings each year from 2009 to 2011. After that—a decent year in 2012 followed by a major three-year dropoff that included a 2014 knee injury before reinventing himself as a finesse pitcher and contributing as a solid back-of-the-rotation starter from 2016 to 2018.

Sabathia would finish his long career in 2019 not only with more than 3,000 Ks and 250 wins but with a 62.5 career WAR that beats several Hall of Fame pitchers and which includes a 10-year peak of 46.8. He put up a 4.0 WAR or better in six seasons and a 3.0 or better in five more. The 116 ERA-plus is a strong number even as it was dragged down during Sabathia's later years—he did a 130 or better six times. Underlying it all—he was a career workhorse who surpassed 200 innings eight times and between 190 and 200 innings three other times.

Measuring by career WAR, 10-year peak WAR, ERA-plus and WHIP, Sabathia rates very close to two of our featured snubbed Hall of Famers, David Cone and Jerry Koosman. So it may seem a bit odd that there's been so much recent clamor for Sabathia as a virtual Cooperstown lock after the other two got no support to speak of. Such is the lure of the 250/3,000 club, apparently. Even the clearly superior Curt Schilling (80 WAR, 3,116 strikeouts, 127 ERA-plus) has been waiting for seven years, though recent trends show he has a good chance to make it soon.

But regardless of any possible voting flaws with other candidates, Sabathia's case is certainly strong. Another pitcher he compares quite closely to would be fellow lefty Andy Pettitte, his Yankee rotation mate for five seasons who we've argued is a close-but-no-cigar Hall of Fame candidate. The quick breakdown:

Wins: Sabathia 251, Pettitte 256
ERA-plus: Sabathia 116, Petttitte 117
Strikeouts: Sabathia 3,068, Pettitte 2,448
WHIP: Sabathia 1.257, Pettitte 1.351
FIP: Sabathia 3.78, Pettitte 3.74
WAR: Sabathia 62.5, Pettitte 60.6

Aside from strikeouts, very close, right? The difference, though, would be that while the two pitchers are similar in career numbers, Sabathia had a longer stretch of dominance—six seasons of no doubt about it All-Star-type pitching to Pettitte's three. Pettitte's relatively lesser seasons were mostly better than Sabathia's relatively lesser seasons, which is what allows to him to keep pace on the career numbers. But if you believe that great seasons ought to largely drive Hall of Fame voting then Sabathia gets the nod over Pettitte, who was more of a compiler.

The verdict: Yes. The great six-year run combined with several good tack-on seasons gets him there.

Robin Ventura

Like his teammate John Olerud, Robin Ventura wasn't a New York player for very long. But also like Olerud, he had an impact. Ventura was a big part of the Mets resurgence that got them to the cusp of the 1999 World Series (though he wasn't as good on the 2000 team that did make it). And he added a very good year for the 2002 Yankee team that won 103 games.

Ventura is largely known for some unique and quirky events that dot his career. He's the guy who set an NCAA record by hitting in 58 straight games for Oklahoma State in 1987, got into a mound-charging scrape with Nolan Ryan in 1993 in which he took a few noogies to the side of his head, and hit a famous "Grand Slam Single" over the right field wall for the Mets in the 15th inning of Game 5 of the 1999 N.L.C.S. to beat Atlanta when jubilant teammates intercepted him near second base and prevented him from completing his trek around the bases (he was credited with a single with the winning run scoring from third, a bizarre 4–3 final instead of 7–3).

What maybe gets lost amid a few memorable events is the fact that this guy could play third base really, really well. He played it better than most people ever played it. And he could hit. It all adds up to a solid Hall of Fame candidate, or so it would seem. But the voters wouldn't comply. Ventura was almost an afterthought when his eligibility came up in 2010, as the BBWAA sent him home with seven votes—1.3 percemt.

Following his standout career at Oklahoma State, Ventura was plucked in the first round of the 1988 June draft by the White Sox. He debuted with the big club in September of 1989 and became the starting third baseman a year later. After a decent but unspectacular rookie year, Ventura hit his stride in 1991 when he started 146 games at third base and popped 23 homers with 100 RBI, 126 OPS-plus and a 5.3 WAR that was second on the team to Frank Thomas and just outside the A.L.'s top 10. That '91 season ignited a run of six All-Star caliber seasons in eight years for the White Sox, and really seven of eight if you count his strike-shortened 1994 season (3.0 WAR, 18 homers, 116 OPS-plus, great defense). Ventura's only other miss came in 1997 when a broken ankle limited his season to 54 games. The run included a six-win season in 1992 and another five-win season for Chicago's 1993 A.L. West championship team when he hit 22 homers with a .379 OBP, 120 OPS-plus while tallying 17 runs above average in the field (the dWAR was 1.9, tops in the league among third basemen and 10th overall). In 1998, he led the American League in zone runs above average with 33 and in dWAR at 3.5

As his career progressed, Ventura's style took hold—quiet, understated, easy to miss by those not based in his home market. He wasn't a monster hitter, he was a good hitter and a monster third baseman.

When Ventura became a free agent after the 1998 season, the Mets, coming off back-to-back 88-win seasons that ended just shy of the playoffs, pounced. The set-up they had in place was perfect: disappointing second baseman Carlos Baerga had played out his contract and was allowed to walk as a free agent, with the flexible rising star Edgardo Alonso sliding from third to second to free up a spot for Ventura. Bingo—the '99 Mets had the greatest infield ever (?). Three of the infielders, Ventura, Alfonso and Olerud, were the Mets' top three players by WAR—ahead of Mike Piazza—as the team won 97 games and narrowly missed the World Series (shortstop Rey Ordonez, a weak hitter but a spectacular defender that year who Fangraphs says was worth 33 runs above average in the field, was the team's number five player by WAR).

Ventura's 1999 season for the Mets turned out to be the best of his career. Defensively, his 27 runs above average and his 2.8 dWAR were both fourth in the National League. At the plate, Ventura hit .301 with a .379 OBP, 32 homers, 120 RBI and a 130 OPS-plus. His 6.7 WAR was also fourth in the league among everyday players behind Jeff Bagwell and the Jones boys from Atlanta, Andruw and Chipper.

Ventura's production faded quite a bit for the Mets over the next two seasons, mainly in the batting average department (though he was still drawing walks and hitting 20-plus homers). After the 2001 season, the Yankees nabbed him as a free agent and benefited from a resurgent year of 27 homers 119 OPS-plus and 3.7 WAR, just shy of the typical All-Star standard. Ventura played another half season in the Bronx before finishing with a nondescript year and a half with the Dodgers before retiring at age 37.

In 15 big-league seasons, Robin Ventura hit 294 home runs with a .362 on-base percentage and 114 OPS-plus. At this point, we're in very-good-but-not-great territory. But then there's defense, a big driving force behind Ventura's seven All-Star caliber seasons, 56.1 career WAR and 47.8 WAR in his 10 best seasons, legitimate Cooperstown range. Fangraphs pegs Ventura at 148 runs above average at third base for his career. That's more than Graig Nettles and Mike Schmidt, considered the defensive gold standards at third in the era just before Ventura's (Nettles wound up playing long enough to see his defensive numbers drop quite a bit in his later years, otherwise he would edge Ventura by a little bit). How about other noted defensive stalwarts at the hot corner? Scott Rolen was worth 153 runs above average, barely ahead of Ventura, while Buddy Bell and Clete Boyer were both worth a little more than 160, also not far ahead of Ventura. There's a bigger gap with Adrian Beltre (196) and of course no one touches Brooks Robinson. But if you believe the numbers, only a handful of third basemen ever played the position better than Robin Ventura did.

The verdict: Yes. A lot of people probably won't like this call, but Ventura is very much the Mark Teixeira of third basemen—right on that cusp of very good and great. It's close, but the elite defense pushes him into the top 20 all-time at his position.

Carlos Beltran

Fifteen years before he became the first Mets manager to never suit up for a game once his role in a Houston Astros 2017 sign stealing saga was revealed, Carlos Beltran held the distinction of being the best free agent signing in the club's history. Beltran was that rare guy who starred as a young player, signed a mega free agent deal in his late 20s, and continued to star into his mid–30s. He was an athlete playing a central position, and a switch hitter who produced from both sides of the plate. During the decade of the 2000s, Beltran could do it all. And he did a little bit more after that.

The Manati, Puerto Rico, native debuted with the Kansas City Royals in September of 1998, three years after the team drafted him out of high school. The Royals started the 22-year-old Beltran in centerfield in 1999 and saw him respond with 22 homers, 108 RBI and a .293 average. The offensive numbers were solid though not exactly great in the context of that hitter-happy season (99 OPS-plus). But there was also the speed and defense. Beltran covered ground in center to the tune of 20 runs above average and a 2.3 defensive WAR, fifth-best in the American League. He also stole 27 bases in 35 tries. He wound up with a 4.7 WAR and the A.L. Rookie of the Year Award.

Injuries limited Beltran to 98 games and minimal production in 2000. But the Royals still liked him enough to trade the popular Johnny Damon to Oakland that winter. Now secure in the center field job, Beltran killed it in Kansas City for the next three years, including a 6.5 WAR in 2001 when he hit .306 with a 123 OPS-plus, 24 homers and 31 stolen bases in 32 tries (advanced stats generally downplay the value of stolen bases, because getting erased on a steal attempt is more damaging than stealing a base is valuable, so you need to be successful about three quarters of the time to add value; but it's worth noting that from 2000 to 2004, Beltran swiped 162 bases while getting caught just 15 times—92 percent! He finished at 86 percent for his career).

In June of 2004, with the financially struggling Royals faced with losing him as a free agent, they dealt Beltran to the contending Houston Astros. What Beltran did over the rest of the 2004 season in Houston became the stuff of legend. During the balance of the regular season he blasted 23 homers with a 135 OPS-plus in 90 games after joining Houston to lead the Astros (38–34 at the time of the trade) to 91 wins and the National League Wild Card. Then came once of the great postseason performances in baseball history: Beltran crushed eight home runs and batted .435 in 12 games against the Braves and Cardinals to lead Houston's push to the brink of the 2004 World Series before they came up a game short (it's always seemed like that epic Houston–St. Louis '04 N.L.C.S never quite got the national recognition it should have, overshadowed as it was by the curse-busting Boston Red Sox historic comeback from a 0–3 A.L.C.S deficit against the Yankees followed by their first title in 86 years).

Beltran's big 2004 season (38 homers, .367 OBP, 133 OPS-plus and 42-of-45 in stolen bases) capped by his unconscious playoff run had him lined up for a free agent bonanza as he headed into his age 28 season. The Mets, newly aggressive under first-year GM Omar Minaya, who had already inked Pedro Martinez that winter, grabbed him up with a seven-year, $119 million contract.

There was that first-year adjustment that many players go through after signing a big free agent contract. Beltran's inaugural season in New York was disappointing with 16 homers, .330 OBP and 97 OPS-plus in 2005 as the team finished 83–79 under first-year manager Willie Randolph.

But everything clicked from the get-go in 2006, for both Beltran and the Mets. The team got big offensive performances from Jose Reyes, David Wright and Carlos Delgado as they ran away in the N.L. East. But Beltran topped them all: 41 homers to tie a club record, .388 on-base percentage, 116 RBI and a 150 OPS-plus, all while rating 10 runs above average defensively in center field. His 8.2 WAR was the best of his career and a close second to Albert Pujols for tops in the league among position players. The 2006 Mets swept the Dodgers in the Division Series and then went to a seventh game against the Cardinals in the N.L.C.S. The set up was in place for the only thing that Mets fans and media seem to talk about to this day when it comes to Beltran: the series ended with him looking at a called third strike on a curveball from Adam Wainwright with the bases loaded in the bottom of the ninth to complete a 3–1 St. Louis win. All the harping over the final pitch of the series, the blaming of Beltran for not being more aggressive, was utterly ridiculous. That final curve from Wainwright was beyond nasty—it would have fooled anyone. Beltran, who had been just about the best player in the league all season and who had a big N.L.C.S. with three homers and a .296 average, practically had his Mets career defined by one pitch thanks to the dramatic overreaction.

But he continued to excel with big seasons for the Mets in 2007 and 2008, and was killing it again in 2009 before a knee injury cost him most of the second half (he wound up with a 144 OPS-plus and 3.6 WAR in half a season). The injury kept him out until July 2010, and then in the middle of another strong season in 2011, the fading Mets dealt him to San Francisco for pitching prospect Zack Wheeler. Beltran signed with St. Louis that winter and hit 32 homers with a 128 OPS-plus and 3.9 WAR for their 2012 team at age 35. That was pretty much his last All-Star-type year as he finished his last five seasons with the Cardinals, Yankees and Astros.

Over a two-decade career, Beltran hit 435 home runs with a .350 on-base percentage, 119 OPS-plus and 69.6 WAR. In his 10 best seasons, the WAR averaged 5.7 and the OPS-plus 135. Much of that prime came with the Mets, where in what amounted to five-plus seasons he averaged just over five wins per year. Defensively, Beltran scores 43 runs above average as an outfielder with a 1.6 defensive WAR. The fielding numbers show that he was mostly outstanding during the first half of his career and then began to tail off at age 32 in 2009, two years before shifting to right field. He'll be eligible for the Hall of Fame in 2023.

A Cooperstown plaque hardly seems like a slam dunk, especially with some voters likely to penalize him morally in the wake of the sign stealing fiasco. Beltran statistically ranks about even with Tim Raines, who waited 10 years to get the call. And as relatively recent center fielders go, he's very close to three players the voters have snubbed—Kenny Lofton, Andruw Jones and Jim Edmonds (of the three only Jones remains on the ballot with a flicker of hope after polling at just over 19 percent in his third year through the voting). Yet at the same time, Beltran was most definitely a bit better than Tony Gwynn and Dave Winfield, just without the narrative that comes from things like multiple batting titles and 3,000 hits. You never know for sure how voters will go, although players with all-around games tend to get short shrift compared to those who excel in one area or reach high profile career milestones.

The verdict: Yes, unless you consider the sign stealing a deal breaker. One of the best players of his time, period.

Roy White

Huh? Yes, Roy White, a guy who got literally zero votes from the Hall of Fame writers. When it comes to underrated Yankees it's tough to top the team's consistent left fielder of the 1960s and '70s. A lot of people probably remember White not as a star but as a solid complimentary player alongside Thurman Munson and Reggie Jackson on the Yankee World Series teams of the late '70s. And it's pretty much accurate, as far as that portion of his career goes.

But his best seasons came before that, when White starred for the mostly nondescript Yankee clubs of the late 1960s and early '70s. As Mickey Mantle was going out and players like Munson and Bobby Murcer were just getting started, White, who had broken in with the team as a 21-year-old in 1965, was the Yankees' best everyday player for the four straight years of 1968 to 1971 and then a close second to Murcer in 1972. He was quiet, reliable, and not a big home run hitter. The only thing about White that seemed to stand out was his unusual switch-hitting approach in which he held the bat up high as a right-handed hitter but held it lower and close to his body as a lefty. But what White could do was hit, get on base, run, and play defense. He was particularly monstrous in 1970 and 1971 when he finished in American League's top eight in WAR, on-base percentage and OPS-plus in both years (White's 6.7 WAR in 1971 was second in the league to his future teammate—Cleveland's Graig Nettles).

But there was something a bit low profile about all of it, driven mostly by the circumstances of the time. Tom Seaver and the Mets owned the city, the Baltimore Orioles owned the American League East and the power hitting Murcer was the Yankee fan favorite. Roy White was something of a John Olerud of his day, a quiet personality who built his value with his all-around game.

A bit later, when the Yankees broke though for their first A.L. pennant in 12 years in 1976, White was an indispensable contributor by leading the club with a .365 on-base percentage and placing second to Nettles with a 128 OPS-plus, while putting up a 5.5 WAR. But with several teammates also having strong years, the big season seemed to get a bit lost in the shuffle. He didn't lead off and steal 43 bases like Mickey Rivers (though White did steal 31) and he didn't hit third and drive in 100 runs like Munson. White was the guy who hit between them, that vital cog in the machine from the two-spot.

White played all of his 14 years and 1,881 games with the Yankees, the seventh-most games in franchise history. He finished with a 121 OPS-plus and a .360 career on-base percentage against a league average of .319 during the same period. Defensively, he wasn't blessed with a strong outfield arm but he was blessed with sure hands and the ability to cover ground. Fangraphs credits White with 54 runs above average in left field and 44 above average overall after factoring in his below par stints in center and right early in his career. His 46.8 WAR and 47.3 in his 10 best seasons (there was that -1.3 in his final year in 1979) rates quite close to a few Hall of Fame outfielders including Enos Slaughter and Kirby Puckett. White was a four-plus win player in seven seasons while coming close in three others.

In the 1985 Hall of Fame vote, left fielder Lou Brock tallied 331 votes to gain induction with 79.7 percent in his first year on the ballot. Left fielder Roy White, also in his first year on the ballot and who outperformed Brock in on-base percentage, OPS-plus, WAR and defensive zone metrics (the last one by a ton), got no votes at all.

The verdict: No. You wanted to see either another big year or a couple of more solid tack-on years to actually hang White's plaque in Cooperstown. But he's darn close, and should be recognized for it.

Rusty Staub

How many players get be adored as an icon as in two cities? Rusty Staub managed to pull it off in both Montreal and New York. He was the third player to come to bat in Expos history on April 9, 1969, when he stepped in against Tom Seaver at Shea Stadium (Staub popped up put but later singled against Seaver and homered off Al Jackson in a wild 11–10 Montreal win). He'd come to Montreal in a 1969 trade from Houston, where he'd broken in as a 19-year-old in 1963 and where he had his first All-Star season in 1967 when he hit .333 with a .398 OBP and 153 OPS-plus with a 5.1 WAR and a league-high 44 doubles.

Staub became the expansion Expos' first star, swinging the bat as well as almost anyone in the league during the team's first three seasons. The lefty-hitting right fielder with the head of orange hair was dubbed "Le Grand Orange" by adoring fans north of the border as he put up six-plus win seasons every year from 1969 to 1971 by averaging better than a .400 on-base percentage and 26 homers. But with the team still not winning much and looking toward the future, management dealt the 27-year-old to the Mets for three youngsters—Ken Singleton, Mike Jorgensen and Tim Foli. Both Foli and Jorgensen went on to become useful players and Singleton became a star in Montreal and Baltimore. But for the Mets, just a couple of seasons removed from their 1969 championship, Staub was the much-needed bat that could potentially get them back to a World Series.

It was working well early on. Staub was hitting over .300 as the 1972 Mets charged out of the gate by winning 25 of their first 32. They were 36–19 on June 18 when Staub was plunked on the hand by a pitch from Cincinnati's Ross Grimsley. A bone was broken, he missed two months, and the Mets faded to third place. Staub had a solid but unspectacular year in the Mets' improbable run to the 1973 N.L. pennant, though he saved his best for the postseason, hitting three homers and making a spectacular extra-inning catch against the Reds in the N.L.C.S and then batting .423 in a tough seven-game loss to the A's in the World Series.

Staub was what baseball followers later came to call "a professional hitter." Not extraordinarily athletic, not a particularly good defensive player, but with a serious approach to hitting and a great stroke at the plate. His at-bats were 100 percent concentration, with everything else tuned out. He studied pitchers and kept copious notes. He closed out the first round of his Mets career with a subpar year in 1974 and a decent one in 1975 before the club traded him to Detroit for veteran pitcher Mickey Lolich. He hit well as a DH for the better part of the next five years in Detroit and Texas (137 OPS-plus for the '76 Tigers followed by back-to-back 100 RBI seasons). The Mets reacquired him in 1981 and watched him renew his love affair with the fans with a five-year run as one of the league's top pinch hitters and top good Samaritans with his tireless charity work. In 1983, he stroked a record-tying eight consecutive pinch hits on his way to 24 for the season, with three homers.

Staub lasted 23 years in the big leagues and holds the distinction of being one of only four players to hit a home run before his 20th birthday and after his 40th. He piled up 2,716 hits, no. 65 on the all-time list, with a .362 career on-base percentage and 128 OPS-plus. His 45.8 career WAR includes a 40.0 in his 10 best seasons. The numbers say he compares closely to Tony Oliva and George Foster, not Hall of Famers but great company nonetheless. Staub lasted for seven years on the ballot, peaking at 7.9 percent in 1994. He sadly passed away from a heart attack on March 29, 2018, at age 73.

The verdict: No. Staub's great run from 1967 to 1971 puts him on the map, but overall a lot of good seasons with few great ones. A consummate pro and fan favorite who comes up short of Cooperstown.

Johan Santana

Another star whose Mets career was fairly brief, but eventful. And despite no real support from voters who gave him a paltry 2.4 percent in 2018, Santana's career body of work—the majority of which he compiled with the Minnesota Twins—stands right there with many Hall of Fame pitchers.

The lefty from Venezuela who relied on a devastating changeup as opposed to throwing major heat came up with Minnesota as a reliever/ spot starter in 2000 and put up mediocre numbers for two seasons. By 2002, in 14 starts and 13 relief outings, he had the changeup going to the tune of 137 strikeouts in 108 innings with a 2.99 ERA and 150 ERA-plus. One season later, as his control continued to improve (2.7 walks per nine innings, down from 5.7 as a rookie), Santana put up his first All-Star caliber year with a 148 ERA-plus, 1.099 WHIP and 169 Ks in 158 innings, with a 4.1 WAR. That '03 season was Santana's precursor for taking over the American League. In each of the next three seasons, he led the league in strikeouts, ERA-plus, WHIP and FIP (yes, no. 1 in the league in every one of those categories in all three seasons) while going 55–19 and tossing at least 228 innings in each season. He took two of the three American League Cy Young Awards over that stretch from 2004 to 2006, and should have easily won all three (Santana's third-place finish in 2005 behind Bartolo Colon and Mariano Rivera was a joke).

After another big year in 2007 in which he led the A.L. in WHIP and finished second in strikeouts and seventh in ERA, Santana, now a pending free agent, was shipped to the Mets for four players and promptly signed a six-year, $137.5 million extension.[4]

His first season after the deal coincided with the Mets' last one at Shea Stadium. He was nothing short of sensational in 2008, leading the National League in both innings and ERA with a 7.1 WAR and 16–7 record. Santana nearly carried the Mets—a flawed team that boasted a few stars sprinkled on top of an otherwise mediocre roster—into the playoffs by winning his final nine decisions, including a shutout of the Marlins on three days' rest on the next-to-last day of the season. But the Mets lost their finale and closed out Shea a game behind Milwaukee for the N.L. Wild Card.

After that came the first shoulder woes that began to slow Santana's career down, although he had a solid 2009 and an All-Star caliber 2010 before missing all of 2011 and petering out for good in 2012. Of course before he left, Santana made Mets history by tossing the team's first-ever no-hitter on June 1, 2012, just over 50 years after Roger Craig threw the franchise's first pitch. A lot of people blamed the 134-pitch no-no for Santana's downfall that came later in that 2012 season, but that's highly questionable. An injured ankle later in the year is what directly precipitated his sudden ineffectiveness. When top pitchers routinely throw approximately 3,000 pitches in a season, what is the likelihood that leaving a guy in for 20 or so extra pitches as he chases a no-hitter is going to make or break him?

Santana finished his relatively brief but brilliant career with a 139–78 record, 3.20 ERA (136 ERA-plus), 1.132 WHIP and 51.7 WAR. His 10-year peak WAR was just over 50, meaning he averaged five wins over that stretch, including four years of more than 7.0.

His candidacy once again brings up the classic dominance vs. longevity debate which has no definitive answer. Generally, having a terrific peak isn't enough without a good handful of tack-on seasons to give the career that extra heft. But what if the peak isn't just terrific but truly exceptional, good enough to stand on its own? The classic example: Sandy Koufax, the former Dodger great whose career length (12 years), WAR (53.1) ERA-plus (131) and WHIP (1.106) are almost spitting images of Santana. Despite light career totals (165 wins, 2,300 innings) Koufax made it to Cooperstown handily on the strength of his historically dominant six-year run during the early-to-mid–1960s—that sweet spot after he found his control and before an arthritic elbow forced him out of the game at age 30.

Like Sandy Koufax from 1961 to 1966, Johan Santana had his own huge six-year run from 2003 to 2008. And if you think that comparing Santana's run to Koufax's is a big stretch, think again:

Annual Avg. WAR: Koufax 7.8, Santana 6.6
ERA-plus: Koufax 160, Santana 157
WHIP (% better than league average): Koufax 24%, Santana 26%
FIP (% better than league average): Koufax 39%, Santana 27%
K/9 (% better than league average): Koufax 68%, Santana 49%

Clearly the edge goes to Koufax based on strikeouts and FIP. But Santana is right there with him in the major categories of ERA and WHIP. That his six-year spree of greatness is even this close to Koufax's puts him into elite company. And remember that Koufax's greatness was entirely bottled up in his 1961–66 groove. Santana's next three best seasons beyond the six-year Superman phase (2002, 2009 and 2010) were superior to any other Koufax year. Ultimately, their careers are about a tie.

The verdict: Yes. Santana's (almost) Koufax-like peak is dominant enough to offset the lack of longevity.

Roger Maris

Finishing out the player category with an old standby. Roger Maris got many more Hall of Fame votes than any other eligible player in this chapter. Across 15 years on the ballot from 1974 to 1988, he got at least 19 percent every year and topped 40 percent in each of his last three. That's still not particularly close to induction, but it's a solid base of support. Many voters clearly placed a big premium on his one-season accomplishment in 1961 when Maris won his much-ballyhooed battle with teammate Mickey Mantle to hit 61 home runs and break Babe Ruth's single season record. Maris was named American League MVP that year even though the overall stats left him trailing Mantle (54 homers, .448 OBP) along with Detroit's Norm Cash and Rocky Colavito. It was actually Maris's second consecutive MVP Award since joining the Yankees, coming on the heels of his 39 homers, league-leading .581 slugging percentage and 160 OPS-plus in 1960.

Roger Maris had a very strange 12-year career—a fleeting greatness for two seasons, solid or average otherwise. Born in Minnesota and growing up mostly in North Dakota, he didn't hail from a baseball hotbed. He put up so-so production during his first three seasons in Cleveland and Kansas City, though he did pop 28 homers in 1958 to finish seventh in the league. Traded to the Yankees in 1960—the Kansas City A's were sending enough players to New York during this period that they were considered something of a de facto Yankee farm team—he suddenly exploded over the next two seasons for 100 home runs and 14.4 WAR (7.5 and 6.9, respectively), not to mention leading the A.L. in RBI in both seasons. And believe it or not he didn't particularly benefit from Yankee Stadium's short right field porch—he smashed 30 homers at home at 31 on the road in the record-setting season.

Across his other 10 major league seasons, Maris totaled 175 homers and compiled a 23.8 WAR. He hit .260 for his career with a .345 on-base percentage that was 8 percent better than league average. He was known as a good right fielder, an assertion that's backed up by the

Fangraphs numbers that say he was 47 runs better than average, or a few runs per year. Offensively he had his moments—four seasons in the top 10 in homers, three in slugging and two in OPS-plus—but not what you would call any sustained excellence. By WAR, 1960 and '61 were his only All-Star caliber years, although he supplemented that with five other seasons that weren't far off, including a 3.6 WAR for the champion 1967 Cardinals in his first year after the Yankees traded him there.

His overall 38.2 WAR and 37.3 in his 10 best seasons don't hold up well to any Hall of Fame outfielders aside from a few controversial old-time Veterans Committee choices like Ross Youngs, Tommy Mc-Carthy and Lloyd Waner. As New York right fielders go, Maris stands statistically about even with Paul O'Neill and a little ways behind Darryl Strawberry. It's understandable that a decent number of Hall of Fame voters wanted to reward him for his 1961 achievement, particularly given all the reports of how he fought through the growing daily public pressure as he pursued Ruth's record and then did it on the final day. But this wasn't a Hall of Fame career.

The verdict: No. Maris had a nice career highlighted by a special season, but he comes up well short.

And Finally, the Managers...

Managers are very tough to figure when it comes to weighing the Hall of Fame. What makes a Hall of Fame manager? With no individual performance stats to sort through, it's mainly about lasting a long time, winning games and bringing home championships. Even on that score, a manager is pretty much only as good as his players. Casey Stengel won championships galore with the Yankee powerhouse teams of the 1950s and then lost all the time with the expansion Mets of the '60s, leaving him with just a .508 winning percentage. But of course he's in thanks to 10 American League pennants and seven World Series titles. The same goes for Joe Torre in reverse order—lousy numbers as a young manager with the Mets and then later six pennants and four titles with the Yankees (with so-so records in Atlanta, St. Louis and Los Angeles mixed in).

Even though most seem to agree that managers tend to get both too much credit and blame for their teams' fortunes, those who stick around to compile a lot of wins, and in most cases pennants and championships too, get rewarded with a Cooperstown plaque. There are currently 22 managers in the Baseball Hall of Fame. For a sense of what a "typical" Hall manager looks like, the median numbers of the 22 honorees break down this way:

Wins: 1,901
Winning percentage: .539
Pennants: 5
Championships: 2

The best overall numbers belong to Joe McCarthy, who took over the tail end of the "Murders Row" Yankees from Miller Huggins in 1931 and stayed through several of the Joe DiMaggio years to lead the team to eight A.L. pennants and seven titles. Overall, McCarthy went 2,125–1,333 (.615) with the Cubs, Yankees and Red Sox.

Four of the 22 Cooperstown managers failed to win a World Series: old-timer Ned Hanlon, who took five pennants in Baltimore and Brooklyn, between 1894 and 1900, Al Lopez, who won at a .584 clip with two pennants in the '50s and '60s with the Indians and White Sox, Frank Selee, another old-timer who won five pennants with a .598 winning percentage in Boston and Chicago between 1890 and 1905, and Wilbert Robinson, whose numbers (.500 record, two pennants) weren't very impressive but who may have benefited from his beloved status in Brooklyn for 18 years—the team was called the Robins in his honor during his tenure from 1914 to 1931.

New York managers are well represented in the Hall of Fame. Seven of the 22 managed the bulk of their games there: Stengel, Torre, McCarthy, Robinson, Huggins, Leo Durocher, and John McGraw. And that's not counting Walter Alston, who won two pennants and a World Series with the Brooklyn Dodgers before going on to manage most of his career in L.A., or Bucky Harris, who won a title with the 1947 Yankees during his two-year stop there.

Against this backdrop, it would be interesting to see how three accomplished New York managers who haven't made it to Cooperstown—Billy Martin, Davey Johnson and Gil Hodges—stack up.

Billy Martin

Record: 1,253–1,013 (.553)
Two pennants
One World Series championship

We all generally know the saga of Billy Martin. Great manager, but short-tempered and overly intense. He turned teams around but always seemed to wear out his welcome. He drank too much, and he clashed with George Steinbrenner and Reggie Jackson too much. He got into fights, including the famous decking of a marshmallow salesman in a Minneapolis bar. Martin managed five different teams from 1969 to 1988, including five separate stints with the Yankees during Steinbrenner's peak circus years.

What's unfair to Martin, at least as far as assessing his Hall of Fame case goes, is the way the highly publicized sideshow aspect of his career came to dominate his narrative at the expense of what he did in the dugout. Martin's ability to turn teams around takes a back seat to no one. His first team, the 1969 Minnesota Twins, was fresh off a 79–83 record in 1968. Martin immediately led them to 97 wins and a division title. Next came the Detroit Tigers, also coming off a 79–83 season in 1970. Martin led them to 91 wins in 1971 and then to a division title with a slightly strike-shortened 86–70 season in 1972. And how about the Texas Rangers? The early Rangers were one of the worst teams of all time during their first two years in Arlington after moving from Washington, D.C., losing 100 games and 105 games, respectively in 1972 and 1973 in a weak division. Martin took over for the last 23 games of that '73 season, going 9–14. Then in his first full year in 1974, Martin's Rangers went 84–76, shooting from last in the league in runs scored to second. And there's no forgetting the "Billy Ball" Oakland A's who rocketed from 54 wins to 83 when Martin took over in 1980 and then to a division title in the 1981 split season (critics legitimately point to a downside of his Oakland tenure—the pitching staff he worked for so many innings wound up burning out a short time later).

With the Yankees, Martin managed over 900 games amid his comings and goings and won at nearly a .600 clip, taking an A.L. pennant in 1976 and a World Series title in 1977. He even slipped in a turnaround job in one of his New York stints, leading the 1983 Yankees to 91 wins after they'd slumped to 79 wins the previous year while blowing through three managers. Overall, his .553 winning percentage beats 13 of the 22 managers who made it to the Hall. Ideally, you'd like to see more than two trips to the World Series and one title, and he might have done that if not for the tumultuous relationship with Steinbrenner that cost him a chance at continuity with those talented Yankee clubs.

But there's also the matter of Martin taking so many clubs further than their talent dictated they should go. Those average clubs he whipped into division champions had already overachieved before losing in the postseason. The 1969 Twins weren't supposed to beat the Orioles. Ditto for the '72 Tigers against the A's, and for the '81 A's against the Yankees. And his 1976 Yankee club wasn't supposed to beat the Big Red Machine in the World Series. So it's hard to find any club that could be said to have underachieved under Billy Martin.

A downside: Martin's career lacked heft to a degree. A managerial run that spanned 20 seasons would have added up to 3,240 games had he gone straight through. Instead, all the various partial or missed seasons limited him to 2,266 games. Martin's winning percentage may beat most Hall of Fame managers, but his 1,253 wins beats just one—Billy Southworth. Still, his numbers show him to be quite even with Hall of Famer Whitey Herzog, who won only 28 more career games than Martin with a lower winning percentage (.532), one more league pennant (three) and the same number of championships (one).

The verdict: Yes. The 2,266 games may be a bit light, but it's hard to find anyone who got more out of his clubs. What could be a bigger test for a manager?

Davey Johnson

Record: 1,372–1,071 (.562)
One pennant
One World Series championship

Davey Johnson easily owns the best record in Mets managerial history. He also owns the 13th best winning percentage of all time among managers with at least 1,000 games, beating Joe Torre, Bobby Cox, Tony LaRussa and Sparky Anderson, among several others enshrined in Cooperstown.

Three years after his playing career ended in 1978, Johnson was hired into the Mets system by Frank Cashen, Johnson's old front office boss from his playing days in Baltimore. He moved up the chain to the big-league job in 1984 and led the resurgence to 90 wins and a second-place finish from 68 wins and last place the previous year. He rolled along in New York for the next five years, winning at least 87 games in every season and 100 or more in two between 1985 and 1989, highlighted by the 108-win championship club of 1986. Yet when he started 20–22 in 1990, Cashen decided to let him go despite a career .588 winning percentage.

Johnson went on to manage four more teams, where, as with the Mets, he kept winning. In all but one stop he won with teams that weren't winning before he got there. In 17 seasons as a big-league manager, including 15 full seasons, he finished first or second 13 times. His first full season with each new club—the 1994 Reds, 1996 Orioles and 2012 Nationals—showed huge improvements from the prior year. Johnson was something of a quiet version of Billy Martin, igniting teams to new heights without the histrionics. A two-year stint with the Dodgers proved to be the only exception, with Johnson putting up a 163–161 record across 1999 and 2000 shortly after a period of upheaval that brought the sale of the club to Rupert Murdoch from the O'Malley family and the trade of Mike Piazza. Johnson's 77–85 record in L.A. in 1999 marked the only losing full season of his career.

Johnson had been a pretty good player in Baltimore and Atlanta while showing signs of future managerial potential. He was known to quiz Oriole manager Earl Weaver during games about moves he made and why. According to baseball author Erik Sherman, who collaborated with Johnson on his 2018 autobiography, Johnson once presented Weaver an analysis showing that hitting Johnson second in the batting order instead of the usual sixth or seventh would optimize the Oriole lineup (the old-school Weaver tossed it in the nearest trash can). A math major in college, Johnson became known in the '80s for using a computer to analyze performance and matchups—quaint by today's analytic standards but somewhat groundbreaking at the time.

Davey Johnson is also something of a poster boy for the "you're only as good as your players" mantra that seemed to follow him around. He was indeed fortuitous in that regard, coming up to the Mets just as the Hernandez-Strawberry-Gooden era was dawning and starting with the Orioles right after they acquired future Hall of Famer Roberto Alomar and solid veteran B.J. Surhoff. Johnson also took over a 2012 Nationals club that was just breaking in super youngsters Stephen Strasburg and Bryce Harper.

But not every team Johnson managed was immensely talented, so call him a push button manager at your peril. His first Mets team in 1984 was a lot better than its immediate predecessors, but it was still a young team that was outscored for the season by 24 runs. Johnson, who had managed and helped to develop some of the players in the minors, led the team to 90 wins, 12 more than the Pythagorean (expected) total based on the run differential. Says Sherman: "He was an excellent talent evaluator and he really knew how to nurture the young guys. He got into the heads of Wally Backman, Lenny Dykstra, and Darryl Strawberry and kept them focused."

You've also got the 1987 Mets, whose pitching staff was beset with injury and suspension following the glory of '86. The rotation's front four—Dwight Gooden, Ron Darling, Bob Ojeda and Sid Fernandez— combined to start 37 fewer games than they did in 1986. Yet Johnson still led the club to 92 wins to narrowly miss the N.L. East title. And how about the 1995 Reds, a team with two All-Star players (Barry Larkin and Reggie Sanders) whose ace was journeyman lefty Pete Schourek, a onetime Met who wound up with a career 66–77 record and 4.59 ERA? Under Johnson, the '95 Reds finished 85–59 (in a slightly shortened sea- son following the 1994 strike) to win the N.L. Central by nine games and then swept the Dodgers in the Division Series before being swept out of the N.L.C.S. by Atlanta.

In the end Johnson only got the one championship. But he won like crazy, kept his clubs in contention year after year and made the playoffs six times. Getting your team into position for a championship is most of the battle—taking it all the way comes down to the crap- shoot of a short series, which can always go against a team through no fault of the manager. When Johnson was placed onto the "Game Era" Veterans Committee ballot in 2018, he received fewer than five votes out of 16. Lou Piniella, who won the same number of pennants and championships as Johnson (one apiece) with a significantly lower career winning percentage (.517), received 11 votes, missing induc- tion by a single vote. Piniella generally seemed like a perfectly good manager, and watching his meltdowns with umpires was entertaining. But it's hard to fathom why anyone would rate him ahead of Davey Johnson.

The verdict: Yes. Johnson is a vastly underrated manager associated with a Mets era that was perceived as a disappointment after it yielded just one championship. But Whitey Herzog and Leo Durocher, with lower winning percentages, also got only one ring apiece. So did John- son's old boss Earl Weaver, whose winning percentage (.583) wasn't that much higher. Yet they got their plaques. It's time for Johnson to join them.

Gil Hodges

Record: 660–753 (.467)
One pennant
One World Series championship

We finish with the beloved Gil Hodges—Brooklyn Dodger first baseman, Miracle Mets manager and strong silent type who secured the admiration of many players and fans. Hodges really built the bulk of his resume as a player more so than as a manager, but in sticking with the Mets-Yankees theme we'll go ahead and slot him here while breaking down both.

There's a lot of sentiment in New York to get Gil Hodges, whose vote count reached as high as 63.4 percent during his time on the ballot, into the Hall of Fame. During the summer of 2019, at the 50th anniversary celebration of the 1969 Mets, several of Hodges's players plugged him for the Hall. Tom Seaver has long lauded Hodges as a leader and a culture changer who molded the Mets into a team that could believe in itself and put the early laughingstock years behind it. At his number retirement ceremony at Shea Stadium in 1988, Seaver spoke of the honor of his no. 41 being on the wall next to Hodges's no. 14, calling Hodges "a man who meant more to me as a professional athlete than anyone else." That's very strong support from an all-time great.

Others who were around then largely agree. "One of the worst oversights ever," is how Howie Rose describes the Hodges Hall of Fame snub. "He was everything that's right about baseball, as a player, a leader, and a man."

Hodges enjoyed a terrific playing career as one of the Brooklyn Dodgers' "Boys of Summer" during the late 1940s and '50s, a big part of the tough lineup that included Duke Snider, Jackie Robinson, Roy Campanella and others. Hodges was a consistent run producer, driving in 100 or more for seven straight years between 1949 and 1955. He finished his career with 370 home runs, popping his last nine for the 1962 Mets. He hit .273 with a .359 on-base percentage (9 percent better than league average) with a 120 OPS-plus. Occasionally he really killed it, twice reaching 40 homers and twice topping a 140 OPS-plus. Defensively, Fangraphs says that Hodges was worth 53 runs more than an average first baseman, so his reputation as an excellent glove man is backed by the numbers.

Hodges exceeded the 4.0 mark in WAR six times and finished with

a 44.8 for his career in 14 full seasons. By all accounts a very good playing career, but not a Hall of Fame one. The numbers place Hodges a good
ways behind Keith Hernandez, a decent ways behind John Olerud and
Mark Teixeira and a hair above Don Mattingly.

Does Hodges's managing career push him to Cooperstown level?
It's tough to say yes when you consider that he managed only 1,414
games with a sub-.500 record before his untimely death from a heart
attack just before the start of the 1972 season. Most everyone agrees that
he was a better manager than his record, considering the weak Washington Senator teams he piloted from 1963 to 1967. The Senators did show
some gradual improvement under Hodges but still never did better than
76–85. When he got to the Mets in 1968, Hodges immediately improved
the win total by 12 from the prior year (to 73 from 61) and then of course
shocked the world with 100 wins and a championship in 1969, the memorable season that would largely define his baseball life.

But the championships didn't last. The Mets followed the "miracle"
year with back-to-back 83–79 seasons before Hodges passed away. They
did take the 1973 pennant under Yogi Berra with a similar 82–79 record,
an unusual year in the National League East with several clubs hovering
around .500.

Gil Hodges was only 47 when he died—perhaps more big years as a
manager awaited him. But the resume he did build wasn't one of Hall of
Fame pedigree. His one title was memorable and it was historic for the
franchise he did it for. But in no other season did his team finish higher
than third.

The verdict: No. Hodges is a big figure in New York baseball history,
and it's understandable that many fans and former players would like to
see him get the ultimate recognition. When you add it all up, though, he
was a fine player and manager whose record just doesn't quite get him
Cooperstown.

Chapter Notes

Chapter 1

1. WPIX Broadcast of Yankees vs. Angels, 17 June 1978, https://www.youtube.com/watch?v=KdY4bmZREeE.
2. Marc Myers, "Where Ron (Gator) Guidry learned to Throw Fast," *Wall Street Journal*, 10 July 2018, https://www.wsj.com/articles/where-ron-gator-guidry-learned-to-throw-fast-1531234826.
3. New York Yankees Channel on You-Tube, "I Was There When: Gator's 18 Strikeouts," https://www.youtube.com/watch?v=oKyxSiTZjO8.

Chapter 2

1. NBC Sports Broadcast of 1978 World Series—Game 3, 13 October 1978, https://www.youtube.com/watch?v=_27zWnz7XGo&t=7102s.
2. Baseball Almanac, https://www.baseball-almanac.com/ws/wstv.shtml.

Chapter 3

1. ABC Sports Broadcast of 1977 World Series—Game 1, 11 October 1977, https://www.youtube.com/watch?v=-UmDVQ1bD8-8.
2. Lee Jenkins, "Randolph, a Son of Brooklyn, Seeks to Scale One More Pedestal," *New York Times*, 2 November 2004, https://www.nytimes.com/2004/11/03/sports/baseball/randolph-a-son-of-brooklyn-seeks-to-scale-one-more-pedestal.html.
3. WPIX Broadcast of 1977 A.L.C.S.—Game 5, 9 October 1977, https://www.youtube.com/watch?v=GFk58Cc0ays.

Chapter 4

1. Fox Sports Broadcast of 1996 World Series—Game 3, 23 October 1996, https://www.youtube.com/watch?v=IlKU5invGeI&t=7613s.

Chapter 6

1. Classic Baseball on the Radio—Radio broadcast of Mets vs. Cubs, 8 September 1969, https://www.youtube.com/watch?v=gKMpYCGiHtU&t=1025s.
2. Irv Goldfarb, *Sabr.org*, 1 July 2009, https://sabr.org/bioproj/person/26133a3d.
3. NBC Sports Broadcast of 1969 World Series—Game 2 (from Sports Revisited), 12 October 1969, https://www.youtube.com/watch?v=kkrgeRIHHB0&t=2559s.
4. Irv Goldfarb, *Sabr.org*, 1 July 2009, https://sabr.org/bioproj/person/26133a3d.

Chapter 7

1. Fox 5 Broadcast of Yankees vs. Expos Game (from MLB Vault), 18 July 1999, https://www.youtube.com/watch?v=wwod7qO4y40.
2. Eric Spitznagel, "David Cone Reveals Vulnerable Side Through Perfect Game in New Memoir," *New York Post*, 12 May 2019, https://nypost.com/2019/05/12/david-cone-reveals-vulnerable-side-through-perfect-game-in-new-memoir/.

3. Fox Sports Broadcast of the 1996 World Series—Game 3, 22 October 1996, https://www.youtube.com/watch?v=IlKU5 invGeI&t=7543s.

Chapter 8

1. Murray Chass, "Doctor's Orders: Rest for Mattingly," *New York Times*, 9 June 1987 https://www.nytimes.com/1987/06/09/sports/doctor-s-orders-rest-for-mattingly.html.

2. Mike Digionanna, "Big Leagues No Big Deal to Him," *Los Angeles Times*, 24 May 1990 https://www.latimes.com/archives/la-xpm-1990-05-24-sp-510-story.html.

3. Spotrac.com, https://www.spotrac.com/mlb/new-york-yankees/mark-teixeira-41/.

4. Associated Press, ESPN.com, "Santana agrees to $137.5M, 6-year contract with Mets," 1 February 2008 https://www.espn.com/mlb/news/story?id=3226412.

Bibliography

Websites

Baseball Almanac, https://www.baseball-almanac.com/ws/wstv.shtml.
Baseball-Reference, https://www.baseball-reference.com.
FanGraphs, https://www.fangraphs.com.
Retrosheet, https://www.retrosheet.org.
Spotrac.com, https://www.spotrac.com/mlb/new-york-yankees/mark-teixeira-41/.

Broadcasts

ABC Sports Broadcast of 1977 World Series—Game 1, 11 October 1977, https://www.youtube.com/watch?v=UmDVQ1bD8-8.
Classic Baseball on the Radio—Radio broadcast of Mets vs. Cubs, 8 September 1969, https://www.youtube.com/watch?v=gKMpYCGiHtU&t=1025s.
Fox 5 New York Broadcast of Yankees vs. Expos Game (from MLB Vault), 18 July 1999, https://www.youtube.com/watch?v=wwod7qO4y40.
Fox Sports Broadcast of the 1996 World Series—Game 3, 22 October 1996, https://www.youtube.com/watch?v=IlKU5invGeI&t=7543s.
Fox Sports Broadcast of 1996 World Series—Game 4, 23 October 1996, https://www.youtube.com/watch?v=IlKU5invGeI&t=7613s.
NBC Sports Broadcast of 1969 World Series—Game 2, 12 October 1969, https://www.youtube.com/watch?v=kkrgeRIHHB0&t=2559s.
NBC Sports Broadcast of 1978 World Series—Game 3, 13 October 1978, https://www.youtube.com/watch?v=_27zWnz7XGo&t=7102s.
New York Yankees Channel on YouTube, "I Was There When: Gator's 18 Strikeouts," https://www.youtube.com/watch?v=oKyxSiTZjO8.
WPIX Broadcast of 1977 A.L.C.S.—Game 5, 9 October 1977, https://www.youtube.com/watch?v=GFk58Cc0ays.
WPIX Broadcast of Yankees vs. Angels, 17 June 1978, https://www.youtube.com/watch?v=KdY4bmZREeE.

Books and Articles

Associated Press. "Santana Agrees to $137.5M, 6-Year Contract with Mets." ESPN.com, 1 February 2008, https://www.espn.com/mlb/news/story?id=3226412.
Chass, Murray. "Doctor's Orders: Rest for Mattingly." *New York Times,* 9 June 1987, https://www.nytimes.com/1987/06/09/sports/doctor-s-orders-rest-for-mattingly.html.

Digionanna, Mike. "Big Leagues No Big Deal to Him." *Los Angeles Times*, 24 May 1990, https://www.latimes.com/archives/la-xpm-1990-05-24-sp-510-story.html.

Goldfarb, Irv. "Jerry Koosman." SABR BioProject, 1 July 2009, https://sabr.org/bioproj/person/26133a3d.

Jenkins, Lee. "Randolph, a Son of Brooklyn, Seeks to Scale One More Pedestal." *New York Times*, 2 November 2004, https://www.nytimes.com/2004/11/03/sports/baseball/-randolph-a-son-of-brooklyn-seeks-to-scale-one-more-pedestal.html.

Myers, Marc. "Where Ron (Gator) Guidry Learned to Throw Fast." *Wall Street Journal*, 10 July 2018, https://www.wsj.com/articles/where-ron-gator-guidry-learned-to-throw-fast-1531234826.

Spitznagel, Eric. "David Cone Reveals Vulnerable Side Through Perfect Game in New Memoir." *New York Post*, 12 May 2019, https://nypost.com/2019/05/12/david-cone-reveals-vulnerable-side-through-perfect-game-in-new-memoir/.

Index